Treats,

Treats, Play, Love

Make Dog Training Fun for You and Your Best Friend

Patricia Gail Burnham

Photographs by Dusty Wasserman
and Gail Burnham

 St. Martin's Griffin ▓ New York

www.stmartins.com

Additional photographs by Peter Baldridge, Maggie Bryson, Sheila Grant, Beth Anne Gordon, Joan Ludwig, and Robert Pearcy

Some portions of this book were originally published in *Playtraining Your Dog.*

Library of Congress Cataloging-in-Publication Data

Burnham, Patricia Gail.
    Treats, play, love : make dog training fun for you and your best friend / Patricia Gail Burnham.—1st ed.
        p. cm
    ISBN-13: 978-0-312-37818-9
    ISBN-10: 0-312-37818-1
    1. Dogs—Training. I. Title.

SF431.B946   2008
636.7'0835—dc22

                                                                            2007039849

First Edition: February 2008

10   9   8   7   6   5   4   3   2   1

*This book is for the dogs—for their companionship,
and for all that they have taught me.*

For decades of people who have told me how much Playtraining
helped them and their dogs. Thank you for your kind words.

*And to the St. Martin's editors: Daniela Rapp, without
whom this book would not exist, and Les Pockell, without
whom* Playtraining *would not exist.*

Contents

Acknowledgments

I would like to thank the talented trainers who appear with their dogs in these photographs. Good work, folks.

Kindness is power.
—John F. Rarey
NINETEENTH-CENTURY HORSE TAMER

The more advanced the mind,
the more it needs the simplicity of play.
—*Star Trek's* Captain Kirk

If it eats, I can train it.
—Gail Burnham

Introduction

Why Write (or Read) This Book?

In 1980, I wrote a dog-training book that was still in print a quarter of a century later. Now it is time for new information and new stories. When *Playtraining Your Dog* was published, the readers' and reviewers' responses were heartwarmingly complimentary. This was great, because writers, like obedience dogs, can use all the positive reinforcement they can get. But one reader had a valid complaint. An automobile accident had left her handicapped, and she correctly observed that playtraining is a very physically active training method. She was right. It is. It encourages the handler to run, jump, and play with the dog. I like very active dogs and I enjoy playing with them.

But what about handicapped, or elderly, or just physically unfit handlers? There should be a way for them to train their dogs without a lot of physical effort. There is a way. It is called food training. I had always trained with food. I just didn't emphasize it in *Playtraining*. But I had shown in breed for years. In breed showing, food is used to get the dogs to perform. Many obedience folks think that show dogs are not trained. Good show dogs are impeccably trained. Every move they make is choreographed and under control, and they perform with obvious pleasure and a speed that should make them the envy of many obedience trainers. There is no place in a show ring for an unhappy or a slow-moving dog.

It was easy to adapt ring-baiting techniques to teaching the obedience exercises. Then I attended one of Dr. Ian Dunbar's (the founder of Sirius Dog Training, Inc.) excellent seminars on puppy training and learned that he was using the food-baiting technique for his junior puppy-training classes in which the dogs are too young to stand much correction. He seemed a little apologetic about the method, using the youth of the puppies to justify it. Over time he outgrew that to become what I already was, an unabashed food trainer.

The late Glen Johnson (the author of *Tracking Dog—Theory and Methods*) used food training for both tracking and obedience training and had a marvelous anecdote about it. He said that a longtime competitor of his asked how he got his dogs to work so well. Johnson replied that he used food to train, and the competitor said that he would never stoop so low as to use food. Glen answered, "Good. As long as you don't use it, you will be placing below my dogs for the rest of your life."

While food training is perfect for inactive handlers and handicapped handlers, it also works for able-bodied folks. In food training, the dog is guided, motivated, and rewarded with food, praise, hugs, and pets. This book describes both food and play training. The best system is to use both food and play for motivation. I have always used both.

Living with dogs should be a joy, not a chore.

Treats, Play, Love

1

Basic Training for Every Puppy

Growing Up Civilized

GETTING WHAT YOU WANT

Dog owners are like other people. They want what they want when they want it. They expect from their dogs everyday doglike devotion, routine heroics, and movie-style intelligence. Not all dogs come naturally equipped with these qualities. They have to be developed. You can create the nearly perfect companion dog, but doing so requires love, thought, patience, and commitment.

I will tell you an important truth right at the beginning: You will receive back from the dog only what you put into him. Dogs that are loved love in return. Dogs that are educated develop their minds. Dogs that are communicated with learn to communicate with their owners. Dogs that are respected gain self-respect and confidence. A dog in close contact with a person will become what that person wishes, if the owner knows enough about dogs to create the dog that he or she wants. It is sad to see well-intentioned owners invest months and years of effort in training dogs only to create monsters of their own design. You get the dog you create. This book is a guide to raising the quality of both your dog and your dog-owner relationship.

A WORD ON THE BREEDS PICTURED IN THIS BOOK

People have asked why almost all of the photos in *Playtraining* are of grey-hounds. Some suggested that my next book—this one—include photos of more popular breeds, such as Labradors and shelties. That misses the point of the pictures. If I can use these methods to train a breed that is not known for its trainability, then you can use it to train whatever type of dog you find on the end of your leash.

BASIC TRAINING FOR EVERY DOG

Through the years I have been asked for training help with the common things each dog needs to know to fit into a family. These include puppy training, housetraining, leash walking, being non-aggressive, paying attention to his owner, coping with shyness, living with kids, preventing aggression over food, and adopting and training an adult dog. I will include all that information here.

But since I love obedience training and performances, toward the end of the book I use the American Kennel Club exercises for the three obedience classes: Novice, Open, and Utility. These exercises are used because they are widely known and standardized. And, since Novice obedience-trained dogs know almost all they need to know to pass their Canine Good Citizen test or to start to compete in the entertaining sport of Rally, I mention it as well. See page 193.

In my teenage days, the animal shelter was on my way home from school. My understanding parents tolerated a steady flow of rescued collies and German shepherds, with each dog trained through Novice before being placed in a home. The training solved the problem of dogs that shuttle through numerous homes due to lack of manners on the dogs' part and lack of control on the new owners' part. The dogs that I trained stayed in their new homes. It takes a minimal

Jeannie Dennard teaching Twist about treats.

amount of training to turn a dog from a pest into a welcome member of the family.

Obedience is not the only thing that dogs can be taught. Dogs can just as well learn gundog work, livestock handling, show ring routines, protection procedures, agility, Rally, or tricks. It is the learning itself that matters, not what is being learned.

Teaching the Dog English

Much of dog training, whether it is for home living or competition obedience, has the goal of teaching the dog an English vocabulary. We want dogs to know what we want them to do when we say certain words. For basic livability I teach my dogs the following: *cookie, kiss, come, sit, stand, down, stay, heel, get back, drop it, give, take it gently, wait, off, get in, stop that, no, feet off, good boy (girl), hush, go home, go to your place, that's enough,* and *get off the bed* (the last only so that I can make it; it is hard to change the sheets with a dog standing in the middle of the bed). On their own, dogs learn "Do you want to go outside?" "Do you want to have breakfast?" "Dinnertime," and "Do you want to go for a ride?"

The Easiest Way to Teach: Naming Behaviors

If you always use the same words, most dogs will learn English vocabulary without formal training. But we can also teach English intentionally in a much shorter time. Most of teaching dogs English is simply naming behaviors. I have a dog that leaps up head high, the same way that Trip did in her flip finish on pages 124–125.

After several years of watching Taupe do vertical leaps, I finally started naming the behavior by saying "Flip" whenever she was about to leap. It took less than two weeks for her to associate the word with the act, so now I can ask her to flip on cue. Dogs offer behaviors all the time. All we have to do is name them to control them. The key to naming behaviors is to use the same word each time.

When Training Isn't Worth the Effort—Engineered Solutions to Problems

Lots of folks ask how to keep their dogs out of the garbage. Can that be taught? Yes, but it is a lot safer and easier to buy a metal kitchen garbage can with a lid. Why bother teaching things that can be more easily taken care of in other ways?

There are two ways to solve dog problems. Training is just one way. The other is what I call an "engineered solution." Engineered solutions are changes in the dog's environment that solve the problem. When I needed to work away from home for long hours, I set up indoor-outdoor living quarters for each pair of dogs. When Lady ate the wood lath fence, I replaced it with chain link. When Love learned to lift the lid of the kitchen garbage can, I put a gallon water jug on top of the lid, which made it too heavy to lift with her nose. When puppies mobbed the door of their room, I installed a baby gate. I built wood fences to restrict my dogs' view of passing pedestrians, which reduced their desire to bark. When old dogs can't walk on slick floors, I lay down rubber-backed bath mats for them. When old dogs start to leak, I put vinyl mattress protectors on the bed. When they can't keep their beanbag beds dry, I change from the usual fleece covers to waterproof Naugahyde ones. Engineered solutions to dog problems are generally less work than training solutions.

Play and Food Rewards

The first requirement for any type of training is motivation. There are two basic motivations for dogs: play and food.

Play: All puppies, and adult dogs that have not been too discouraged, want to play with us. Dog games, whether with a person or another dog, are structured. The handler can make obedience a series of games

Arriba wrestling with Afghan hound Bubbie.

with food rewards and then gradually shape the games into the obedience exercises. Does this sound like a lot of work? It had better not be, or the dog will decide not to play. I once complimented a trainer on the work that he must have put into his training. He said, "No. It was not work. If it had been work, I wouldn't have done it. It was fun." He was right. Ultimately, obedience is not taught because the dog refuses to come or he will not lie down. Obedience is taught because it is fun for both the dog and owner.

According to *Webster's,* play is "the spontaneous activity of children." But why does the dictionary restrict play to children? Adult people and animals all play. I finally found a good definition of play from a photographer. He said that "play is a spontaneous activity that produces pleasure, creative satisfaction, and self-fulfillment. Play often involves a structure with rules, setting, beginning, and outcome agreed upon by the participants." Nothing was said about the age or

species of the players.

The most common way for an adult to play is to have children and to play with them and their toys. This leads to

Arriba playing keep away with Saturn and Tempest.

jokes about children who cannot get near their train set on Christmas morning because their dad is playing with it. But having children is quite an investment for the privilege of being allowed to play. There are more readily available playmates for us in the form of pets. Dogs are not picky. They will play with other dogs, cats, or people.

Why does throwing a stick for a dog to retrieve please the owner and engross his or her attention? It is a basic game of catch. Why is it fun to run away from a dog that you know from experience is going to run you down and smile as he passes? It is the essential game of tag, and the moment the dog goes by us is a delight for both participants. Tug-of-war, keep away, and just plain wrestling are also high on dogs' list of play skills.

Food: Why do I use food training? Because it is a nonviolent training method that has been proved effective on everything from people to pigeons, with dogs and dolphins fitting between the extremes of that range. It provides a way to teach through strictly positive motivation. Food training creates dogs that will nag me for a training session because, in their minds, training equals rewards for work well done, as well as an opportunity to interact with me and show off their initiative and learned skills.

Why do some trainers object to the use of food? And what is the truth about their objections? The objectors never say that food training does not work. If it did not work, nobody would be using it. So the food foes admit that food training is effective, but they have several objections.

Objection: Dogs should work for love, not food. My dogs love me. And whether I food-train them or not, they will continue to love me, because their affection is based on the time we spend together and our interpersonal relationship. It is not based on whether all their food is dropped in a bowl at the end of the day, or if some of their food arrives in the form of small treats they can earn.

Objection: Food training is unnatural. What are the primary motivations of a wild (natural) dog? What motivates wolves and coyotes are food and sex: food to keep themselves alive, and sex to provide the next generation. But sex is a once-a-year event, while food is a daily pursuit. They hunt. They travel to look for game. They devote most of their nonsleeping time to the search for food.

Zoo animals are happier if their food is not simply delivered in a bowl. Animals need to have an activity that keeps them from going brain-dead, or from resorting to destructive behaviors like fur chewing and aimless pacing. So zoos have added ingenious food delivery systems that both feed and entertain the animals.

What zoos seem to have overlooked is that they have always had an interactive food delivery system for the animals that take food from visitors. Do bears at zoos beg for peanuts from the visitors because their diet is deficient in peanuts? If that were true, it could be remedied by adding peanuts to their dinner. Or is what they crave the interaction with the crowd? The bear does a trick and the crowd behaves like a Skinner food dispenser and throws a reward. It helps pass the day.

Dogs come to us with a wide variety of food-gathering skills. My dogs are really good at searching out food in the house. I have lost untold loaves of sourdough bread, packages of dog biscuits, and cookies. When we deliver their dinner on a plate, we deprive them of any chance to use their detective skills. Food training gives them the opportunity to use their intelligence and energy to perfect new food-gathering skills. Instead of ambushing elk, they learn to recall or heel. Or they learn to track a scent trail or perform trick routines. The precise detail of what they are learning is not important. What they are doing is earning their food through their actions. And that gives them the conviction that they control their own destiny.

Objection: Food trainers starve their dogs if they don't perform. If a dog is not fed regularly, its blood sugar falls and its performance abilities decrease. Some professionally-trained animals work for all their food. They need to have access to frequent food-training sessions. The performance schedule at an animal park lends itself to this. The lives of most dog trainers do not. The dogs would be happy to work for all their food. It is the trainers who do not have that much training time available. So their dogs are fed just like regular dogs, and the training food is made up of treats—special interest items like liver or jerky.

Do I withhold food if the dog has not mastered a particular skill? No. Instead I help the dog to perform correctly so that he can be rewarded for success. With time and repetition, the dog graduates beyond the need for help. The sport of tracking is the perfect example of failureproof training. There is never any question that a dog will successfully reach the end of a practice track and be rewarded for it. The only question is whether the dog will do it independently or whether I will help him. But every track will be completed successfully and the reward given.

Sometimes I decide that a particular dog needs to receive all of his food on the track to improve his motivation. It is no inconvenience to the dog, whose food intake stays the same. He gets his usual dinner; he just gets it at the end of the track. But it is a substantial commitment on my part. It means that I have to track that dog every single day for a month. Even if it is only a fifty-foot incentive start, there has to be a track for him every morning.

Objection: Dogs cannot think in the presence of food. I generally hear this from people who have never taught their dogs that food can be earned. When they offer food, their dogs mug them for it. If I hold up a piece of food, or just reach into a pocket, my dogs will line up and ask, "What do you want us to do?" They are thinking like crazy about which of their routines will cause my hand to deliver the treat to their mouth. First, we need to teach them that food can be earned (see pages 10 and 13).

Objection: The use of food somehow makes the resulting learning inferior. Everyone draws information from his or her own life. I learned to swim at an early age with the inducement of a half dozen Kasper's hot dogs and a few Edy's hot caramel sundaes. The hot dogs were pungent with their astronomical garlic content and a trade secret dusting of celery salt, and the sundaes were served pristine and white in big goblets with glass pitchers of warm caramel sauce on the side. Did such bribes lead to later swimming problems? They didn't interfere with my becoming a competitive swimmer in college or taking up scuba diving after that.

Once acquired, any skill is enjoyed just as much as if it had been gained for nonfood motives. How much we use and enjoy a skill has to do with how good we are at it, not with the original motivation for learning it. And being rewarded for grades seems to have left my curiosity about the world undamaged, or I would have run out of subjects to write about years ago.

Objection: Food-trained dogs are not reliable in competition. They can be made perfectly reliable in competition by teaching the final step in food training (see page 194).

My friend Betty Lou had intricately trick-trained greyhounds. Her dogs learned that if I was talking to Betty Lou, they could get me to reward them by offering some of their trick routines. I was so well trained to reward cute behaviors that I generally rewarded each of them several times before I noticed what I was doing. What they were saying was, "Here is Gail, the easy touch. She rewards every trick." Betty Lou rewarded only every third or fourth trick.

The Treats Have to Be Worth the Effort It Takes to Earn Them

Betty Lou used kibble or puppy biscuits to reward her dogs once they had learned a trick, but to teach something new she brought out the good stuff: roast chicken or Jarlsberg cheese. If you want your dog to make an extra effort, the treat needs to be exceptionally good.

Since greyhounds are generally unimpressed with run-of-the-mill treats, I start out with their favorite: boiled lamb liver. I special-order it in ten-pound lots (frozen in two-pound packages, sliced). When boiled, each package will get me through a training morning with four large dogs in Novice. They work harder for lamb liver than beef liver because lamb liver has a higher fat content, and the higher fat content makes lamb liver taste better. Lamb liver's fat content is halfway between beef and chicken livers. I have also used cold roast beef, corned beef, lamb heart, beef heart, and, of all things, Cheerios, which they are very fond of. There are also many commercial premium dog treats, ranging from rolls of meat loaf–type treats, which

work well, to a bewildering variety of tiny packages of overpriced dog treats.

For extreme motivation, like getting Sheena to show, I used boiled lamb tongues. They look a lot like fingers or male body parts. Some people at shows asked in horror what I was using for bait.

Chris wanted to make sure I didn't forget his treats.

But liver is cheaper and works 95 percent as well as tongue. Unfortunately, the prices for both lamb tongue and liver have gone up dramatically in recent years. So I offer a cheaper substitute that is highly motivational and easy to make.

Gail's Liver Freezer Treats

1 pound chicken livers, undrained
2 eggs
16 ounces Jiffy corn muffin mix

1. Preheat oven to 350°.
2. In a blender, mix the chicken livers and eggs—shells and all—until smooth.
3. Pour the blended chicken livers into the corn muffin mix and stir completely.
4. Cover a jelly roll pan with parchment or waxed paper. Spread out the liver mixture.
5. Bake for 35 minutes or until firm.

I turn off the oven and leave the liver overnight. The treats cut best with a large pizza cutter, which won't scratch the pan's surface under the parchment. I cut the treats into rectangles or diamonds that measure about ½" by ⅜". Makes about one hundred treats.

Important: Freeze baggies of the treats. You can take them straight out of the freezer and feed them. No thawing is needed. They don't freeze hard. But, like real liver, they will go moldy in a day or two without refrigeration. I keep them in the freezer and grab a bag whenever they are needed.

Salmon Variation: For variety you can replace the chicken livers with 1 pound of canned salmon and increase the eggs to 4. The advantage of salmon is that you can keep cans on the shelf for times when you need to make treats and get caught without fresh chicken livers.

One day I was training with these treats when a trainer in the next ring with her advanced Doberman had run out of treats. I gave her a handful of mine. She gave one to the Dobe, and the dog snapped to attention and executed the exercise flawlessly. Her owner was so impressed at the improvement in her dog's motivation and performance that I handed out the treat recipe and sent it to the training club newsletter.

Shaping Behavior

Betty Lou created her trick-trained greyhounds by training them in her living room during television commercials. She trained them to do intricate behavior chains the same way that Skinner trained his pigeons. (For more on Skinner see page 70.) She started out by rewarding her dogs with extraordinary treats. She used food to lure the dogs into the first stages of the action that she wanted, and rewarded that first learning step.

During the next commercial, she repeated the cue and the dogs would have to do something more than they had done the last time to be rewarded. Once the dogs had learned that they could earn treats, then everything else was taught by breaking actions down into small steps and chaining them together to get the finished action that she wanted. The more a dog learns and is rewarded, the more he wants to learn to be rewarded again. Dogs that understand the concept of working for treats often offer new behaviors in a learning situation, to see if those moves will be rewarded. The actions that are rewarded are repeated. And, when the action has been repeated enough times, it becomes a habit, which is our goal.

The First Step

The first step in food training is teaching the dog that you will provide food. The second step is teaching him that food can be earned—that he controls the food and that, by his behavior, he can make you open your hand and deliver the treat. As a training method, it means giving apparent control to the dog, which might be why the discipline-based trainers hate it so much. They have to be "in control." I figure that as long as the dog is doing what I want, then I am in control. It is just a more subtle level of control.

Training Puppies

I am often asked at what age a puppy should start his training. The answer is simple: What age is the puppy you want to train? Whatever age he is, you start training now. This does not mean that you put an obedience collar on a four-week-old puppy. It means that puppies learn constantly and that you can teach them useful things at any age. The training methods just have to match the age of the puppy. Very young puppies need gentle and loving lessons. We train young puppies with play and food and kind handling, and omit discipline (except for teaching them to inhibit their bites).

If you wait until a puppy is half grown to start his formal education, you have wasted the most productive learning period in a dog's

life. Dogs will never learn as fast as when they are puppies. If they were wild dogs or wolf puppies, they would have eighteen months in which to grow from helpless pups into fully

Twist learning to sit for treats.

Puppies should be raised in the house, in this case in the shower.

functional adults capable of hunting for themselves and surviving in a hostile world. They learn from the time they are born.

Since there is no way to prevent growing puppies from learning, the only question is whether we will allow them to learn at random, or whether we will guide their education. Everything a puppy is going to see or be exposed to later in life he should meet in his first year. There are lots of reasons why people fail to do this: fear of disease, fear of frightening the puppy, simple lack of time, or not wanting to see the puppy startled by strange new things. It is true that new situations are stressful, but that does not mean that all stress should be avoided. Much of a young dog's training includes subjecting him to the moderate stress of new situations

and, by successfully meeting each challenge, enabling the puppy to build his own confidence. A puppy never knows what he can do until he tries.

The ideal puppy-raising situation is to have them grow up in a corner of the kitchen,

Glen Grant with Saturn and Tempest. Puppies should get to meet men.

Aurora, Fiver, Frolic, Goldy, Doc, and Juliet try out their couch. A tired puppy is a good puppy, and a sleeping puppy is no trouble at all.

with men, women, kids, and household activity all around them. Plus some stable adult dogs. If all of these ingredients are not readily available, a thoughtful breeder will try to import them.

Beth Anne bred two litter sister bitches in the hopes that one would take, and of course both of them did: fifteen puppies! Here was a household with an adult of each sex, plus a kitchen alcove big enough to raise the puppies in. The only thing they needed were children. Fortunately, it was summer vacation and they managed to hire a teenager to puppy sit during the day. She brought along her young brother and sister to watch them at the same time. I saw a lot of photos of the youngsters buried in puppies.

Toward the end of the summer, Beth Anne asked if she could dispense with the puppy sitter, as the puppies were nearly old enough to ship to new homes. I suggested that she keep the puppy-sitting trio; simply having the children there was valuable. I took a puppy from each of these litters home to my childless household and, at the age of eleven months, they would drag me down the street in pursuit of young children. Child-oriented dogs really like kids.

What do you do if you suspect that your chosen puppy is not being raised in a household situation? Bring him home as young as possible and do the socializing yourself. Talk to the breeder and see how much he or she knows or cares about socialization. Will the puppy be around men, children, other dogs, and animals? Will he know what

Puppies should get to meet children.

the inside of a car and house look like? Will he know what a vacuum cleaner, dishwasher, and smoke alarm sound like? I use a noisy shop vacuum in the house. The first time I vacuumed the puppy room, they all ran for their closet-whelping area. In a week or two, I had to push some of them aside to vacuum under them.

Dogs can get used to anything, but they have to be exposed to it first. Guide dog puppies are given to families to raise because the guide dog training schools know that a home is the best place to raise a young dog. And a good family home is better than the best possible kennel.

Mom Is Both the First Environment and the First Trainer: Once the chromosomes are united and the puppy embryo is developing, what is its environment for the next sixty-three days? The inside of the mother's womb is its complete life-support system.

For the rest of the pup's life, its living conditions will never be that totally dependent on a single being again. Is mom a flighty bitch? Then every time she gets upset, the puppies are flooded with adrenaline. And they may suspect for the rest of their lives that the world is full of unpleasant surprises. Is a female puppy packed into one uterine horn with four brothers? Then their male hormones can act on her and cause her to grow up to be more aggressive and outgoing than if she had been sharing her space with four sisters.

Then, after sixty-three days, the big day arrives, and the puppies are squeezed out into a fairly cold world. Here, Mom's personality becomes even more important. Does she keep them warm, fed, and clean? How good a teacher is she? This is important because she is their first teacher.

Dogs roll over on their backs to show submission because their mother taught them to do it. Young puppies are unable to urinate or defecate unless their mother rolls them over on their backs and licks their genital area. Many young puppies do not like this, and some of the more determined ones really resist. But since a puppy weighs one pound while Mom weighs eighty pounds, she wins. She has to win or the puppy will die. By the time she has wrestled them onto their backs a few times, they learn what is expected. They also learn that it is useless to resist and that, when a very large animal approaches them, it is a good idea to roll over on their backs and pee to show submission. By the time puppies are old enough to wean, they have been rolled over on their backs dozens of times. They have learned not to resist.

Betty Lou took her nine-month-old greyhound Lancelot to his first dog show. There he met an Italian greyhound mother that had left her puppies at home to attend the show. Lancelot weighed nearly one hundred pounds. The Italian greyhound weighed ten pounds. She sniffed noses with him as he towered over her and then barked at him sharply. Recognizing her authority, Lancelot fell on the ground at her feet, assuming the position that said that he was just a puppy and she was the boss. The onlookers were amused. Puppies come to us knowing how

Puppies should learn from adult dogs. Arriba training Tempest and Saturn.

to submit to authority. It is up to us to finish the job their mothers started and to keep them practicing submission as they grow into adult dogs.

When the puppies are older, Mom teaches them other things. Most of the brood bitches I have watched were extremely well organized. Fancy ran an especially tight ship. Dinner was offered at certain times, and when it was over, that was it. She was willing to play with the kids, but if they bit her hard enough to drive their needlelike puppy teeth into her, then her answer would be a large and intimidating woof that ended the play session. They listened to her.

I once had the misfortune of having a new mother fall ill and die several weeks after whelping. On her way to the vet, she looked at me as if to say, "I've done all I can. Take care of the kids." So I raised the puppies as orphans from the age of seventeen days. When they were grown, the vet asked me if the orphan puppies had grown up more people oriented than the usual pups. They hadn't. They loved people, but not more than usual. What was unusual about them was that they were a very undisciplined and rowdy litter. They hadn't had a mother there to teach them manners, and people are not very good at teaching puppies manners. Puppies are so cute that we tend to let them get away with everything.

Their early lack of maternal training was correctable. When the rest of the litter had gone to their permanent homes, the two that I kept were introduced to their eight-year-old maiden aunt. Sunny had them well organized in no time and served as a stepmother all of their lives. Stable adult dogs make some of the best puppy trainers, but they are rarely given the opportunity. Often adult dogs are not allowed near puppies. It has been said that a male dog will kill his own puppies. That may be true in some breeds, or for some individuals (after all, there are deviant humans who kill their own kids). But the rule in both people and dogs is benevolent fatherhood. I like to raise puppies confined to their own area, but the responsible adult dogs can hop over the door barrier and visit when I am there.

What does an adult teach? A grown dog entertains and plays with the puppies. He will wrestle with them, pin them, and play tag with them. Many adults will pretend to be a rabbit, running large circles with the kids in hot pursuit. They will teach them where to dig, and where to potty, and what to bark at. And the adults teach the pups what it means when an adult says, "That is enough." They teach them to submit to authority. My first two males did this without any perceptible show of force. Whatever they did was very quiet.

Then Chris came along. He did not see a puppy until he was four years old and did not have the opportunity to train a litter until he was six. His technique was more direct, and it disconcerted me at first. When the puppies were about six weeks old, they ran up to greet him at the door partition, and one nipped him on the nose. He reached over the barrier, took Star's entire head in his mouth, squeezed a little, and emitted a deafening bark. Poor Star ran shrieking into the closet that had been their whelping area. She was followed by the rest of the litter. I picked her up and comforted her, fearing the worst, and found, once she had calmed down, that she was totally unhurt. So we went back to playing in the puppy room. About fifteen minutes later, Chris walked by the door and looked in. And all the puppies ran for the closet. Not only had he taught Star that he was the pack leader, but the rest of the litter had learned from watching.

In the following weeks he did the same disciplinary move to three other puppies. He disciplined about half the litter over a two-month period, but no puppy was ever disciplined more than once. I was a little irritated at first because I considered him heavy-handed when compared to his sire and grandsire. But the puppies all adored him. Until they were adults, I occasionally needed to raise my voice to get their attention, but Chris never did. All he had to do was utter a virtually inaudible growl or lift a silent lip and he had their total attention. And obedience. Did they have a bone? He would probably take it, not because he wanted it but to prove to them that he could and that they were subordinate to him. People are often advised to practice taking bones and toys away from young dogs to remind the dogs that they are subordinate. But most people could use a lesson from Chris.

He never suddenly grabbed anything from them. Instead he moved very slowly and gave them a chance to realize that they were going to lose it and to give it up gracefully. He drilled them on submission every day. He was a much more conscientious trainer than most human owners. The result was that when Chris was eight years old and Traveler was two and in his prime, Chris could still walk up and, with a glance, ask Traveler to drop in submission. Did Traveler hate Chris? He idolized him, followed him around the yard and doted on him. Dogs love their pack leaders. And when Traveler had had enough of Chris's demands, he would squeeze his body between me and the kitchen counters when I was cooking, confident that I would tell Chris to move along and find something else to do. Whenever I found Traveler's thirty-one-inch shoulders squeezed between me and the wall, I knew without looking around that Chris was right next to us.

What did Chris know about training young dogs? He knew that young dogs benefit from lessons in submission. That gentle daily reminders of who is in charge are needed. That it is easier to train puppies than to wait until they are adults and then fight them for pack leadership. That once you have their attention, there is no need for loudness; very subtle cues work if puppies are watching. That it is a good idea to regularly practice taking toys and bones away from puppies. And that, when you take a bone or toy, you do not snatch it away but take it slowly to give the pup time to consider his response. If he considers his options carefully, he will let you have whatever you want. If not, then you are back to teaching submission. Chris did not start teaching submission at six months of age. He started teaching it at eight weeks, an age when puppies naturally submit.

Training Baby Puppies: Puppy training is not formal training. At first it is simple imprinting of the human presence on the dog. It is easy to tuck a well-fed puppy in the crook of an arm while reading or watching television. When the puppy is four weeks old, this turns into puppy play, encouraging him to chase and come to me for mock wrestling matches and hair-biting games. When the puppy's vaccinations are complete, it is time for him to meet the public, taking along a calm older dog to set a good example.

When puppies are in the cute stage, there is no shortage of people to help socialize them. A pair of puppies soon attract a circle of volunteer petters who think that I am doing them a favor by letting them touch the puppies.

It is half as much work to raise a pair of puppies than just one. They provide companionship, exercise, and entertainment for each other. With a single puppy, you have to provide all that companionship, exercise, and entertainment. While sisters often scuffle as adults, a brother-sister pair can grow up into the kind of devotion that Sunny and Tiger showed each other.

By the time the puppies are two months old, we start gradual and low-key Novice training with lots of play. The conditioning from three weeks to two months is used to develop the dog's personality, orient him toward people, and instill in him confidence and the desire to please. A stable temperament and the desire to please are the most important assets to later training.

The job of puppies is to learn about the world. One of the joys of raising puppies is watching them as they first see the world. We can see the world through their eyes. At the same time we can teach them to come, sit, down, submit, and work for treats.

Puppy Classes: Is there a puppy or Novice dog-training class near you? Adult obedience classes are full of dogs that have reached their teenage months before their owners decided to train them to correct adolescent problems. Why wait until there is a problem, when puppy

The tough part about training young puppies like Souri, Rush, and Timba is that they are short. So Jackie Root, Henry Bohunek, and Jim Musci get to bend a lot.

class can head it off? In the puppy class the dogs learn to sit and stay and come and do a little heeling. More important, they learn about other people and other dogs, and that they are expected to behave in public. They learn to pay attention to their owners. Sunny and Tiger became the first Champion–Utility Dog–Tracking Dogs of a breed that is not noted for its obedience potential. They started learning obedience when they were two months old.

On the other hand, Chris and Love started out young in tracking class, but I neglected formal obedience. Then, when they had their tracking titles and championships and I was looking around for something else to keep us busy, I thought it might be time for obedience. Chris was cooperative if not terribly enthusiastic. But Love looked me in the eye and said that this was not in her contract. She

In handling classes, puppies learn to get treats from strangers (and their owners). This is Lu Anne Spencer-Hartle with Sunnie.

Jackie Root with Souri learning to take treats in a handling class.

had not signed up for obedience as a puppy and did not intend to do so now.

So my next generation of puppies started out in puppy class. I didn't want to let them know that obedience is optional. If your area does not have a puppy-training or Novice obedience class, or if you have watched the available classes and their methods are too discipliary for you and your dog, that still does not mean you have to give up on class forever. Is there a conformation class available? These are also called breed, show, and handling classes. I like them for older puppies because a good conformation class includes very little discipline and lots of food rewards, along with the opportunity to meet lots of other people and dogs.

What to Teach Puppies: *Teaching the early down while teaching the puppy to submit to people* (Mom will have already taught the puppies to submit to her). Years ago, a friend asked me to help hold her dog while he was tattooed for identification. What followed was twenty minutes of strenuous exercise as two of us tried to hold him down in the face of his determined resistance. Alex did get his tattoos. We all got a lot of exercise. But this incident really startled me. Why was he resisting so much?

Then I had a flashback to my orphan litter. The vets who tried to save the mother kept asking me if the puppies were okay. As one way of testing the puppies, they asked me to place each of them on his back and see how quickly he would turn over, how hard he would fight to regain his feet. I turned the first puppy over, and he lay perfectly still, not because he was ill but because I am in the habit of holding puppies upside down in the crook of my arm to pet their stomachs. No puppy in that litter, or in any litter I have raised, will make any attempt to turn over if he is placed on his back. From the time they are two weeks old, they learn that flat on their back is a good place to be, that it gets their tummy rubbed. These puppies were all healthy, but my early training had invalidated the diagnostic test. They wouldn't struggle to regain their feet.

The early training also had produced adult dogs that did not resist lying down or being rolled over on their backs. And that was the real secret to why my dogs didn't fight being tattooed. I had spent years accidentally training all my puppies to relax when they are held on their backs.

Sometimes teaching submission was even deliberate. When Sunny got to act as stepmother to the orphan puppies, she enjoyed the job. But when I brought the puppies in to visit her, they were so excited that they ran laps in the bedroom, and they occasionally ran over her body. She didn't like that. Love was the worst offender, so I took to asking her to settle down, and if she didn't, I laid her on her side on

the bed. I held her front legs in one hand and her back legs in the other until she settled down. She caught on quickly. Years later this procedure proved to be invaluable when

Puppies should learn to relax on their backs.

it turned out that in a vet's office I could hold her full-grown legs the same way and she would relax and not move. Greyhound legs are very strong. One person does not have enough strength to hold an adult greyhound still. Love remembered being held as a twelve-week-old puppy and she did not resist.

When elephants were trained in India, it was customary to chain a youngster to a large log and let him try to pull free. Once he found that he could not pull free, he could be kept for the rest of his life on a light chain. As long as he remembered being helpless, he would not fight again. I had taught my youngsters the same thing: that humans were stronger than greyhounds, and they might as well submit.

In a world where thousands of dogs get euthanized for trying to dominate their owners, early submission is a good thing to teach. Even if there is no pack leadership problem, it is helpful to have an adult dog that will lie down without protest to allow for tooth and nail care, first aid, vet work, and tattoos. And for the dog's sake, being calm in the down position reduces his stress and anxiety.

Turn your puppies on their backs. Pet them until they relax. Lay them on their sides and hold their paws. Stroke their bellies and the undersides of their paws. Make it a game. Remember that they already know how to do this. They have been taught it by their mother. Your job is to transfer that training to yourself.

Teaching the come for treats. Puppies are born knowing how to come. They need their mother's warmth, milk, and protection. As soon as they can walk, they follow her. When I start feeding them, I start calling "Come" when I put their food pan down, and they come running to wade into the food dish. Then I start to carry treats, call "Come," and reward them with the treats when they come running. Every breeder has some word that he or she uses to call puppies. A friend was using "Puppy, puppy" to call her litter until I suggested that she use "Come," as the call that meant come for treats. That way she would be teaching the puppies not only to come but also the word that goes with it. They were also learning that they could earn

*They learn to sit
for treats.*

treats by responding.
And the ability to earn
treats is the foundation
on which all incentive
training is based.

*Teaching the sit for
treats.* Because it is an-
noying to have a whole litter of puppies jumping around my feet, I
teach them to sit for treats. I do this by concealing a treat in my
closed hand and holding my hand above the puppies' heads. A sitting
puppy can reach higher with his nose than a standing puppy can, so
they sit in order to reach up for the treats. As soon as they sit, I open
my hand to give them the treat. You can teach a puppy to sit in two
days and an entire litter in a week. They are cute all lined up in a row
waiting for their treats. They learn quickly that they *all* have to be sitting before the treats arrive, so you see the ones that sit quickly glanc-
ing sidewise at the others to see who is holding up the treats by being
slow to sit.

Responsible breeders educate their puppies. By the time a puppy
leaves his litter, he should know how to come, sit, and lie down without resistance. He should know that treats can be earned. Then the
new owner can continue the training to produce a well-trained, well-
behaved adult dog.

Lead Training Puppies: Natural submission is one of the problems
with lead training puppies. When a puppy first feels a collar tighten,
his reaction may vary from panic to simply collapsing on the ground.
Some owners misinterpret the puppy's collapse as defiance. The
puppy is not defying the owner by flattening himself on the ground.
He is trying to appease the owner. So the calmer you can keep the

They learn to play with their owner and they learn to let go on request.

puppy, the more he is going to learn.

I hate to see people lead training puppies on choke chains and narrow nylon choke collars. Lead training is best done with a wide plain collar. A puppy's normal response to the first pull on his neck is to fight the strange sensation. And the more punishing a collar is, the more pain he will inflict on himself if he decides to struggle. The more pain he feels, the more he is likely to panic. This is crazy. Nobody starts out to train a young horse in a punishing bit. Colts are trained in heavy breaking halters and hackamores that don't have bits—equipment that can control them without inflicting pain on them. The idea is that a young horse or dog may need to thrash around a little without being hurt.

The doggy equivalent of a snaffle bit is a plain buckle collar. The lesson to be learned is not that resistance is painful, but that it is useless and there is nothing to fear anyway. The first lesson or two should be brief, and don't be surprised if the puppy uses his options of backing up, sitting down, and in general moving every way except forward. I like to have an older dog with us to set a good example. Most young dogs are more willing to follow another dog, especially their mother, than to follow their trainer.

*They learn to come
for treats.*

What do you do if
the puppy collapses?
First you make the leash
slack, because the tight
leash is what the puppy
is resisting. Then you
talk happily to the
puppy. You kneel down and offer him treats. You walk with a treat held
in front of his nose. You walk only a short distance with lots of rewards.

Even with the lead dog and the trainer there to encourage the
youngster to move forward, it may be a couple of days before he finds
his forward gear. I once trained three puppies that had come from another breeder and reached the age of five months without walking on
lead. Two of them were fine the first day, but the third one tended to
throw herself on the ground in dramatic tantrums. I mentioned to
Betty Lou, who was particularly fond of Sable, that I was having
trouble with her favorite girl. A week or two went by and I had occasion to take Sable in for a vet visit. I was astonished to find that she
walked quite reasonably on leash.

I called Betty Lou to report Sable's progress and wondered
whether she had thought over the early lessons and learned from
them. It was almost as if she had been lead trained when I wasn't
looking. Betty Lou confessed that she had dropped by twice to give
her private coaching. She couldn't stand that I would think her
puppy was the slow learner. And she was right. A little private tutor-
ing brought her right up with the rest of her class. But if you do not
have a friend who will sneak in and leash-train your puppy, it is up to
you. Once puppies have the basic idea that forward is better than
backing up, it is time to move on to longer walks.

Any puppy larger than a toy dog and older than four months can probably walk you into the ground, so a stroll of a mile or so should not be a problem. What do they learn from the long walks? They learn human walking patterns. Dogs out for a walk are led by their noses. They turn and twist to check interesting scents. But people walk in long straight lines, with changes of direction at corners. Puppies need to learn to walk in straight lines, stay out from underfoot, and watch out for those changes in direction.

When Sable and her sister and brother were trained to the point where they did not hang back and fight the leash, they still dithered around and braided their leads into knots, dodged underfoot, and generally made walking inconvenient. So we went to a nearby recreation lake and walked for a couple of miles along the dirt roads. When we went back to the car I found that, while bending over to pet and encourage the puppies, I had dropped the ignition key. So we appealed for help from some dog club members who were working in the area (which meant more walking) and waited for a locksmith (more waiting and walking). By the time we got home, all four of us were tired and the trio was walking on lead like veterans.

At a match, an old-time show trainer and I were watching another exhibitor working with an adult bitch who was hanging her head against the lead, weaving around, and moving everywhere except in a straight line. He said, "Do you know what that dog needs?" And my answer was, "Sure, a long walk." What do long walks do? They give the dog time to build the habit of walking in a straight line, of carrying his own weight. The least tiring way to walk is willingly, on a loose lead, in a straight line. As the walk gets longer and longer and the dog starts to tire, he discovers the easiest way to walk with a person. The long walk gives him the opportunity to discover those things for himself.

Car Training: You don't want to travel with your puppy because he gets carsick? Car sickness can be prevented with lots of short car trips

*Betty Lou and Lancelot
both liked car rides.*

that take the puppy somewhere fun, like a park or conformation class. Fair Oaks Park is a mile from my house. Trips there have taught generations of puppies to love car rides. The objective is to keep the dog from getting apprehensive in the car. Ideally he will get bored instead and fall asleep. I also like dog travel arrangements that allow them to look out a window. I would get sick in a car if I were closed into a crate and looking at nothing but the interior of a van. Dogs should be able to see out the window, curl up, and take a nap. Most of my dogs will be asleep before we have driven a mile.

It is also helpful to teach a cue, like, "Get in," to tell the dog to climb into the car. Beth Anne had driven to a dog show to pick up Dusty on Saturday. On Sunday she said that she was having trouble getting Dusty to leap into the crate in her rather tall van. I patted the crate bottom and said, "Get in," and Dusty leaped into the crate. She knew what "Get in" meant. But I hadn't told Beth Anne the right cue. The whole purpose of teaching a dog English is to be able to tell him what you want him to do, instead of wrestling with him.

Night Barking: Dogs and wolves are most active at dawn and dusk for good reasons. At dawn and dusk there is enough light to see prey, and it is cool enough to run it down. I like the dusk running period and try to let my dogs exercise then. But the dawn run can be a problem for the neighbors. Fortunately, most dogs can learn to sleep in. Some get so good at it that they will stay in bed with a sick owner all day.

Baby puppies sleep a lot. But eventually the night arrives when the puppies are twelve weeks old. It is two in the morning and they want to bark and play. You can discipline them and they may well shut up. But you can also sit with them, play with them, or do a little training: teach them to sit or shake hands and they are just as likely to shut up. Both the disciplinary and the nondisciplinary measures work by distracting the puppies. With the most recent pups, I avoided the late-night play sessions by taking a pocket full of dog biscuits and holding a brief food-training session before bedtime. Not only did they go to sleep afterward, but they learned sit, down, sit up, and shake hands in the process. People discipline puppies because they want to change their behavior, and they find that discipline does work. But it works by distracting the puppies, and it does not work any better than friendly distractions.

Pups that are separated from you at night often learn that if they bark, you will come to them. And once they discover that, they will bark for attention. When the latest pair of ten-week-old puppies arrived, I settled them in their quarters, which included a run and doghouse inside the garage, plus a yard of their own. Then I took out the lawn mower and started on the main lawn. It is a big lawn. It takes a couple of hours to mow. Before I was done, the puppies had given up on barking for attention and gone to sleep. Over the next few days, every time they stood at the gate and barked for attention, I turned my back on them and went into the house. I also visited with them a lot, but at times of my choosing, not theirs. In two days they realized that barking for attention made me go away. It produced the opposite of what they wanted, so they stopped doing it.

In that same forty-eight hours, I could have taught them to bark relentlessly for attention just by going to them when they barked. They still bark. They bark when they are playing together. They bark when they are digging or running. But they do not bark to summon me. And that reduces the potential barking by 50 percent. Now they are adults, and if they forget and bark when I am headed toward their gate, I turn my back and take a few steps away. That silences them. When I turn back to them, they don't make a sound. They think that barking drives me away.

What is another solution to barking? Exhaustion works nicely. Sleeping dogs are quiet dogs. Being tired can solve more dog problems than training ever has. Tired dogs are generally good dogs. And sleeping dogs are no problem at all.

Housetraining: We make such a major project of what is a fairly simple process. There are entire books devoted to the subject. When people ask me how long it takes to house-train a puppy, I ask them a couple of questions. What do you actually want to teach? Do you want the dog to use papers in the corner of the room? Do you want him to scramble through a dog door into the backyard when nature calls? Do you want him simply to wait with his legs crossed for eight to twelve hours until you arrive home to take him outside? Do you want him to develop some sort of signal to ask you to open the door so he can go outside? Do you want the dog to bark, scratch, or ring the doorbell?

The Joy of Dog Doors

The use of a dog door is easy to teach. Dogs are born inherently clean, not wanting to soil their own living area. And the cleaner they are kept as puppies, the more they will retain of their natural tendency toward cleanliness. Puppies raised in filthy conditions learn to tolerate filth, and that can make housetraining difficult later on. But puppies that have access to a yard usually establish a designated potty area and use that consistently. Each puppy may have his own designated area.

All you need to do is accompany them to the area you want them to use until they accept that destination and make a habit of using it. That means watching each new dog like a hawk for the first two days.

Every time the dog drinks, eats, wakes up from a nap, starts to pace aimlessly, or has played hard, you take him outside to the designated spot. And then you stay with him until he performs and you can praise him. My youngest dogs have been praised so often for going outside that they all urinate in response to a heartfelt "Good girl." My actual cue for going is "Find a place," but whatever works is welcome and the house stays clean.

The wonderful thing about a dog door is that it gives the dog control over his own actions and allows him to be as clean as he is naturally inclined to be. One pair of very experienced dog owners returned a beautifully bred adult bitch to her breeder because she was leaving puddles just inside their sliding glass door. I asked why they didn't just put a panel with a dog door in that location. These are the easiest possible dog doors to install. They cost far less than the entry fees that had been paid for this bitch, and they install in minutes. She was a veteran kennel dog that did not know how to ask to be let out, but she was getting as close to the outside as she could. If there had been a dog door next to her, her owners would never have seen another puddle. But she had no way of opening the glass door. And they were adamantly opposed to dog doors, so she went back to the kennel.

Asking to Go Out

For apartment dwellers and folks who are renting houses or otherwise can't install a dog door, there are other options. Like teaching the dog to tell you when to open the door or take him out for a walk. What many people mean by housetraining is that the dog will tell them when he wants to be let out. That is an abstract concept. What the dog needs is to potty, but what you want him to do is give you a signal. Most signals are not intentionally designed. They are arrived at by chance. Some dogs pace back and forth between you and the offending door. Some bark. Others just stand and stare at the doorknob, which is not really effective if you are in another room.

The Bell Signal

The easiest way to teach a dog to signal you when he needs to go outside is to hang a bell from the doorknob. Then, when you are going to take the dog outside, you ring the bell and then open the door. Most dogs learn quickly to ring the bell themselves to bring their owners for doorman service. The bell is a less objectionable noise than barking and easier to teach.

Teaching them to signal you when they want the door opened should not be confused with the actual housetraining. The housetraining is done the same way it was with a dog door. You anticipate your dog's needs, take him to the designated place (ringing the bell on the way through the door), and praise him for correct performance.

No Mistakes

The most important part of housetraining is preventing mistakes by anticipating them. Usually each of my young dogs has made a single attempt to squat in the house. That is met with a shriek and being rushed outside to the designated area. You can almost see their eyes rolling back as they decide that I disapprove of what they tried and that, if I am hysterical, they had better not try it again. And they don't. But it is important not to let untrained dogs have the run of the house. If you are not with them, then you don't get a chance to make that shriek and rush them outside.

Timing

Experienced dog folks develop a subconscious clock that tells them when a dog needs to go outside. I was visiting a litter and chatting with its breeder when I became anxious because my automatic timer was telling me that one of the puppies had been playing for long enough to need to head outside, but I was a guest and didn't say anything. When he suddenly squatted, the owner shrieked and whisked him outside, but what startled me was that she was surprised. Some people's automatic timers work better than others, or perhaps my being there had distracted her.

How Long Can a Dog Hold It?

It amounts to dog abuse not to allow your dog access to an allowable potty area for long periods of time. When a dog is shut indoors, forbidden to relieve himself in the house, and then denied access to the outside, I am baffled at what the owner expects the dog to do. The dog is in a no-win situation. For a dog to learn to behave properly, he has to have the opportunity to behave properly. I suggest that if you expect a dog to cross his legs and wait for thirteen hours between relief stops, you should try it yourself. From the time you leave the dog in the morning, to the time you return to the dog, no restroom stops are allowed. None. You won't make it through the day, and the attempt is educational.

Some adult dogs between the ages of two and ten may be able to sleep away the day, not move around much, and make the wait successfully, as long as they are on a low-residue diet and in perfect health. But young dogs and old dogs, and dogs with upset digestive systems, are not going to make it.

Puppy Output

Pound for pound, puppies eat much more than adult dogs do. Puppies have to process a lot of food to grow their adult bodies. As a result, puppies are eating and pooping machines. I once counted the piles of feces produced by a trio of four-month-old puppies. In twenty-four hours they produced eighteen piles. That means that each day they each defecated six times, and that translates into a pile from each puppy every four hours. With that kind of output, you can't expect your puppy to wait for long periods of time. The time when you are trying to house-train him is the very time that he requires the most frequent relief stops. This is good because it gives you lots of opportunities to practice his signal and to accompany him outside for rewards.

New Dogs

I try to arrange my schedule so I am home with a new dog for at least the first three days, both to reassure him and to make sure that the new habits he forms are the ones I want.

But you can't be with the dog all the time, so eventually it becomes important to have a dog area, somewhere damageproof for the dog to stay while you are away. This can be either outdoors with a doghouse and run, or indoors with access to a dog door or utilizing a crate or a closed-off area. The usual choices of closed-off areas are the bathroom or kitchen, to take advantage of their washable floors.

Old Dogs

Old dogs need to potty often. It is like having puppies again. And they have very little warning between when they realize that they need to go outside and when it is too late. My senior dogs have their own room and an oversized dog door that leads to a small yard. The room has industrial short-nap carpeting for old dog traction. The old dogs also have vinyl beanbag beds instead of fleece-covered ones.

People often complain that old dogs can't stand up on vinyl or tile floors. Or that they are becoming incontinent. I have bad news for them: The same thing happens to old people. As a dog or person ages, nerve impulses are transmitted more slowly. The longest distance for a nerve impulse to travel in your body is from your lower body to your brain. Or from the dog's back end to its brain. The result is a loss of continence and walking ability. This is the same reason that many old people wind up in wheelchairs. Some people have their dogs euthanized when this happens. I prefer to engineer solutions to the problems. A good dog door and rubber-backed bath mats on slick floors go a long way toward keeping the house clean (see page 297).

Submissive Urination

It is always fun to impress your coworkers. One came to me with a dog problem. When she greeted her cocker spaniel at home, the dog would run up to her happily, and when she bent over to pet it, the dog would pee on the floor. She had tried disciplining the dog, but that made him pee even more. I explained that the dog was peeing to show her that it was subordinate to her. When a large human leans over a smallish dog, that dog can feel challenged, just as if a large dog were standing over it. So the small dog pees to show its submission. The cure is easy. I told her to watch the dog, and the moment he started to squat, she should turn her back on the dog and walk away. This works because it eliminates the threat the dog feels. There isn't any point in showing submission to a big dog that is walking away from you. Walking away worked so well that the owner decided that I was a dog guru.

Food Manners: If you watch dogs being temperament tested on the animal cops shows on *Animal Planet,* the most common reason for failing the test is food aggression. The tester puts down a bowl of food, allows the dog to start eating, and then pushes a fake hand into the bowl. Some dogs keep eating. Some leave the bowl. Some growl. Some bite the intruding hand. What would your dog do?

Most children are told by their parents not to bother the dog while he is eating. That is a good rule, but children are forgetful.

So you want your dog not to defend his food bowl. The easiest way to teach the dog that hands in his bowl are not a threat is to feed the dog in installments. Divide his dinner into halves or thirds. Feed the first part, and when it has been eaten, give the dog a small dog biscuit, pick up the empty bowl, and refill it for the next serving. The dog learns that giving up his bowl is a good thing: It will be returned with more food.

When I put down a food bowl, I run a hand down the dog's back. If you have been doing this from the time he was a puppy, he won't object. Preventing food aggression is easier than correcting it. But if you have to correct it, hand-feeding is another choice. When Chris was an adolescent and decided to guard his food bowl, I hand-fed him for two weeks. He was not allowed to reach into the bowl; instead he had to watch me reach into the bowl and pick up a handful of food for him. It quickly cured his objections to my reaching into his food bowl. Another method is to put down an empty bowl and then reach toward it to drop treats into it one at a time.

Does your dog snatch food from your hand? From the first time I hand a puppy treats, we work on having him take treats gently. If he tries too hard to snatch the treat, I close it in my hand, and say, "No, take it gently." When the dog stops trying to grab the treat, I give it to him. The dog learns that grabbing for treats will not get him one. Don't reward bad behavior by giving treats to a pushy dog. It will only teach him to be more pushy. Warn him off and teach him to be gentle. His mother has already given him lessons in asking gently for food. Puppies that fling themselves on their mother will make her move away, taking the milk bar with her. Puppies learn to approach her gently. In fact, they learn to sneak up on her.

When dinnertime is over, I pick up the bowl and we move on to the next step: to sit for treats. A dog is happy to give up his empty bowl when the next step is treats. And it reinforces his willingness to mind me around food.

Hand-Feeding

When thirty dogs were released into a rescue group, I got a call for help. The dogs had lived alone with their owner and were unsocialized and shy. In order to reshape the dogs' behavior, I recommended having the foster folks hand-feed the dogs. It is the quickest way to form a bond with a new dog. And it lets you establish boundaries about how the dog receives treats from your hand. It makes each meal a learning experience, and it teaches the dogs to be gentle.

Don't Trade Bowls

One of the quickest ways to start a dogfight is to let one dog push his nose into another dog's bowl at dinnertime. To solve that problem, my dogs eat either separated in different rooms, or tethered to their own eating area. I started doing this when Sheena began pushing her adult littermates out of their bowls. Their food wasn't any better than hers. She was just pushy. You don't get named after Sheena Queen of the Jungle when you are three weeks old for nothing! I tied a leash and collar to a doorknob and, after that, Sheena ate on lead. A friend had a dog that was displaying food aggression toward her children and would chase them. I suggested that she put him on leash to eat. It worked for her and made feeding time far less exciting.

Why don't I feed dogs in crates? It is another effective solution, but I admit that I don't crate-train my dogs unless I am going to fly somewhere with them. But crates are good for letting multiple dogs eat without competition.

Disgusting Munchies: The Internet is full of anguished pleas from dog owners who want to know how to stop their dog from eating feces. Some dogs eat their own feces. Others prefer the feces of other dogs. And nearly all dogs love to clean up the cat's litter box. Most dogs have a taste for horse droppings. Human feces are incredibly popular too. I learned this when I was teaching tracking to my dogs in an open field where the neighborhood children played. The kids didn't see any reason to go home to use the bathroom, and my dogs, who did not normally munch on feces, were entranced with their souvenirs. I found another area to train in.

The technical term for eating feces is coprophagy. In Greek, *phagy* means to eat and *copr* means feces. An unrelated but similar problem in dogs is the eating behavior called pica. Pica means eating various inappropriate nonfood objects like stones, plastic, fabric, stuffed animals, planter mix, garden soil, etc. When upset owners ask for help in getting their pet to stop eating feces, there are three kinds of advice generally given:

1. Clean up after the dogs frequently to remove the source of temptation.
2. Sprinkle feces with hot sauce to teach the dog to avoid them in the future.
3. Add things like meat tenderizer or the commercial product Forbid to the dog's food to make his feces unattractive to himself and other dogs.

The first measure is aimed at prevention, while the latter two are aimed at changing the dog's behavior. I am all for rapid cleanup— good dog care requires rapid cleanup. Even if the dogs aren't interested in reprocessing the feces, flies will be.

So why do well-fed dogs eat feces? Coprophagy is a normal dog behavior that is rooted in wolf behavior. The first time food goes through a well-fed dog or wolf, digestion removes only half of the nutrients. If a wolf is injured and can't hunt for food, it can live until it heals by eating the feces of its better-fed and able-bodied pack mates.

All nursing female dogs are coprophagic. Every dog and wolf had a coprophagic mother. All canine mothers consume their puppies' feces. That both keeps the nest clean and adds to Mom's calorie intake. When they are older, the dam continues to gain calories by reprocessing puppy poop. It is her own partially digested milk.

When a mother wolf is denned up to nurse her cubs and cannot be away for long periods of time to hunt, the feces of her puppies and her pack mates help her survive. When I raised my first litter of greyhound puppies, my ex–significant other phoned me at work to notify me that there was a pile of puppy feces on the back step. I obediently rushed home at noon to clean it up, only to find that the dam had beaten me to it. There were no puppy feces on that porch. I never told him what had happened to them. Over the years I have gotten quite good at racing dams to puppy piles. The mothers regard my interference as competition for their rightful food source.

Some dams stop cleaning up after their puppies as soon as the owner starts to feed the puppies. While they are eager to reprocess their own digested milk, they are reluctant to digest secondhand kibble. Others go on cleaning up after their puppies until after they have completely stopped nursing.

The romantic version of the domestication of dogs pictures an early human adopting an orphaned wolf cub. But what actually attracted early dogs to humans was the chance to scavenge human feces when times were hard. Humans are resourceful and omnivorous eaters. We store food for hard times. In such times we are likely to be better fed than the local wildlife. The better fed an animal is, the more nutritious its feces are.

We can only digest so much food at a time, and we can consume far more food than we can digest. As our food intake goes up, the percentage of undigested food in our feces also rises. Fortunately for our waistlines, only a small percentage of a Thanksgiving dinner is digested and converted into fat. The rest passes on unused through our digestive tract. That makes well-fed human feces a useful source of food for the weaker and smaller members of wolf packs that were already used to eating the feces of other animal species. You could think of human feces as the first dog kibble. Certainly the dogs thought that it was.

Dogs are attracted to horse feces because they contain partially digested plant foods. Dogs are intensely attracted to cat feces because of the high protein and fish oil content of cat food. Since we don't feed cat food to dogs (and we shouldn't, because cat food isn't properly balanced for dogs), the dogs try to obtain it secondhand.

The last time I had coprophagic dogs, they were not interested in the feces of dogs that were fed the same additive-free, high-protein kibble that they were fed. What attracted them on our walks were the feces of dogs that were fed soft-moist foods, which are preserved with sugar and colored bright red with food dyes. Since my dogs were living on a healthy diet, what they wanted was secondhand junk food.

What was the advantage to humans of having dogs living around their camps to eat human feces? Since many diseases are species specific, the canine cleaning crew benefited its human neighbors by decontaminating human feces with a trip through the canine digestive system. Both dogs and humans have intestinal tracts that host communities of bacteria that help us digest our food. Feces, like an animal's body, are 60 percent water. But with the water removed, nearly 50 percent of the dry weight of feces consists of intestinal bacteria. The dog's digestive tract bacteria have adapted to processing feces without making the dog sick. Pariah dogs hang around villages to act like little sewage treatment plants. They have survived for millennia on garbage, feces, and dead bodies, which is one of the reasons that some cultures considered dogs to be unclean. Other cultures, however, ate dogs. For them the dog was consuming a waste product and returning edible protein.

Pariah dogs are small. Their average weight is less than thirty pounds. The pariah dog's small size is an adaptation to scavenging for food. A small dog requires less food to survive than a large dog. A wolf needs its large body size and strength and very large teeth to pull down large game, but a scavenger has no need for strength. When wolves went from hunting to scavenging human camps for food, natural selection reduced their size.

Present-day dogs are provided with kibble and canned food. Coprophagy is no longer necessary for survival, but it is still a retained behavior. These dogs don't have depraved appetites. They are throwbacks to the days when eating feces saved their ancestors' lives. Frequent cleanup is the best prevention.

Health Issues

What about the health issues? A coprophagic dog munching on the feces of his own living group is probably not going to be exposed to any parasites or diseases to which he hasn't already been exposed. I try to keep my dogs from dining on the feces of strange dogs to reduce their exposure to outside parasites and diseases. I also try to keep them from dining on the feces of cats, horses, and geese, but if they outwit me, I rely on interspecies immunity to protect the dogs. There are only a few parasites that can be transmitted from one species to another; it is one's own species that carries the parasites and diseases you have to worry about. That's why it is safer for me to kiss a dog on the lips than another human. I am immune to most dog diseases while I am susceptible to all human diseases.

Some owners think that coprophagy indicates a mineral deficiency. But feces are low in minerals. When my dogs feel a need for extra minerals, they eat garden soil. They dig off the top layer of grass and happily eat the grass roots and dirt. When I see my dogs eating dirt, I add some bone meal to their diet, or provide them with knucklebones to grind into their own bone meal.

Dogs that eat feces are not craving minerals, so giving mineral

---

GAIL'S RULES FOR COPROPHAGIC DOG OWNERS

1. Keep the yard and litter box clean. Don't leave snacks lying about. Prevention is the best solution.
2. Don't kiss a coprophagic dog on the mouth.
3. Don't reach into a coprophagic dog's mouth to remove an unknown item in the dark.
4. Don't get upset about having a coprophagic dog. It is a natural behavior.

supplements doesn't stop coprophagy. Owners have reported some success with food additives like meat tenderizer or one of the specialty products like Forbid. Coprophagy is contagious. Once you have one coprophagic dog, the rest of its pack mates are likely to think he is eating something good and will try the new snack.

House Manners for Older Puppies and Adults

More Useful Things to Teach

Once a dog comes when he is called, is at ease around other dogs and people, understands housetraining, controls his barking, does not bite his owners over food, is organized on lead, rides in the car, and responds to a few simple cues like sit and down, most owners consider the dog civilized enough to be worth living with. But I find the following house manners well worth teaching.

GO TO YOUR BED (OR PLACE OR RUG)

This is one of the least taught and most convenient directions for a dog in the house. First you need to arrange an identifiable place. This can be a dog bed or just a small rug. Dogs are territorial, so this is easy to teach. You tell the dog, "Go to your place," and take him there. If he leaves, you take him back, repeating, "Go to your place." Give him a treat. Most dogs pick this one up quickly, and it enables you to put the dog out of the way when there is a lot of activity in the house.

Sable and Julia and their cousin figured out beds for themselves.

Sunny and Tiger relaxing on their foam bed. If you want to keep dogs off the furniture, make them a comfortable bed and teach them to go to it on request.

GET BACK

Put the dog on leash, stand directly in front of him, and say "Get back" while stepping forward. The dog backs up a step and gets rewarded. The next time he backs up two steps and gets rewarded. This is good for both getting the dog out of your way and keeping him back when you open a door.

DON'T RUN OUT THE OPEN DOOR

Lots of dogs have been hit by cars after they ran out an open door. Teach your dog not to rush out the door when you open it. At first, don't open the door wide enough for the dog to run through it. When he moves toward the open part of the doorway, use the "Get back" cue that he already knows. Or use a "Sit" cue. Do this with the dog on leash. Open the door. Tell the dog to get back or sit. Repeat several times and then repeat each time you open the door. Reward the dog when he doesn't charge the door.

WAIT

Since dogs want what they want right now, it is a good idea to teach them the meaning of "Wait." It seems like an abstract concept, but dogs learn it fairly easily. Hold out a treat and say, "Wait." Then give the treat seconds or minutes later. Increase the time that they have to wait before they are rewarded.

WAIT FOR THE LAST BITE

A trio of magazine editors was visiting me. I planned to serve cookies and juice, and wondered just how Sheena and her young daughter, Kira, would take the invasion of strangers. I was hoping that Kira wouldn't help herself to the visitors' cookies. I was pleasantly sur-prised. Kira and Sheena sat in the middle of the living room and watched us with interest but made no cookie raids. I hadn't been aware of teaching them good party manners. What I had taught them (by giving them the last bite of my meals and not giving them any food before the last bite) was that I would always give them the last bite of anything I ate. That meant they had learned to wait until I came to that last bite. And that is exactly what they were doing. Se-cure in the knowledge that they were always entitled to the last bite, they were waiting for it. They got the final cookie.

JUMPING ON PEOPLE OR NOT

Lots of owners say they want their dog not to jump up on them. But then they regularly reward the dog by hugging him when he jumps up. Why do dogs jump up on us? Because our faces are a long way above the ground and dogs greet each other face-to-face. Dogs treat us like their mothers, and a puppy greets his mother by licking her lips. In order to do that to us, dogs need to stand on their back feet. One way to reduce jumping up is to give the dog your hands to greet instead of your face, or just bend down and greet him on his level. I gave up teaching my dogs not to jump on people when I realized that most of the people they met wanted to be hugged and rewarded them for hugging. Now I just warn the people and, if it is an inappropriate person, I tell the dog to sit for treats. He can't sit and jump up at the

We want control of jumping up. Many obedience folks teach the dog to jump on cue and use it as a reward. They also teach a cue to not jump. LEFT: *This is Patty Nicholas with Belgian Malinois Halley.* RIGHT: *Pat White with golden retriever, Riot.*

same time. I don't teach the dog never to put his feet on a person. Instead I teach him the cues that let him know when he can hug and when he can't. What you want is verbal control of the behavior, not to eliminate it entirely.

Ringo loved to be hugged. When he first put his front feet on top of the washing machine, instead of on me, I hugged him to his heart's content. He quickly learned to put his front feet on the washer to get his hugs. And if I wanted a hug, I tapped the top of the washer and he put his feet up.

FEET OFF

I do teach a feet-off cue for when I am dressed to go out and don't want a muddy footprint in the middle of my chest. I teach it verbally when I am wearing clothes that my dogs can put their feet on. I push them away and say, "No feet." They still leap around me, but they learn fairly quickly to keep their paws tucked in, since touching me gets them a verbal reprimand in a warning tone. This can also be used to keep them from jumping on inappropriate people.

WARNING TONE

For verbal warnings, I rarely use the word "no." Instead I use a throat-clearing noise that sounds like the *a* of *cat* or *rat*. It is easy to say and dogs respond to it better than they do to "no." It is the human version of a warning growl, also known as the universal caution *A*.

The flat *a* verbal correction works on more than dogs. I am a devoted thrift store shopper. I was once shopping about eight feet away from my shopping cart when I saw a man reach into the cart and begin looking at my items. I automatically gave the flat *a* correction sound, and he snatched his hand out of the cart as quickly as if I had

Digging is normal dog behavior, a lot of fun, and good exercise. The best we can do is restrict it to a nondamaging area.

touched it with an electric prod. I don't know exactly why the flat *a* correction sound works, but it seems to be a universal caution sound.

And speaking of voice tone, cues get their authority from being enunciated clearly, not from loudness. At a public-speaking class at work, each of us was supposed to sit after our presentation, while the class critiqued us. One young man was nervous after his speech and kept walking around the classroom in spite of the teacher's repeated requests that he sit. As he past me, I said distinctly, "Sit," in my carefully enunciated dog-training voice and he dropped into a chair as if I had shot him. Then he realized that he had responded to a dog-training cue, so he held up his hands like paws and panted like a happy dog. That triggered my automatic response. I offered him a Milk-Bone leftover from saying good-bye to the dogs that morning. (I often arrived at work with a Milk-Bone or two in my pockets.) The class nearly fell down laughing. You never know when a dog treat is going to be useful. Keep rewarding those good dogs. And pronounce your cues clearly.

A TIRED DOG IS A GOOD DOG

The challenge is to get the dogs tired each day. While puppies are charming, they have formidable energy levels. Dogs (or, for that matter, wolves) were not designed to sleep away their lives in our living rooms. They were designed to cover large amounts of ground in the pursuit of their dinner. Since we have taken their life's work away from them, what can we substitute for the hunt? The answer is long walks, short walks, playing catch, Frisbee sessions, runs in the park, anything that gets them moving and keeps them moving long enough to burn off excess energy.

I had a neighbor whose Lab barked every morning when the young man left for work. He was a jogger, but he never took the dog along. If he had taken the dog on the morning run, then the dog would not have worked off his extra energy by barking. The dog didn't have a training problem. He had an exercise shortage.

So how much exercise does a puppy need? After the age of four months, he absolutely needs to be tired out at least once a day, preferably twice. This is where you may begin to regret your choice of a breed. Bulldogs get tired a lot faster than Chesapeake Bay retrievers. It doesn't take much of a walk to wear out a Pekingese. Border collies are supposed to be able to run a hundred miles, and do it again the next day. Even among the active dogs there are differences in the energy requirements. The high-speed dogs, like the sight hounds, are sprint dogs. You can wear them out with a fifteen-minute walk and a hard three-minute run.

On the other hand, the sporting breeds like pointers were designed to run for hours at a time, and retrievers were designed to swim for long periods. Herding breeds like the border collie are the ultimate long-distance runners. A dog that is supposed to be able to hunt or work sheep all day is not going to be impressed with a fifteen-minute walk and a brief run.

TRAINING FOR EASY NAIL CARE

Dogs that hate having their nails cut, hate it in different degrees. They range from moderately annoyed dogs to dogs that struggle and bite to prevent anyone from trimming their nails. Some of them fight so hard that it is necessary to have them tranquilized before cutting their nails. Veterinarians are used to seeing dogs come in with long nails.

Betty Lou's first two greyhounds were both strongly opposed to having their nails cut. Sheba could have her nails trimmed as long as she was muzzled; otherwise she reached for the hand that held the clippers. Image fought so hard that he had to be taken to the vet to have his nails cut. Both dogs lived long lives, which gave my friend years of practice in cutting a resisting dog's nails. When she got her next greyhounds, she resolved not to go through more decades of fighting over nails, so she did two things. She changed from clippers to a nail grinder. And she set out to teach the new dogs to let her grind their nails without resistance.

She broke down nail care into a series of small steps and then rewarded the dog with food for successfully completing each step. It takes a week or two to teach the procedure. You should start to teach it when there is time to complete it, not the night before a show when you decide that your dog's nails need cutting right now.

There are three reasons why dogs hate to have their nails cut. If you cut nails while the dog is standing up, then he is standing off balance on three legs while you work on the fourth. If you cut nails while the dog is lying down, then he may object to having to lie on his side in a submissive position. And no matter what position you cut the nails in, you are likely to pinch the quick and cause the dog pain.

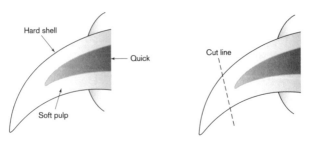

FIGURE 1. *Parts of a nail*   FIGURE 2. *Cutting a nail beyond the quick*

In order to cut or grind nails painlessly, you need to know a little bit about nails. At the center of the nail is the quick, which is flesh that is well supplied with blood vessels and nerve endings. A dog that fights having his nails cut is trying to protect the quick. Surrounding the living quick is an insulating layer of weak fibrous tissue (soft pulp), and over that is the hard outer shell of the nail. All the strength of the nail, and its resistance to wear, is in the outer shell, which, like the fibrous cushion, is made up of dead cells. You can do anything you want to the outer shell and the secondary fibrous layer as long as you don't pinch, cut, or grind into the quick.

No amount of training is going to teach a dog to willingly let you cut into the quick. That is like running a needle under your fingernail. Could anyone reward you enough for you to let them do that? But if someone were to offer me five dollars, or even a homemade cookie in exchange for letting her file my fingernails, that is a bargain I would accept. And that is the bargain we make with our dogs.

Dog toenails come in two basic colors, black or white. The white nails are transparent and you can look through them to see the quick, which is made pink by its blood supply. That makes it easy to avoid cutting or grinding near the quick. Black nails seem to be made of harder horn and are certainly more challenging to grind because you cannot see where the quick is. The solution is to cut black nails conservatively, making sure to leave room for the quick. I trim a white nail much closer to the quick than I do a black one.

One of the reasons I prefer grinding nails to clipping them is that a grinder can remove the hard outer nail shell without cutting across the quick. When using a grinder, I don't grind the nail straight across. I grind through the hard outer shell starting on top of the nail and ⅜" back from the point. Then I grind the strip down to the nail point and up the underside of the nail for ¼". This destroys the structural strength of the outer nail shell, so that the nail wears back

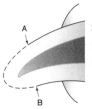

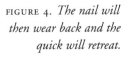

FIGURE 3. *Grind through the hard shell in a strip over the nail tip.*

FIGURE 4. *The nail will then wear back and the quick will retreat.*

to the start of the strip over the next few days. If you are dealing with really long nails, grind the outer strip, let the nail wear back, and then grind a new strip for further shortening.

You need to make three major decisions before cutting a dog's nails for the first time. The first is an equipment decision. Are you going to clip or grind? And if you are going to clip, are you going to use a guillotine-style clipper or a scissors-style clipper? For medium-sized to large dogs, I strongly recommend grinding using a Dremel Moto-tool with a number 8193 grinding stone. (There are dozens of grinding attachments for the Moto-tool. Only a couple of them are suitable for grinding dog nails.) Oster makes a nail grinder that is lighter weight than a Dremel. You can find Dremels in hardware stores and Osters in pet stores. My first Dremel outlasted generations of dogs. While the basic tool lasts a long time, you need to replace the grinding heads often.

If you prefer to clip nails, and have medium to large dogs, I recommend using a sharp scissors-type clipper. The guillotine clipper that most pet stores sell is best suited to small nails. I showed my neighbor who had a Chihuahua with long nails how to trim the nails and gave her my last guillotine clipper, since it wasn't useful on my dogs. The guillotine clipper applies pressure to large nails and pinches the quick even without cutting into it. And, while the blade can be replaced with a sharp one, most people never bother to replace it.

The second decision is whether you are going to cut nails with the dog standing or lying down. Racing greyhounds always have their nails trimmed standing up and most groomers clip dogs that are standing on a grooming table with their head tied. Tying the dog gives better control. I have cut nails both ways. I had always ground nails with the dog lying down with his feet in my lap until Annie arrived as an adult.

The first time I tried to grind her toenails resulted in a major wrestling match. The next couple of times were not much better. Then I took her to a tattoo clinic that happened to be held at a grooming shop. After she was tattooed I asked them to cut her nails. They put her on a grooming table, picked up a foot like she was a horse being shod, and did her nails with no struggle at all. Watching her calmly having her nails cut, I realized that she had stood up to have her nails cut all her life. When she resisted my attempts to cut her nails, it was not the manicure she was resisting, it was being laid on her side. After this I did Annie's nails her way, standing, and had no further problems.

The third decision is whether the time spent to teach a dog to allow his nails to be trimmed is worthwhile. Basically, you have the choice of teaching the dog to allow happy nail care, or of looking forward to years of wrestling matches whenever the nails need cutting. Dogs are not born hating to have their nails cut. We teach them to hate it or to like it, starting with the first time we try to cut their nails. If we hurt them and punish them, they learn to hate nail care. It is so unpleasant to cut the nails on a dog that fights and resists that I strongly recommend taking the time to teach the dog to relax and look forward to having his nails cut as a rewarding experience.

I once took a seven-month-old puppy in for a hearing test, and the vet, after making sure that he could hear, suggested also cutting his nails. He had been tranquilized for the hearing test and was woozy but not unconscious. She brought out an old pair of guillotine clippers and pinched his first nail. He came up off the floor and made a very creditable pass at her cheek. I suggested that we not cause him pain when he was not in control of himself and said that I would do the nails at home.

It was the closest I have ever come to having a vet bitten. In his groggy condition, the dog considered the nail pinch to be an attack and defended himself against it. But what the vet was about to teach him was that having his nails done hurt, and I didn't want him to learn that. It is much easier to teach a dog the correct way to do nails than to retrain a dog that has been hurt.

I don't recommend starting your relationship with a new dog by trimming overlong nails. If you get a dog with overgrown nails, either have your vet cut them under anesthesia or wait a while. Then set out to establish a relationship with the dog before you ask him to let you do his nails. When the University of California at Davis released nineteen greyhounds to be placed as pets, I went down to inspect them. I asked the veterinarian in charge if I could visit before the dogs were released in order to grind their overlong nails back to normal. I didn't want the new owners' first experience with their dogs to be a struggle to cut back overgrown nails. Racing dogs are used to having their nails ground, so I knew they would let me grind them, but the new owners might not have nail grinders available. When I offered to grind the nails, the vet directed his kennel people to grind back the nails before the dogs were released, since they should have been keeping the nails short as routine care. The new owners received dogs with properly short nails.

Toenail Drill

First, put a large number of really good treats in a baggie. If you want your dog to have his nails cut lying down, pad the area where you want him to lie (a beanbag or foam dog bed works well). Put a leash on your dog and teach one of the following drills.

DOG LYING DOWN

1. Lay dog on his side. Give treat.
2. Gently hold dog on his side. Give treat.
3. Pick up and rub paw. Give treat.
4. Repeat step 3 with all paws at least twice. More treats.
5. While you are at it, lift the lips to expose the teeth. Give treat.
6. Hold paw and individual toe. Give treat.
7. Repeat step 6 a lot of times.
8. Tap each toenail a few times with your fingernail. More treats.
9. At this point you should be able to clip or hand-file the nails. Give treats for each nail.

DOG STANDING

1. Tie the dog using a short leash and a nonchoke collar. Give treat.
2. Pick up one foot at a time and hold so the dog balances on three feet. Give treats.
3. Pick up and rub paw. Give treat.
4. Repeat step 3 with all paws at least twice. More treats.
5. While you are at it, lift the lips to expose the teeth. Give treat.
6. Hold paw and individual toe. Give treat.
7. Repeat step 6 a lot of times.
8. Tap each toenail a few times with your fingernail. More treats.
9. At this point you should be able to clip or hand-file the nails. Give treats for each nail.

GRINDER

In order to use a grinder, teach either of the above drills and separately teach the following:

1. Start with lots of small treats, one dog, and one nail grinder held at arm's length away from the dog.
2. Give a treat.
3. Give another.
4. Turn grinder on and off quickly.
5. Give treat.
6. Repeat steps 4 and 5 until the dog looks for a treat when the grinder turns on. This may be ten to thirty times.
7. Turn grinder on, give treat, turn grinder off.
8. Repeat step 7 until dog ignores the grinder and eats while it is on (another ten to thirty times.)
9. When dog is full, stop.
10. Run through the sequence more quickly another day. (It may take more than one day to get through the sequence at first.)
11. Move the grinder closer gradually and repeat on subsequent days.
12. When the dog will stand or lie on his side relaxed and also take treats when the grinder is running, then touch a toenail with the grinder, just tipping the nail and rewarding the dog as each toenail is finished. After the dog is happily allowing you to cut or grind his nails, you can eventually reduce the rewards to a treat for each completed paw.

It is possible to retrain a dog that has learned to fear having his nails done, but the drills have to be done in small increments and repeated over a much longer time. Retraining can take more than a month, while the initial training takes a few weeks. But the benefits last for a dog's entire lifetime. When Star Traveler was obviously going to grow into a hundred-pound dog, I was careful to teach him to like having his nails done. For the next ten years, whenever I got out a nail grinder, he would come to me and insist that I do his nails first.

HELPING THE SHY DOG: RINGO'S LESSON

The first genetically shy dog that I ever saw was a huge male German shepherd at a dog-training class. It was sad to see him try to crawl under a picnic table when he felt threatened. At least he was in the right place. Training can help the shy dog function in a world of strangers.

I raised greyhounds for twenty-five years before I bred my first shy one. Ringo was gorgeous and a beautiful mover, easily the prettiest male in the litter, but as he reached the age of three months, he started to back away from people. Everybody who had seen the puppies wanted Ringo, but once I realized that he was turning shy, I kept him. I had been training dogs for forty years and showing them for twenty-five years, and I like a challenge.

I hadn't anticipated just how much of a challenge it would be. When he was four months old, I started taking him to Jackie Root's Thursday morning obedience training practices. The other trainers were happy to give him treats while their own dogs were practicing sits and downs. I trained him in obedience. I took him to conformation classes. I did not show him as a puppy. You can't train in the show ring, and I didn't want him to display shyness in any situation where I couldn't reward him for nonshy behavior. We went for lots of walks where I could give Cheerios to strangers to give to Ringo. He learned to take treats from strangers.

I recruited other trainers to do show exams on him. One helpful older lady let me talk her through judging procedures for conformation. We were doing fine as she went through the hands-on exam, until I said, "Now you feel his testicles." There was a pause. She said slowly, "I . . . don't . . . think . . . so." It was very cute. I suddenly realized that she kept only female shelties and had never shown in breed. The fact that conformation judges routinely grope male dogs' testicles was news to her. Come to think of it, I haven't seen a lot of testicle exams on televised dog shows. They must edit those parts out.

By the time Ringo was eighteen months old, Jackie commented that he wasn't shy anymore. She said that he didn't look worried when she examined him, and that was true. But it didn't mean that he wasn't shy. What had happened was that she had stuffed so much turkey jerky into him that he no longer considered her a stranger. She had been accepted into his inner circle of friends. And he was never shy with his friends.

It seemed like a good time to start showing him. At first I entered him only under women judges at outdoor shows. Many dogs are shyer of men than of women. They can smell the testosterone on men. Then, at the shows, I started walking him around the indoor rings late in the day when the buildings were empty.

Ringo was a regular at Tanya's conformation classes. He had

learned to stand still for a judge's exam. But even when he kept all his feet in one place and didn't lean away, he looked at approaching judges like they were Jack the Ripper, and his expressive face transmitted that opinion to the

"He didn't look shy." Ringo with his sister Jirel. The stays, whether stand, sit, or down, are wonderful for letting you photograph dogs singlehandedly. There wasn't another person within miles of us in the High Sierras.

judges. They often responded by trying to help. They crouched down and approached slowly. What does it mean to a dog when another dog crouches low and approaches slowly? It means he is being stalked. From Ringo's point of view, the helpful judges were stalking him, which made him sure that they meant him harm.

What should you do when approaching a shy dog? Stand up straight, walk normally, offer the dog your hand, and examine the dog without putting your face nose to nose with the dog. Face-to-face confrontation is a threat in dog language.

At the shows, Ringo met Ron and Bev, who were showing their greyhound bitch, and he discovered that Bev routinely microwaved sliced hot dogs into treats, and that Ron always carried some of them. Ringo could be bought. He made friends with Ron and Bev. He liked their dried hot dogs so much that I tried to make some for him and managed to microwave them into miniature hockey pucks. But, with Ron as a male friend, he improved enough so that I started to enter him for male judges, and it went well. A male judge gave him Reserve at the Greyhound Club of America's western specialty. (But the next day's judge approached him wearing a hat, and he completely lost his composure.) After that, we did hat training. I trained him while wearing several different hats.

He was also trained in Novice obedience, where he learned to do the stand for examination. I could pose Ringo, stand six feet in front of him, and the judge would walk up to him and run her hands down his back. In his obedience career he failed the stand for exam only once, when a very tall male judge, wearing a hat, leaned over him.

One day I was shopping at a dog show booth owned by a very large man with a well-developed tummy. I had been talking to him for a while and Ringo became bored. He looked at me and then reached up and poked his muzzle into the man's paunch with a very definite push. Then Ringo looked at me to see if I had noticed. I fell all over myself praising him and giving him treats. It was the first time he had voluntarily touched a stranger.

Ever after that, if I was talking to spectators at a show and Ringo was feeling neglected, he would tag them with his nose and then look at me to see if I would reward him. I always did. And when I explained what he had done, the stranger would ask to see him do it again, so we got additional practice. By then I had put words to the trick, and he knew that "Touch a stranger" meant to tag a person in exchange for treats. He was pushing a lever to get treats, but the lever he was pushing was the stranger.

He occasionally reached up and tagged me to see if that would get him treats. I always said, "No, Ringo, touch a stranger." And he would then tag the stranger. He was just testing to see if it was the tag itself that was being rewarded or the fact that he was tagging strangers.

Ringo taught himself this trick. I suspect that it started with him nudging Ron to get his hot dog treats, and then he generalized it to strangers. It got him a lot of happy attention from strangers, which helped him. If you have a shy dog, this is easy to teach. It takes less than a half hour to teach a dog to touch a target like the end of a stick in exchange for treats. You touch the target to his nose and treat him half a dozen times while saying "Touch." Then you hold the target in front of him and say "Touch," so he reaches to touch the target. Once he is good at tagging the target, you place the target on a stranger's body and have the dog tag the person in exchange for rewards. When he knows "Touch a stranger," you eliminate the target.

The last step in Ringo's show career was to start showing him at indoor shows. When I took him to the huge and crowded Golden Gate benched show and he handled it well enough to be Winner's Dog, I thought of how far he had come from the shy puppy. He was still shy, but he had learned ways of handling his shyness. He was also, like many shy dogs, incredibly sweet with the people he liked.

Finally, Ringo beat several champions to finish his championship. I took him out of the ring and commented on how glad I was that he was finally finished. A spectator asked, "Why?" and I said, "Because he is shy, and showing him has been a challenge." And, bless her, she said, "He didn't look shy in the ring." It was the perfect finish to his show career.

Yes, he had finished his Championship, but would I breed him? Never. Hereditary shyness is just that, hereditary. For thousands of years dogs have been bred away from shyness, yet it still turns up occasionally. We don't need to encourage it. Enough shy dogs turn up from nonshy parents.

However, moderately shy dogs are often very affectionate with their owners. Ringo was a great pet and companion. I described him as being as "sweet as sugar," which was appropriate because he also had a major sweet tooth. He never met a doughnut he didn't like, or a peanut butter cookie, or ice cream. And when he was ten and a half years old, he started going back to dog shows to show in Rally.

I was showing the young dogs in Rally when I remembered how much Ringo had loved obedience and entered him a few times in Rally. He received the highest scores of any of my dogs. He seemed to enjoy his late in life visits to dog shows. And he still tagged strangers for treats.

3

Learning from the Past

Compulsive Versus Inducive Training, and B. F. Skinner

Most of the dogs enrolled in obedience classes are not there to be trained for trial competition. Neither are they there to be helped in rounding out their personalities. They are in class because the owner has discovered that he or she has a problem on the other end of the leash. Since he or she is more conscientious than the average dog owner (the average dog owner with a problem sends the dog to an animal shelter), the trainer-owner resorts to obedience training in an attempt to correct the problem.

What you find at many obedience classes is either an incentive-based training program or a series of corrections intended to redesign the dog's behavior. In most cases, these corrections were designed for use on problem dogs and were patterned on the knowledge gained from training of defense and police dogs. Many professional trainers spent a good deal of their time being paid by the only available large customer for their services: the armed forces. This creates a problem. In a defense-training program, large numbers of dogs have to be trained in the shortest possible time. Only a minority of dogs love to be corrected. These are masochists. The more they are corrected, the more they love their owners and the better they work.

If quite a few of the more normal dogs wash out under the training pressure, replacements are always available. Before the program even starts, the shy and less assertive dogs are culled. Training methods developed to train tough, aggressive dogs in minimum amounts of time do not work well on most dogs.

Food training (incentive training) never harmed any dog. Compulsive training has ruined many dogs by destroying their willingness to be trained. For a hundred years there has been a division between these two major camps of dog trainers. It took two world wars to create the division in training.

ENGLISH VERSUS GERMAN DOG TRAINING

World War I was the first great market for organized dog training. Both the English and the Germans established large dog-training programs to supply dogs to their troops. Each side developed techniques suited to the kinds of dogs they were training and to the kinds of work the dogs would be used for. The resulting training systems could not have been more different. The Germans based their training system on the use of compulsion. The English used food rewards and inducive-training techniques.

The opposing sides used different training methods in their war dog programs because both their dogs and their goals differed. The Germans were predominantly training sentry and patrol dogs, while most of the early English training was devoted to messenger dogs. Later in the war, the English started training watch and patrol dogs, but by then their training methods were established.

The Germans were training working breeds (mostly German shepherds) that had been bred for police and army use. These dogs had been selected and bred for generations to accept a lot of discipline without either defending themselves or giving up.

The English were training donated pet dogs in a wide variety of breeds and crossbreeds. They needed training methods that would work on dogs with a wide range of temperaments. The most commonly used breeds were Airedales, border collies, and lurchers. (A lurcher is a cross between a greyhound and another breed, usually a sheepdog.) A roll call of forty-eight students in the messenger service shows that half of them were made up of those three breeds, with the remainder a motley collection that included one Bedlington, two whippets, two setters, two spaniels, two Old English sheepdogs, four terriers, and a bloodhound. Turning this group into effective messenger dogs required different training techniques from those that were being applied to German war dogs.

Fortunately, the English and German training directors both wrote about their methods. On the German side we have Colonel Konrad Most. Most was a police commissioner who started training police dogs in 1906. At the outbreak of the war, he formed the Canine Service. Between wars he was head of the Canine Research Department of the Army High Command. He again organized war dogs for the Second World War and afterward he was head of the Experimental Institute for Armed Forces' Dogs as well as being principal of the North German Dog Farm. In 1910 he wrote *Training Dogs, a Manual,* which has been in print in a variety of languages ever since.

On the English side we have Lieutenant Colonel E. H. Richardson, commander of the British War Dog School in the Great War and the author of *War, Police and Watch Dogs, British War Dogs, Their Training and Psychology,* and *Watch Dogs: Their Training and Management.* Most of these books are old, rare, and available only in collectors' bookstores and large libraries. So, while Konrad Most is well known to this day, especially among the fanciers of German shepherd dogs, Richardson is a rare find.

Most's training was based on what he terms "compulsion." The dog is motivated to seek the cessation of pain. In Most's words, "Disagreeable experiences which we impose upon the dog for educational purposes are known as compulsion. . . . Agreeable experiences include the always abrupt arrest of compulsion the moment the dog shows the least sign of performing the service required."

He also warns that "training should take place from the beginning, not in a so-called training room, but in open country, at different and frequently changed places. In a training room a dog remains permanently in a state of intimidation because while there he is continually reminded of the compulsion he has undergone in that place in the past. The effect of such recollection is that the moment the dog enters the place he becomes apprehensive. His ability to learn is thus prejudiced and he can take no pleasure in the work." This is an interesting warning. An inducively trained dog also needs to be trained in a variety of locations because of his tendency to work *best* in his familiar training grounds. The inducive trainer has to work in new locations to make the dog as reliable when he is away from his home ground as when he is performing there.

The German dogs were not trained through the use of food for a simple reason. To poison proof the dogs, they were taught food refusal by the following method, "Food is held out to the dog, and as soon as he snaps or only merely sniffs at it he is given a smart blow." Once a dog has been trained to equate the offer of food with a blow, it is impossible to use food to motivate him.

Most had only one solution for a dog that objected to compulsion: "In the exceptional case in which the dog snarls at the trainer and a heavy cut with the switch does not stop him, a beating must follow. Such treatment will in such a case stimulate the submissive instinct. As in a pack of dogs, the order of hierarchy in a man and dog combination can only be established by physical force, that is by an actual struggle, in which the man is instantly victorious. Such a result can only be brought about by convincing the dog of the absolute physical superiority of the man."

This, however, is a technique that is inappropriate for the majority of American dog trainers, who happen to be women. It is both difficult and dangerous for a hundred-pound woman to try to convince a hundred-pound dog of her absolute physical superiority.

Colonel Richardson's philosophy was the opposite of Most's. Richardson writes, "What is really required is that the dog's intelligence should be trained. Most of its faults will arise in the first place from ignorance of the result of its actions, and of what is required of it. Gentleness of handling, therefore, is most important, otherwise the poor animal only becomes bewildered."

Richardson goes on, "The correct method of training is by reward and encouragement, and the tricks should be entered into as an amusing game. Under this aspect the dog will readily respond, and my own experience has been that such diversions have always been thoroughly enjoyed by both pupil and master. Some people imagine that the animal is starved beforehand, and performs under the goad of starvation. This is, of course, nonsense. Such cruelty may be practiced by stupid trainers, but is certainly not necessary, as a dog will learn to walk on its hind legs, turn somersaults, do sums, etc. etc., just after a hearty meal, for the sheer pleasure of entering into a game with its master, even without a reward; but no healthy, normal dog thinks lightly of ginger-snaps or a piece of sugar, and will do a good deal for either."

Richardson starts his training by teaching the basic down. "Teaching a dog to lie down, when told to do so, is a very useful method of disciplining. This lesson has a very settling effect on its character, and is the preliminary to many other lessons where obedience is required."

He continues: "The dog should be pressed down to the ground with the hand and held there till told to rise, and should then be rewarded with a tit-bit, and this lesson can be continued daily until it has learnt to lie down itself, at a word of command, and without being touched. Vary the length of time of lying down, and on no account over-do the lesson, so as to tire the dog and make it bored. Little and often is better. After a time teach it to remain lying down while the owner goes out of sight . . . Never forget the reward for good service, and never strike the dog, but indicate by the voice what is required."

Once the down has been mastered, the next step is to teach the come. Richardson advises: "The next thing is to teach it to answer the whistle or call. A good method of teaching this lesson quickly is to make a game of it. Let one person take the dog away and hold it while the owner whistles and calls to it. It can then be immediately released, and must be rewarded with a pat and a piece of biscuit on coming up. The next stage is for the dog to be held in leash out of sight of the master, but within sound of his voice, and to be released in the same manner. This exercise is to be repeated until the lesson is thoroughly learnt. It is one which will be entered into by the pupil with great zest.

"Unreasoning discipline, especially for young things is not desirable, and has a bad effect. This method is an excellent one to follow in the case of a dog with disobedient ways and bad habits. Simply checking such an animal and perhaps striking it does not really train it. What is required is to place a fresh impression in the dog's mind, and a new thought of approval, which is conveyed through the presentation of a little reward, will bring out a different attitude.

"This system of training by reward can be applied to various necessities. Thus if a puppy or young dog does not seem to be learning obedience very satisfactorily it can be called, and if it does not come, persist, until it does so. Then pat it and reward it with a tiny piece of biscuit. It will soon learn to associate obeying with its master's approval and something pleasant."

Richardson's graduates sent him testimonials to the effectiveness of his training program. Keeper Goodway reported: "The two are doing well, the black lurcher bitch especially. She is splendid, takes no notice of the guns or anything; they have both been running regularly day and night this last fortnight from advanced H.Q. to the rear. They used to do it in about seven or eight minutes, where it takes a man over half an hour. The officers think they are splendid, and I know they have sent in a good report. One thing I was rather afraid of was the runs at night, when there is generally more shelling, but it makes no difference; they run quite as well in the dark as the daylight."

Most and Richardson both have their disciples. You are likely to hear reminders of Konrad Most whenever you have contact with German shepherd fanciers. Electronic collars can also help you identify compulsive trainers, because they are strictly a compulsive training tool. The cessation of the shock (compulsion) is what the dog has been taught to seek.

WHEN COMPULSION HAS ITS USES

I don't have any difficulty in accepting the use of compulsion on dogs of those breeds that the Germans programmed to accept compulsive training. These are German-bred rottweilers, German shepherds, giant schnauzers, and Dobermans. But what the advocates of compulsion neglect to mention is that compulsion was developed for use on police dogs that had been bred for generations specifically to withstand it. It was never intended for use in the general dog population and it is inappropriate for use on the average pet dog. To be used effectively, it requires a dog with a high tolerance for discipline and a high pain threshold.

Now when I encounter particularly intense advocates of compulsion, I like to point out that they are still fighting the world wars. That they are fighting it on the side of the Germans. And that they lost.

B. F. SKINNER AND THE RISE OF OPERANT CONDITIONING

Because Richardson has been out of print for a long time, his disciples are often unaware of his existence. But his tradition of training with kindness and food was given a shot in the arm by B. F. Skinner. Skinner was a psychologist who never trained a dog. But he trained a lot of pigeons and rodents, and his research into the psychology of behavior and training resulted in the development of the science of behavior. Skinner gave scientific proof that food training works. He provided us with a whole new vocabulary of behavior that included things like primary and secondary reinforcers, behavior shaping, and operant conditioning. This is not light reading, but it was the basis for the explosion in marine mammal training in wildlife parks.

Early marine mammal keepers were biologists, so they were more likely to know of Skinner's works than Most's. Besides, it is impractical to apply compulsion to a killer whale. So they trained everything from porpoises to tigers through behavior modification and inducive methods. Karen Pryor wrote accounts of their training methods in *Lads Before the Wind.* She later wrote *Don't Shoot the Dog!* for dog trainers, but I prefer *Lads* as the more thoughtful training book. In the 1990s, the most eloquent spokesperson for inducive training was Dr. Ian Dunbar, who was a popular seminar speaker in the United States before he became host of a television series on training in England.

4

Understanding Your Dog's Personality

We Love Dogs for Their Personalities

WHY DOES PERSONALITY MATTER?

What makes us fall in love with individual dogs? Animal shelters are filled with cast-off dogs, so what makes a single dog so special that we remember him fondly for a lifetime and grieve over his loss for years? What is the special bond that forms in the best relationships between a dog and his person? What lets you look into the eyes of a dog and find a soul mate: a dog whose personality fits your personality so well that it is as if he has been created for you? (Kathy Leyba said that "Slick fit into my life like the missing piece of a puzzle.") And when that happens, the fifteen years of a dog's life span will not be long enough. Even fifteen years of perfect love is not enough. Dogs teach us about love, but their short life span means that they also teach us about loss and the need to find love again. The best thing about dogs is that it is possible to find love again, especially if we know what we are looking for.

Children are better at this than most adults. Most children know that they are looking for a dog that is really a friend and playmate. Adults get misled by the books that describe dog breeds and try to give guidelines to fit those breeds

Children understand that what matters about dogs is the love they give us. This is Angel McClendon holding Twist.

to the reader's lifestyle, housing, age, and interests. But they miss the point. And often people who buy a dog based on its appearance are disappointed when they later discover that they can't stand the inner dog that goes with those outward good looks.

In the old days, a person buying a dog was looking for working ability. He or she wanted a pointer that could point, a sheepdog that could herd, a sled dog that could pull, or a greyhound that could hunt. But working dogs have become rare. Now prospective dog owners want dogs that fit their personality. We want a dog with which we can have a significant emotional relationship for a decade and a half. Or, in the case of a family dog, we want a dog with which the kids can have a significant emotional relationship. In this age of divorce and single-parent families, the dog may be the child's second strongest emotional attachment (after the parent he or she lives with), so when I see parents dispose of a child's dog as inconvenient, it makes me cringe.

HOW TO FIND A DOG TO MATCH YOUR PERSONALITY

Beware of Puppy Charm

How do we find a dog with the temperament that we need? First, it is a mistake to look at puppies. Puppies have their personality buried in their puppy charm. Many of the behavioral and physical

Raye Lynn at a dog show with Starlite and T.G.

traits of adult dogs are those of wolf cubs. The dog is basically a wolf that was never allowed to grow up. When wolves evolved into dogs, the ones that behaved like puppies the longest were the ones that could live with people the longest and thus were the ones most likely to reproduce. So dogs have been selected for immature wolf behavior for as long as they have been domesticated. This is another reason that animal shelters are full of eleven-month-old dogs that have outgrown their puppy charm. And it is the reason why the pet store in your mall has cages full of young puppies. The store owner is hoping that they can charm you into buying them before they lose their adorable puppiness.

If looking at puppies is not the way to find a soul mate, what is? Actually a lot of people fall into the best solution by accident. I did.

Linda Transhel with two litters of puppies. Tiger's puppies interacted with visitors more and stayed with them longer than the other litter's puppies. Temperament is hereditary.

The best way to find a breed that suits you is to find an individual dog that suits you. Then look at members of the same breed for the individual personality that fits into your life. If you ask folks who are happy with their dog how they happened to select that breed, many of them will say that they had a dog of that breed as a child, or a friend of theirs had a dog of that breed that they admired. This is how I found greyhounds.

I had the perfect collie as a teenager and practiced my training skills on him. He looked like Lassie, and was an intelligent, good-hearted dog, but when he died at twelve, I had brushed all the long hair that I ever cared to see. My next dog would have a short coat. Then I went to a party and met a whippet named Amanda and her daughter Fauna. Amanda and I communed on her cushion near the woodstove, and I found her delightful. I wanted a dog with her personality. But I had always preferred large dogs. That made me want a bigger dog with her personality. And the larger version of a whippet is a greyhound.

At this point I had never seen a greyhound, but I was rescuing collies at my local shelter. Within a few months they had a middle-aged male greyhound. The day before he was to be put down, he went home with me and stayed for eight years. I had thought that my collie was smart and sweet, but that first greyhound was nearly human. Traveler was incredibly intelligent, gentlemanly, worldly, charming, and courtly. He was as good a sales dog for his breed as the whippet had been for hers. He even won over my mother, who had never owned a dog in her life and considered them health hazards. When I came home from work one day and found him lying near her on a bath mat in the kitchen, I knew that he had raised charm to new levels.

Hereditary Personality

Thirty years ago, I believed that I was a good enough trainer to create a puppy's personality. But five generations of breeding down from the original Tiger have taught me that at least 90 percent of personality is hardwired into the puppies' brain before they are born. The charming personalities of Tiger's descendants owed far more to his genes than to my training.

There are three kinds of inherited personality in dogs: breed personality, gender personality, and individual personality.

Breed Personality: Each breed has its own personality. Shelties are temperamentally different from greyhounds or golden retrievers. We like certain breeds because we like the general personality of that breed. How is breed personality formed? It is formed by the work that the breed was expected to do when it was created.

I will use greyhounds as an example of the development of breed personality, but a similar account could be written about every breed.

Greyhound minds and bodies were created by coursing, by the need to pursue game at high speeds through open country. The speed required for successful coursing developed the sight hounds as the ultimate athlete, a streamlined, light-boned, heavily muscled dog with greater heart and lung capacity than the average dog. It also formed their personality.

Intelligence

It takes a fast mind to control a fast body. The greyhounds' speed made it necessary for them to be quick thinkers. They needed to be

Chris running at greyhound speed. Greyhounds are the fastest breed of dog because they can expend more energy in a few minutes than other breeds can.

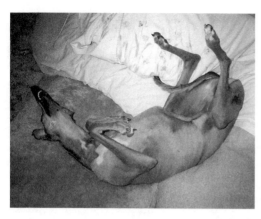

Then they lie around with their feet up, storing up energy for the next day's run. This makes them popular pets.

able to run through rough terrain at forty miles an hour without breaking a leg or running into a tree. In order to keep game in sight, a greyhound has to be able to process a great deal of information very quickly. He has to keep track of the quarry, avoid the field hazards, and cooperate with another dog to outflank and pull down the prey animal. There isn't time for a mistake.

The heart of their independence is their need to make decisions on their own initiative. They don't look to you to make their decisions because, when they are running, they can't. This enables them, when somebody tries to force-train them, to decide that they will not participate in an activity that they find unpleasant.

Aggression Levels

What about aggression levels? In competitive coursing, it was common for English gentlemen to place sizable bets on who had the better coursing dog. To resolve the bet, the two dogs would be judged together in pursuit of a hare. If either dog made an aggressive move toward the other dog, it forfeited the course and generally would be killed for its misbehavior.

That doesn't mean that greyhounds never fight. All dogs will contest pack rankings with each other and with their owners. But the different breeds challenge for rank with varying degrees of frequency and intensity.

Denise Nelson with Fury. A border collie's energy can be channeled into obedience. Heeling is a lot like herding.

The Influence of Racing on Temperament

After coursing had created intelligent, independent greyhounds with low aggression levels, greyhound racing came along in the 1920s and it modified greyhound temperament. Racing dogs live in very close quarters. At a typical racing kennel, they are crated in large boxes. They are turned out in exercise paddocks every four hours in batches of several dozen, and they wear kennel muzzles to prevent disagreements among the dogs.

This is a highly restricted lifestyle and a nervous dog is not going to tolerate it well. If a racing greyhound cannot stay within one pound of his racing weight, then he is not eligible to race until his weight is stabilized again. Nervous dogs, demanding dogs, aggressive dogs, and fretful dogs could not hold their weight and were not bred. So the last eighty years of racing have had the effect of selecting racing dogs for relatively undemanding temperaments. An acquaintance who breeds both racing and show greyhounds said that the show dogs are more demanding and attention seeking than the racers.

There is one quality in the greyhound personality that coursing and racing did not account for. That is the intensity with which they are devoted to people. Ex-racers have lived as kennel dogs with just enough human contact to keep them socialized. When they find themselves in a pet home, they bond quickly to their new owners and react with intense affection. They know the meaning of gratitude.

A similar account could be written for the personality development of every breed. The requirements of the work they did formed both the bodies and the personalities of the breeds.

Even Related Breeds Have Different Personalities

There are personality differences even among breeds that were created to perform similar work. The herding breeds have the greatest range of temperament. A border collie is nothing like a collie or a Belgian Malinois. In the sporting dogs, the biggest differences in temperament are those among the highly trainable retrievers, the independent pointers, the more biddable setters, and the more excitable spaniels. But even within each of those subgroups, there are individual breed differences. Each breed has its own limited gene pool, and those genes affect not only the dog's appearance but also its breed temperament.

Breed Personality Can Change Over Time

Now that many breeds are selected for companionship, instead of for their original work, breeders can select for different temperaments. Sometimes this is an improvement. Sometimes it is not. Fifty years ago, cocker spaniels were calm, reasonable family dogs with relatively short coats. In five decades, show breeders have changed them into excitable piles of fur. I loved the old-fashioned cockers.

The German protection breeds like rottweilers and German shepherds that were first imported into this country had very hard temperaments. They were originally bred to be professional police dogs, but in this country they have been bred to be more user friendly, so that they can fit into American family life.

The Division Into Show and Field Dogs

When breed personality and body type change over time, a breed often splits into one group of working dogs and another group of much different show dogs. Sometimes the breed registries are split so that the two types of dog can no longer be bred to each other to produce registered puppies. The setters and retrievers have had the most dramatic split between their working and show dogs.

Gender Personality: Dogs and bitches are not the same. How they differ varies from breed to breed. In the German working breeds, the males are generally more aggressive and dominant than the bitches. In greyhounds, the girls tend to be smart and demanding while the boys are more relaxed and gentlemanly.

My longtime optometrist owned a succession of male Bouvier des Flandres. Then a time came when he chose a puppy from a litter that was all female, so he bought his first Bouvier bitch. He was astonished at the difference between his previous boys and the new bitch. Bitches tend to be smart and, well, bitchy.

The best male greyhounds are gentlemanly and chivalrous. When people say they want to do obedience with a greyhound, I recommend that they look for a small male. Small, because the jumping of advanced obedience is easier on a small dog, and male because most males want to please their owners and take good-naturedly to obedience training. The girls learn faster, but they get bored easily and they want you to make the work worth their while. They want to know what is in it for them.

Individual Personality: Every single dog has a distinctly individual personality. So in one litter, you can have a bold puppy, a shy puppy, an alpha bitch, a thoughtful puppy, and any other combination of personality traits. Once you have chosen a breed and a gender, how do you choose from a litter of active puppies?

If you are dealing with a breeder who knows her breed well, your best choice would be to tell her the kind of personality you are looking for and let her tell you which puppies would be a good choice. The best skill that a responsible breeder can have is the ability to match each puppy to a home that will appreciate its personality type. That means that she has to observe the puppies enough to know their individual personalities and know enough about dog behavior to recognize personality traits.

While no two puppies in a litter will have exactly the same personality, there are common variations in basic personality that turn up again and again. These are the charismatic dog, the comedian/humorist, the organizer, the sweetheart, the sovereign, the calm dog, the nervous dog, the shy dog, and the thinker.

The Charismatic Dog

Often a male greyhound turns up that simply oozes charm. Christopher was such a dog. He was handsome and he knew it. He loved going from person to person in a crowd, allowing each one to pet and admire him while he was already eyeing his next admirer. My sister said of Christopher that he had the kind of charismatic personality that the best actors had. I often thought of him as the canine equivalent of Errol Flynn. Years later, big, black Lancelot, who was Chris's younger brother, became the resident charmer. He had Chris's trick of working a crowd, picking out his next admirer and making eye contact while the current person is still petting him. In the human world, these would be the movie stars, models, gigolos, and lady killers. In a dog, that level of charisma is entertaining and amusing. It also makes them very popular with strangers on the street.

The Comedian

Beth Anne asked me why I described some of my dogs as having a sense of humor. I could understand her bafflement: I knew her dogs, and none of them had a sense of humor. It is a quality that has to be seen to be understood. These dogs deliberately do something ridiculous and then look at you expectantly to see if you got the joke. Their facial expressions are exuberant and happy. Tiger Jr. rolled his eyes and mugged for his audience as successfully as Michael J. Fox did in *Back to the Future*.

When we were at his first obedience trial, a longtime dog judge broke out laughing at Tiger's body mannerisms and facial expression. She said that he was plainly a dog that got a lot of fun out of life. And she was right.

To dogs with a sense of humor, the world is an amusing place. Star would come sailing past me in the kitchen, carrying an alarm clock. Her mother used to accompany other dogs to the kitchen to steal butter cubes and come out with a metal fork as her prize. These dogs see the world differently and derive great amusement from it.

The Organizer

Littermates can have very different personalities. Star was a comedian, but her sister Sheena had no sense of humor at all. To Sheena, the world was a very serious place and it was up to her to keep everything in order. It was a task that she took on with formidable intensity. I wanted to say, "Hey, Sheena, lighten up." But she was devoted to organization. She was the last dog to climb into bed at night. If she came to bed and found that her sister or brother was still on the daybed in the living room, she would go back to the living room and herd him or her into the bedroom so they would all be in their designated places before she crawled under the covers.

Sheena's behavior was not unique. When Sheila and Glen and Sheena's half sister, Arriba, were houseguests, I met another organizer. At about ten P.M., Arriba trotted into the guest room and then back to the living room, where she looked at her owners and barked once, sharply. I asked what that was about. Sheila said that Arriba wanted them to go to bed, so that she could go to bed too. She wanted her people in bed before she settled down.

The Sweetheart

These are the romance novelists of dogs. While most greyhounds are demonstrative, these are exceptionally loving. They love you, and their entire goal in life is to get you to love them back. In a way these are the feminine equivalent of the charismatic males. These girls flirt, charm, and work hard to please you. All of this makes them easy to live with and popular with the public.

The Sovereign

Dog trainers in Germany idolize a character in dogs that they call "sovereignty." This dog owns the ground he walks on and assumes without question that he is the leader of whatever pack he finds himself in. He truly fears nothing. It is not a common trait in greyhounds, but does exist.

When we were evaluating for adoption the nineteen greyhounds that had spent a year as potential research dogs at the University of California, the veterinarian in charge warned us about Mr. T because he had been grabbing the kennel help. We checked his ear tattoos and, when we turned to leave, he gently took Susan by the elbow and held her to keep her from leaving. We both laughed. Mr. T was extremely alpha but not vicious. He wasn't biting aggressively. He was trying to show her that he didn't want her to leave. He went to a home with an old, blind boxer male that idolized him, and in a short time he organized the family's life, including their teenagers. The main trait of dogs with sovereignty is that they are absolutely fearless. Given the chance, they may also decide to dominate their owner.

The Calm Dog

My first greyhound was exceedingly calm. Traveler went through life with optimistic thoughtfulness. Nothing upset him. Golden retrievers are popular because they are calm. It is a great personality to live with. The dog's calmness has a calming effect on the owner. When a group of young hippies asked if they could take Traveler with them to a hot springs for the afternoon, I let them take him. I knew that he would not get into trouble because he never got into trouble. He observed the world and made reasonable decisions about what he should do. Everyone had a fine time at the hot springs and they happily returned him that evening. I can't imagine agreeing to let them take any other dog that I have owned.

The Nervous Dog

The opposite of the calm dog is the nervous dog. Contrary to popular opinion, the nervous dog is not usually created by abusive upbringing. It is a hereditary condition where the dog's body dumps too much adrenaline into his system when he is stressed. His body is overreacting to stimuli. Some people make the mistake of breeding a nervous dog to an aggressive dog, thinking that the two qualities will average out into one normal dog. They think that the range of temperament has the fearful dog on one end and the aggressive dog on the opposite end, with the normal dog in the middle. But that is not true.

Fearful dogs and aggressive dogs are both overreacting to stimuli. The actual scale of temperament has the fearful and aggressive dogs grouped together on one end as overreactors. On the other end of the temperament scale is the calm, unreactive, sensible dog. So when a fearful dog is mistakenly bred to an aggressive dog, the degree of overreaction to stimuli is increased. If overreactors need to be bred at all, they should be bred to exceedingly calm dogs.

The Shy Dog

Akin to the nervous dog is the shy one. Worried dogs fear the world in general. Shy ones worry only about people. This is simply a throwback to wolf cub behavior. Wolf cubs have to bond to their pack mates before they are four months old. After that age, anyone they meet is considered a dangerous stranger and is avoided. Some dogs inherit the wolf trait of fearing strangers once the cub is past the bonding age. Often puppies don't appear to be shy when they are in their bonding stage, and the shyness shows up only when they grow older. This leads folks to say it was poor upbringing that caused the shyness, but it isn't. It is the combination of genes and maturity. Shyness can range from extreme to moderate. When you are socializing a group of dogs in a crowd, the moderately shy dog will move behind you, while the braver siblings advance to meet the strangers. (For help with a shy dog, see page 59.)

The Thinker

Sunny was a cerebral, thoughtful dog. She was affectionate without clinging. She considered herself my friend and equal. She analyzed life and acted on the results of her analysis. She wasn't interested in striving with the other dogs for pack status. She was one of the most rational, intelligent dogs I have ever met.

After she had done years of lure and open field coursing, I thought she might like to try oval track racing. We went to a greyhound training track. The lure was attached to a steel cable that ran along the inside rail of the track. The cable was driven from a derelict auto with the cable attached where its rear axle should be. Sunny watched several sets of dogs run before it was her turn. Then the operator had me release her.

She took off running down the straight, but when the lure went out of sight around the turn, she slid to a halt. The operator told me to release her at the turn. Sunny was dancing around and having a fine time. I caught her and held her on the corner as they brought the lure around to us. She looked up and down the track in both directions. When I slipped her, she immediately ran to the rail and turned left, watching the moving cable above her and running the reverse of its direction. She had neatly deduced that the lure was traveling a circle and the quickest way to catch it was to meet it head-on. The operator cut the power—had she succeeded in meeting it, she could have been badly hurt. I laughed at one more demonstration of Sunny's reasoning ability and took her home.

Socialization

Most dog books warn you against getting a puppy that has not been extensively socialized. Socialization means exposing the puppy to a wide range of people, environments, and experiences while he is less than twelve weeks old. Much bad adult dog behavior is blamed on lack of early socialization. But that brings up an interesting question. How do thousands of retired racing greyhounds move into pet homes without a backward glance?

Nobody intentionally socializes greyhounds as puppies. Yes, people take care of the litter, but after they are weaned, they are raised in huge paddocks with their littermates. That gives them room to establish their pack hierarchy though running games. When they are about a year old, they start race training.

Their unusual upbringing produces dogs that are able to bond quickly and firmly to their new owners. It is amazing to see retired racers that have never lived in a house move into a home and adopt a new family as their own. Bringing a newly retired racer home is like hosting a visitor from another planet. Everything is strange to him: stairs, couches, houseplants, other pets. The newly adopted racer is plainly astonished at everyday household routines, but he quickly figures out that couches are softer than floors to sleep on and that a real family is preferable to kennel help. This is a breed that wants to sleep not only in the same room with you but in the same bed.

How do they do this when nobody sets out to socialize them? They learn their basic behaviors from their mother and their littermates. They are the only breed of dog that gets to grow up in family groups.

When we separate puppies from their mother and littermates at eight weeks of age, we then need to provide all the training that mom and the siblings would have provided. (See Puppy Training on page 21.)

Inherited Behaviors

In addition to personality traits, dogs can inherit certain behaviors.

Play Styles: Dog play is based on either universal puppy play or the work that a breed is bred to do. Herding dogs love to herd. Retrievers love to retrieve. Sight hounds love to chase. They all like to play games that use their working instincts. Basic puppy play that is common to all the breeds includes wrestling, stalking, chasing, tug-of-war and keep away,

Prey Drive: Hunting dogs have a fairly wide range of prey responses. If a small animal runs, the average greyhound is going to chase it. While many sight hounds and sporting dogs can be taught to live peacefully with cats, rabbits, and small dogs, it is a good idea always to remember that there are several thousand years of selection behind those breeds for the drive to pursue and bring down prey. Individual owners and dogs can overcome that, but it never goes away. It is part of what makes the hunting dogs what they are. Don't leave a small, vulnerable animal alone with a large, predatory, dog. The same applies to infants. One of the most tragic types of dog attacks are those where a dog mistakes his owner's new infant for a small prey animal. Babies are about the right size for prey. They make a lot of distressed noises. And they squeak when you squeeze them. Do not put your baby on the floor with a dog.

Talking: Talking is a vocalization that is neither barking nor whining. Dogs that are talking sound like they are trying to imitate human speech. They use a wide variety of tones, broken into what sound like syllables. When a dog is getting ready to talk, he puts a lot of effort into arranging his lips and mouth in the required position. I have no idea what function talking serves. Some dogs do it naturally. Betty Lou taught her dogs to talk on cue. In order to do this, she selected puppies that talked naturally when they were still with their litter.

Johnny Carson's television show featured a "singing dog" contest. Most of the dogs howled. Sheba Meadow was a dog that talked a lot.

*Beth Anne and John
Gordon with Shadow
and Beauty. Shadow
couldn't resist smiling
for the camera.*

She qualified at the audition and was chosen to be the lead-off contestant. Betty Lou decided to introduce her by having her sit and offer to shake hands with Johnny.

She had not counted on Sheba's love of hamming it up in front of an audience. Sheba grinned at the audience, towed Betty Lou across the stage, and greeted Johnny by nosing him firmly in the inseam, giving him a chance to respond with one of his famous double takes for the camera. I have known several greyhounds who were notorious crotch greeters, but Sheba had never done it before and would never do it again. With a star's flawless timing, she picked her moment.

During one of Tiger's adventures as a sire, the bitch participated in a backyard mating and then trotted inside to where her owner was sitting at the kitchen table. She sat down in front of her owner and proceeded to talk earnestly to him for five minutes. It sounded like she was giving him an account of the events out in the yard. She had amazing vocal range. When she was through, I asked him if she talked often and he said that he had never heard her talk before. Perhaps it was the first time that she had anything worth telling him.

Smiling: Smiling is a partly inherited, partly learned behavior in which a happy dog lifts his upper lips and shows his teeth. It is easy to mistake it for snarling. The first smiling dog I saw was a greyhound with a litter of puppies that I was puppy sitting for. After a few visits, Mimi took to greeting me with all her teeth bared. Since she had puppies to defend, I was properly respectful. After a week, she met me at the gate, plainly delighted to see me, wiggling with joy and showing every tooth in a wide ivory grin. I had never heard of genetic smiling, but I no longer mistook her toothy grin for a threat. It was obviously a greeting.

So how do you tell if all those teeth are a threat or a greeting? Look past the teeth at the rest of the dog. Is he bouncing up and down with a wagging tail, happy to see you? Or is he backing up the tooth display with a growl and raised hackles to let you know he is serious? When in doubt, ask the owner.

Smiling dogs can be intimidating to the general public. Betty Lou lived in a tough section of town because the landlords there allowed dogs. But with Sheba smiling in her front yard, nobody came into her house uninvited.

The original Tiger did not smile and most of his children did not carry the trait. But his daughter, Star, not only had a sense of humor, she was both a talker and a smiler. If your dog tends to smile when he is happy, you can encourage him by showing your own teeth. The smilers learn to smile back. I always warned visitors that Star would be smiling at them and not to mistake her toothy grin for snarling.

Response to Training: In their responsiveness to training, border collies have a huge advantage. Working sheep has to be done under the precise direction of the shepherd. Herding breeds are genetically programmed to pay attention to commands. They do it very well.

Charlene Vincent with her three utility dogs: Eureka, Caboose, and BillyJoe. Any breed is trainable. Some breeds just require more ingenuity than others.

Greyhounds, on the other hand, have to be able to make decisions on their own initiative, which is the heart of their independence. They don't look to you to make their decisions because, when they are running, they can't.

Other breeds vary between being highly trainable and wanting to know what is in it for them. But if you make it worth the dog's effort, any dog is trainable.

Aggression Levels: Aggression levels vary both for different breeds and different individuals. Some dogs are far more likely to bite you than others. When I moved back to Sacramento in the 1980s, the pit bull craze had struck. They were everywhere. I occasionally met a pit bull out for a walk with his tattooed owner, and the owner would say, "Hey, lady, you want to have your dog fight mine?" I would explain that for two hundred years, his dog's ancestors had been selected for fighting, and those that wouldn't fight had been killed. But during that same time, greyhounds that would fight in the presence of game had been killed and the ones that would rather chase than fight had been bred. This usually sent the pit bull owners away happy.

Protective Behavior: There is a whole range of protective behavior, from dogs that will invite Jack the Ripper into your parlor and show him your jewelry, to dogs that can put on a formidable threat display, to dogs that actually attack strangers. Threat displays are also learned behavior, so once you have a dog that barks at strangers, he will pass that behavior on to succeeding generations of dogs.

Some greyhounds have no interest in barking at strangers. Then there are ones that can put on an impressive threat display. Sheena was one of these. I have a large window in the living room and she loved to stand on the daybed, stick her head through the drapes, and warn off intruders. I wouldn't try to walk past a dog that looked as threatening as she did. And her sister and brother tended to back her up.

One day I flew home from New York. This was before the flight restrictions that followed the 9/11 attacks, so the airport authorities made me check my pocket knife instead of confiscating it, and it arrived the day after I did. I was trying to catch up on my sleep when Sheena put on one of her best threat displays at the window. An airline employee was walking across the front lawn to deliver the wayward knife. I whistled the dogs into my bedroom, and all but Sheena came. She knew that if she went into the bedroom, she would miss her chance to meet the delivery man. I decided to let her come to the door while I reached around the screen to take the knife. She had stopped barking and was standing behind me. I opened the door and reached an arm around the screen. Quick as a snake, Sheena stepped in front of me, reached her long neck around the screen door—and kissed the man on the hand. Only seconds before she had been screaming threats at him through the window. I called her a fake, and she looked pleased with herself.

Her reaction is not unusual. One night around midnight I was dozing in the living room when a loud crash woke me. It was followed by the sound of lots of voices. I went outside to find that a huge teenager had run his car into an oversized power pole. He had been on a beer run for a nearby party, and the whole party group was now standing on my front lawn looking at the car and trying to decide what to do. I asked if the driver was hurt and was told that he wasn't, so I suggested that they get the car towed away before the police came. The driver asked if he could phone his folks.

I had him follow me to the house, intending to leave him on the front porch and hand him the phone. But when I picked up the phone and turned back toward the door, I saw that he had followed me into the house. He was standing in the living room, surrounded by greyhounds that were licking his bare knees. He was so upset about his car that he didn't even notice the dogs. He made his call, went back outside, and soon his parents arrived. Dad was even bigger than the son. I was impressed. The dogs were entertained. There is nothing like having an enormous distraught stranger come into the living room at midnight.

I don't know how dogs can tell when an intruder is or isn't a threat. On three occasions during his life, Chris, who loved people, warned off people who were approaching me. He did this before I had seen them, so he couldn't have taken his cue from me. In each case he was right. They were people I was glad to have warned off.

On the other hand, I was once escorting a young air conditioner repairman into the main yard, thinking that I had secured all the dogs. Chris bounced against his gate and it opened, allowing him to charge toward us at greyhound speed. I was standing close behind the young man and could hear him suck in his breath as he halted, but there was no time to intervene. It gets all your attention to have a hundred-pound dog approaching you at thirty miles per hour. Chris cleared the steps to the patio in a bound, veered slightly around us without slowing down, and gave us a quick smile as he passed. He leaped through the dog door and went directly to the couch in the living room. We found him waiting there after we had taken care of the air conditioner. The service man turned out to be quite fond of dogs.

There is a wide variation among the breeds and individuals as to how protective each one is. And this doesn't really correspond to aggression. Even nonaggressive dogs can be protective. In terms of dog bites, the safest dog to have is a nonaggressive dog that will protect. When people buy an aggressive dog for protection, what they really need is protection from lawsuits when the dog bites someone who is not a threat. (Or who even bites someone who is a threat.)

Lady was a twenty-six-inch, sixty-three-pound girl who was a talented lure courser. When she was five years old she went to a home where she could be the only dog. A nice-looking young woman adopted her, and when I drove by a few weeks later to see how things were working out, Lady was pleased to see me but plainly thought

she belonged with her owner back inside her house. She didn't want
to hurt my feelings, but she was just fine, thank you. What made me
a little concerned was the half dozen motorcycle fanciers working on
bikes in the garage, but I know bikers can love dogs too.

Then I received a phone call from the new owner saying that Lady
had threatened her boyfriend. I was dumbfounded because Lady had
always been a total cream puff. She had never challenged anyone, dog
or human, in her entire life. I could do anything with her without
protest and so could every kennel mate she had ever lived with. I
asked if they wanted to bring her back and the young woman said
no, she really didn't want to.

Another week passed and the phone rang late at night with the
owner almost in tears, saying she had to bring Lady back right now
because she was afraid her boyfriend would kill her. I didn't quibble.
All Tiger's kids are welcome home, and Lady was a special favorite,
because a sweeter dog never lived. But I was curious and asked for de-
tails of what had happened. It turned out that the boyfriend had been
out of town when the young woman got Lady and he had not returned for two weeks.

During that time, the new owner and Lady became friends.
When the boyfriend moved back in, Lady had taken to growling at
him. I couldn't have been more surprised if they had said she had
turned into a werewolf. But by the time the young woman and Lady
arrived, I thought I had the answer to the mystery, or at least the right
question to ask: "He is violent, isn't he? He abuses you physically?"
And she said in almost a whisper, "Yes."

So that was the answer to the puzzle. Lady was trying to protect
her newly bonded mistress, and the miracle is that a small pacifist
dog could stand off, even temporarily, a large, violent man. That was
also why the woman didn't want to return Lady. Long after she had
given up defending herself, Lady was trying to do it for her. I wished
her luck. She would need it. She would have been smarter to keep the

dog and dispose of the abuser. Lady moved back in, finished her Field Championship, charmed her way into my bedroom, and appointed herself the willing puppy sitter for her younger half brothers and sisters. She played with them endlessly and patiently. Sometimes I wonder how the young woman is doing.

5

Preventing Dog Bites

Dominance, Fear Biting, and Pack Leadership

FIVE RULES TO KEEP YOUR CHILDREN FROM BEING BITTEN

To keep your child from being bitten by strange dogs there are a few rules to teach the child.

1. Do not approach a dog that doesn't have an owner with it.
2. If a big dog approaches you without an owner, try to put a gate or door between you and the dog.
3. Never scream and run from a dog.
4. If you want to pet a dog that is with its owner, ASK if you can pet the dog before you touch it. My parents taught this rule to me and reminded me of it every time their dog-crazy daughter asked if she could pet a passing dog.
5. This rule applies to your own dog: If your dog shows signs of wanting to discipline your child as if the child were a puppy, you have a perfect right as his pack leader to tell him that is not acceptable behavior. It is a pack leader's *right and duty* to intervene in fights between his pack members. I once accidentally kenneled together two bitches who hated each other. When I realized

what I had done and called them out of their giant dog house an hour later, they emerged accompanied by Tiger. They were all perfectly calm. Why hadn't the girls fought? Because Tiger was their pack leader and he wouldn't let them fight in his presence. He would simply shoulder between them and discuss it with them. If you can't do this because your dog doesn't consider you his pack leader, move to the section on regaining pack leadership.

WHEN IS A DOG BITE NOT AN ATTACK?

Everybody knows what a dog bite is, right? The usual definition of a bite is any tooth-skin contact that breaks the skin, but is that correct? What if a dog pinches and bruises you with his teeth but does not break the skin? What if you cut yourself on your dog's teeth while playing with him, when he had no intention of closing his mouth? To health agencies the important part is whether the skin was broken. To dog owners and dog trainers, the important part is the dog's intention.

Why the difference? Health officials are concerned that diseases like rabies can be transmitted through a break in the skin. Animal trainers are concerned about whether the dog is likely to attack a

person in the future, so they need to know what the dog's intentions were. Is the dog an uninhibited biter?

Dogs play with their teeth. This is Jade and Taupe doing what I call "tooth wrestling."

Is he one of the many types of inhibited biters? Or was there even a bite at all?

The majority of reported dog bites are not all-out attacks but are inhibited discipline strikes. It is easy to tell the difference by the amount of damage that is done. An all-out attack by a medium to large dog will cause major lacerations. Discipline strikes cause small tooth marks.

Uninhibited bites are the darlings of the news media. They are the all-out, full-strength attacks. They are often very serious and can be fatal. And they are extremely rare, which is fortunate, because they give a graphic demonstration of just how much damage our domesticated wolves can do to anything as soft skinned as a human being. An encounter with an uninhibited biter can make a person appreciate how much we trust our dogs never to use their full strength. If dogs did not routinely restrain their bites, nobody would want to live with them.

INHIBITED BITES

The vast majority of dog bites are inhibited, which means that the dog is using less than his full strength. Inhibited bites are usually either discipline strikes or play holds. And a fair number of bites are not bites at all—they are normal dog activities that are mistaken for bites.

Annie and her puppies had a bedroom all to themselves, with a low barrier that allowed the other dogs to visit. Annie was an experienced mother and rarely disciplined her puppies until they cut their puppy teeth.

Puppy teeth appear when the puppy is three weeks old. They are replaced by adult teeth at the age of four months. When the puppy teeth first come in, they completely fill the tiny puppy jaws. But puppies grow fast. By the time the big adult teeth start to appear, the jaw has grown enough to leave huge gaps between the puppy teeth. In

Brother and sister, Chris and Love, playing toothy games.

order for the first teeth to fit into the three-week-old mouth and give the puppy the tearing power it needs to eat when it is young, those puppy teeth are as sharp as needles. And this creates a problem for their mother.

When Annie's puppies wanted to nurse with mouths full of little needles, Annie did a good deal of disciplining of any that bit down too hard. The puppies quickly learned that if they wanted to keep nursing, they had better not bite down. That was their first lesson in how to inhibit the strength of their bites. They learned precisely how hard they could bite before Annie would react. When they were larger and started to play with each other, that training was continued by their littermates.

Instead of pushing, grabbing, and wrestling like children do, puppies nip and tag each other with their teeth and play a game that I call "tooth wrestling." They take turns gently biting each other's muzzle. Adults also tooth wrestle with their friends, but they are even more careful not to bite hard.

When Annie felt like playing with the puppies, she bowed down on

Chris is hugging Love to keep her teeth away from his throat.

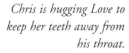

her elbows and pinned them to the ground by taking their entire head in her mouth. They loved it and she was very gentle with them. When they played with each other, sometimes one would forget the lesson about biting gently. Then his playmate would scream and go off in a huff and refuse to play anymore. That reminded the biter that he should not be so rough, because now he had nobody to play with.

The adult teeth are much blunter, so a puppy with adult teeth could bite harder. But the puppy has learned just how much strength it is okay to use. Most dogs go through their entire lives limiting their bites to that degree of strength. And that is fortunate for us, because along with the blunt adult teeth comes adult jaw strength, so the potential for bite damage increases with age.

Every properly raised dog has an inhibited bite. He *could* bite down full strength, but he has been taught first by his mother, then by his littermates, and finally by his breeder that he had better not, or things he does not like will happen to him: Mom will push him away from a nipple, his littermates will stop playing with him, and his breeder will tap his nose and tell him, "No."

Two Inhibited Bites

At one dog show I found it particularly fortunate that most dog bites are inhibited. A fellow exhibitor had a very large komondor that was known for having munched a few people. This dog was the pack leader, and komondors were bred to fight wolves.

High temperatures make even good-natured dogs irritable, and this dog was not noted for his good nature. I came back to my shade to find him monopolizing my dogs' shade and water. Without thinking, I approached him from the rear, told him to move over, and bumped him in the hip. For all his size he had deceptive speed. I know how surprised wolves must have been when they first encountered members of his breed. He spun around and bit me with nice pinching, inhibited bites, twice in the body and once on the arm before I could lift a hand, or his owner could pull him off.

The dog knew me and had recognized my voice when I told him to move over. That is why the bites were inhibited. He was just demonstrating that he was not to be pushed around. I was impressed by his speed but not by his manners. Like most unmannerly dogs, he paid a price for it. He lost the use of my shade. When approaching a dog of dubious temperament, let him see you. Do not surprise him from the rear.

If a dog's temperament is really poor, do not be too surprised if he bites you even if you do approach him from the front. The only time I was bitten by a dog that I didn't know was very educational. It taught me three things: that temperament is the responsibility of the breeders who produce the dog, that there is only one real solution for a dog with very poor temperament, and not to take my eyes off an untrustworthy dog.

In this case, a friend who was a Great Dane breeder said that a woman had requested one of her adult dogs as a pet. She was willing to let the dog go but did not know whether his temperament was good enough for him to be safe outside the kennel. She asked me to help her test the dog to see how he would react to strangers. I readily agreed. I knew this breeder's dogs and had found them to have delightful temperaments. I did not know until later that she had not bred the dog in question. She had purchased him and his brother from another breeder. If I had known that I would have been more careful, because the brother was crazy. He was both aggressive and fearful, and the fact that he had seen me visiting for most of a year had done nothing to calm either his aggressiveness or his fear.

The breeder and I walked up to the four-foot paddock fence. The dog came right up to us, looking distrustfully at me. She petted his head and he settled down, but he never looked at her. He only had eyes for me. I offered him a hand along with some dog talk. He accepted both and let me stroke his head. So far it was going well.

A greyhound ran up to the adjoining fence and I glanced at her.

The moment eye contact was broken, the Dane grabbed my arm in his teeth. Dogs that bite and hang on were a new experience. It was a little like having a great white shark hanging onto my arm. The teeth had very little cutting action, but the pressure was tremendous. (By the way, this was a big dog's idea of an inhibited bite. I have never experienced an uninhibited bite. I have never been bitten by a dog that was trying to do more than communicate with me.)

The breeder was sensitive about having her dogs disciplined, and I was weighing the options of possibly losing her friendship by striking the dog on the muzzle below the eyes to make him let go, or waiting to see if she could make him release me. At her third outraged yelp, he let go. In the next week, my arm turned bright green and purple, but the damage was minor, just scrapes and bruises.

The real loser was the dog. Having failed the first part of his temperament test, he was kept at the kennel where he quickly developed a hatred for one of the female kennel helpers who was about my size and had similar long hair. Apparently he had decided that long-haired women were fair game. He was put down. Who was to blame for it? His breeder was. The difference in temperaments between the rest of the kennel's dogs and these two dogs from a different breeder was striking. There are dogs that should not live among humans, just as there are men who belong in jail.

WHEN IS A BITE NOT A BITE?

Even a dog with a fully inhibited bite reflex can do normal things that people may interpret as a bite attempt. Many kinds of communication between dogs involve the gentle use of their teeth. To the general public, these other uses of teeth can be misinterpreted.

The Play Snap

"She snapped at me!" My houseguest had come into the kitchen and was oohing and ahing over Sunny and doing a very excited greeting. Sunny found the lady pretty amusing and entered into the spirit of the game by dropping her elbows on the floor in a play bow, turning her head *away* from the woman's face, and snapping her teeth closed on empty air. The visitor heard the crisp snap of the closing teeth and, not being very knowledgeable about dogs, thought automatically, bite attempt. I explained that a play bow and an empty air snap to the side were a doggy invitation to play, not a predecessor to an attack.

Toothy Greetings

A lot of dogs that are delighted to see visitors may take a grip on part of their body without meaning them any harm. Sally Perry had two impeccably trained obedience dogs. One was a golden retriever and the other was a Belgian Malinois, which is a herding breed. They would each escort me from the gate to the front door in their own way. The golden would proudly hold my elbow in his mouth and retrieve me into the house. I preferred his greeting, because the Malinois's idea of a greeting was a brisk nip on the rump, herding me into the house as if I were a sheep. She never put any strength into the nip; it was just hard enough to let me know that she was there, and that she wanted me to move faster.

Finger Nibbling

When Annie arrived from England as a mature bitch, she had a habit that I found rather quaint. If she was hungry and thought I was too slow with dinner, she would fuss around me and take my hand in her mouth to nibble it gently. She wouldn't bite down—it felt like being nibbled by hungry fish—but her intent was clear: "Hurry up and feed me. I'm starving."

WHY DO DOGS COMMUNICATE WITH THEIR TEETH?

Dogs most often use their teeth for communication, not for attack. They use their teeth because they don't have hands. So the things that we do with our hands, they do with their mouths. As long as the dogs are dealing with folks who know enough about dogs to understand them, there is no problem. But the majority of people in the world are not students of dog behavior, so perfectly harmless actions can be misinterpreted, just as my visitor misread Sunny's invitation to play. With the increasing number of vicious-dog laws, it would be a shame to have a dog condemned as vicious for actions that are normal behavior for friendly dogs.

KNOWING WHEN A DOG WILL BITE

One of the most effective solutions to dog bites is education. People who are knowledgeable about dogs and are exposed to lots of dogs are rarely bitten, and almost never bitten seriously. One of the contributing factors to dog bites is that folks who have no experience with dogs not only may think they are being bitten when they are not but also may ignore the warnings of a dog that does intend to bite them. Dogs are not mysterious phantom attackers. Their behavior is relatively predictable, and they usually communicate their intentions. The problem is understanding them. And the solution is education.

UNINHIBITED BITES

The Deprived Dachshund

What happens if a puppy's dam and littermates do not teach him to inhibit his bite? As a child, Betty Lou's family dog was a dachshund, which gave her a lasting fondness for them. She called me to say that she had been shopping at the local mall and had found a dachshund in the pet store there. At first she was not sure whether he was a young standard dachshund or an older miniature. But he was a smooth-coated red puppy and he was in the shop's special petting enclosure.

The pen was open on the top to invite prospective buyers to reach in and pet the puppy. She reached in and he bit her firmly, very firmly for a young puppy. Then another customer came by and said, "Oh, look at the cute puppy." She reached in and was surprised when he fastened his teeth in her sweater sleeve and tried to pull the rest of her arm into his den. The lady left, no longer even moderately interested in the aggressive puppy.

Betty Lou asked the salesman how old the puppy was. She found that he was not a young standard-sized dachshund. He was a four-month-old miniature dachshund and had been separated from his mother and littermates and shipped to the pet store before he was six weeks old. Before that he would have had no contact with people, since puppy mill puppies grow up in raised wire cages. The only human contact would have been when the automatic food and water dispensers for their mother needed to be refilled. And after he was shipped, there would have been no opportunity for his mother to use her big teeth to teach him not to use his little ones.

So he arrived at the pet store without having learned that it was not acceptable to bite hard. And what happened at the store? He was put in a small enclosure and strange people reached in to touch him. When he was little, he would take hold of their fingers with his teeth and the customers were delighted to have the puppy nibble their fingers. But he had the misfortune of not being sold, and every day he grew larger.

As he got stronger, so did the bites. People still reached into his enclosure. But now when he bit them, they squealed and pulled their hands out. He decided that was a fun game. People reach in to you.

You bite them firmly. They squeal and back away. Then you wait for the next customer. He was treating the hands that were thrust at him as if they were squeaky toys. Dachshunds are attractive dogs and popular pets, but they were bred to go down rodent burrows and bite and pull out badgers. Badgers are big, tough animals with formidable teeth and irritable tempers, so it takes a dog with a lot of willpower and jaw strength to subdue one.

Genetically our little dachshund came with the courage and hunting instinct to bite down. That, followed by his endless opportunities to bite the customers, had taught him to bite hard. In his case, human profit had interfered with the lessons he should have learned when he was tiny. Now, through no fault of his own, he had become almost impossible to sell unless somebody walked into the store who liked being bitten. Don't laugh. There are dog owners who are bossed around by tiny dogs who bite them and still love the dogs.

If he was lucky, someone who knew enough about training to teach him that his biting was unwelcome would take a fancy to him. It would not be difficult. The new owner would just have to go back to the beginning, take the place of his mother with the big teeth, and make it clear to the puppy that biting hard is no longer acceptable. And at the same time he should be provided with new games to take his mind off his teeth. If he was not lucky, then he would soon join the "Free Dachshund" ads in the newspaper or end up at a shelter.

One of the risks of buying a puppy from a pet store is that the entire puppy mill–pet store environment is an unnatural one in which to raise a dog. The chances are good that these puppies may miss some of the lessons they should have learned from their mom and their littermates and their breeder.

Private breeders who wean their puppies and remove their dam as soon as possible are also doing their puppies no favor. A lot of folks were astonished that I let Annie run with her puppies for as long as she wanted to. She was a devoted mom. She nursed her puppies until they were twelve weeks old and educated them until they were adults.

Young dogs were not intended by nature to be weaned and shipped away at six weeks of age. At that time they are learning about life at an astonishing rate, and I was more than willing to let Annie teach them. If puppies are separated from their family group at an early age, then their new human foster mother has the job of providing all their education.

The Two Types of Uninhibited Biters

Aggressive biters are either defending a treat, their turf, or their puppies, or they are challenging for pack leadership. Aggressive biters can be disciplined out of biting in the future. When they understand that biting has unpleasant consequences, they stop biting.

When Fancy arrived from England as an adult, she had a small cut on her paw. She was also incredibly alpha. When I reached for her paw to treat it, she growled. I said, "Fine. It is a minor cut and will heal while we work out our pack ranking. And the next time you have a cut, you will let me treat it." So the first rule is don't push a dog that thinks he outranks you. Work on the relationship first. Once the dog thinks that you are in charge, life gets easier. The next time Fancy had a cut, she did let me treat it.

Fear biters are different. Virtually any dog can be turned into a fear biter if he is treated badly enough. Every dog has a fight-flight boundary. Fearful dogs have a fight-flight boundary that covers a really large area. Calm dogs have a boundary that is much closer to their bodies. Faced with a threat that is outside the boundary, the dog will watch it carefully, give an alarm bark, and try to frighten it off. When the threat crosses the fight-flight boundary, the dog will take action either to flee or defend himself. He defends himself by biting.

Discipline makes a fear biter worse. When you discipline a fear biter, you reinforce his belief that you are a threat to his survival. Any animal will fight for his life, and that is what a fear biter is doing.

LEFT: *A comfortable kennel muzzle is not punishment. It is insurance against fights, bites, and leash or upholstery chewing. Chris is modeling the old-style racing kennel muzzle.* RIGHT: *Chris likes the old leather muzzles for their chewability. Modern kennel muzzles are bright colored plastic and not nearly as much fun to chew. Plastic is lighter, less durable, and cheaper.*

The only solution to fear biting is prevention. If you know you have a fear biter and you are going to do something that will frighten him or cause unavoidable pain, the dog should be physically restrained. The dog should be muzzled or crated or otherwise disarmed so that he cannot bite anyone. One writer said that all biting is fear biting, but that is not true. I have met plenty of dogs that were willing to bite to improve their pack status or to defend their treats, home, or puppies. It is much easier to handle an aggressive dog than a fear biter. It is true that normal dogs can be pushed into fear biting by a real threat or abuse. But the chronic fear biters can't be cured.

They can only be somewhat desensitized by being exposed to low levels of whatever frightens them and rewarded for behaving well. Serious, chronic fear biting is grounds for euthanasia.

PACK BEHAVIOR

Anyone with more than two dogs has a pack. Even the person with two dogs will see elements of pack behavior in the dogs' relationships with each other and with their owner. Pack behavior is often anthropomorphized and misinterpreted. Horrors, the puppy grew up to fight with his father and brothers! Or the pack gangs up to attack a misfit member. As much as this bothers us, dogs have been running with packs a lot longer than they have been running with people. Our dog-master relationships are based on the dog's ability to substitute a person for the pack leader.

The pack's major interests are food, sex, play, and dominance. Both food and play are essential to good dog training. Play is generally either mock fighting or mock hunting. The practice hunt can be one of the most successful incentives for obedience. And every owner has a place in the dominance order of his or her pack, so it is a good idea to learn about dominance. Otherwise, you are engaged in a game without knowing the rules.

In Praise of Good Pack Leaders

Being a pack leader means more than dominating the other pack members. Pack leadership is a civil service job. The leader exists not for his own sense of power but for the benefit of the pack. He sees that the pack survives, that it stays safe and fed and sheltered from the weather. He provides protection and makes the decisions that are responsible for the health, diet, comfort, safety, and activities of the pack. When a person assumes pack leadership, these responsibilities go with the position.

I was exercising the pack by jogging along a shoreline path with the four trotting ahead on leash like a chariot team. We passed a young family, and the father called out a frequently asked question, "Are they all yours?" But this time an answer different from the usual yes occurred to me. "That is only one way of looking at it. Actually, I'm theirs." And that is the truth. The pack leader exists for the well-being of the pack and not the other way around.

Dominance

A pack with multiples of each sex will have a separate dominance ranking for dogs and bitches. The top dog and top bitch generally get along quite well with each other. The top dog defends his position against challenges from what is usually his second in command. Dogs from the bottom strata of the pack do not challenge the leader. If they are ambitious, they work their way up through the levels of the pack until only the leader is left above them. Then they try for the leadership. This does not usually mean a dogfight. Dogs have an intricate series of competitions that establish rank among themselves.

In a pack that started with two puppies and a retired coursing dog, the scenario went like this: As a youngster, the low-ranking dog was the male puppy, Tiger. His sister could outrun him, and the grown dog could outrun both of them. With adolescence, Tiger moved up one notch when he became both larger than his sister and able to show a speed edge on power runs. At ten months of age, he started a game that I

Trip and Kitty Hawk testing their pack ranking.

misunderstood. He took to making sudden runs at the coursing dog. The objective was to hit the older dog behind the shoulder and roll him over.

I was indignant. Where was Tiger's respect for age? My protests were ineffective, and by the end of the month the older dog had become a master at giving Tiger a broadside target and then pivoting at the last moment to let him charge on by. By that time the game was tapering off, and I finally realized what had been happening. The game ended because it had served its purpose. For the first time, Tiger was top dog in the pack, having taken the position without a growl or snap. He took it with tests of strength and speed. When he was clearly faster and stronger, the old dog yielded the leadership. If a dog's activity is so restricted that he cannot use speed and strength as means for determining rankings, he is likely to resort to fighting. Fights don't take much room.

Dogs check constantly to see if the pack rankings have changed. The photo on the previous page is of a pair of two-year-old litter sister bitches who are checking their rank. The raised heads, ears, hackles, and tails signal aggression as they stand as tall as they can and push against each other's neck in a strength test. The white bitch is stronger and heavier, and she initiated the challenge, but the fawn bitch is dominant. The white bitch has started to drop her head and tail in submission and is giving ground. This illustrates the reason why, if you stand tall and stare at a dog, it usually drops its head or turns its head to the side to break eye contact and acknowledge your dominance.

The Trainer as Pack Leader

I have known several instances in which people were subordinate pack members to large male dogs. In these situations the dog was physically stronger than the human owner. The attraction that very large dogs hold for moderate-sized people may sometimes not work out well. In both packs, if the owner displeased the dog, the owner was disciplined by being first warned and then bitten. Having one subordinate human pack member already, neither dog was reluctant to bite strangers. Why would anyone keep such a dog? Each owner seemed to admire his dog's strength while not being terribly fond of its personality. In fact, each owner had gone through extraordinary difficulties to avoid being separated from his dog. It would seem that there is indeed a dog for every type of owner.

I recommend that the owner of a pack of dogs any larger than toy poodles be the pack leader. One difficulty with maintaining the leadership is that many owners do not recognize a challenge when it is offered. The dog is not going to pounce on you in the middle of the night. Instead, one day you will make a normal correction and hear a quiet, calm growl that says very clearly, "Hey, you, knock it off. I do not acknowledge your authority."

What he is actually doing is testing the owner's leadership, because the leader has the right to discipline any pack member without resistance on its part. If you back off and try to be reasonable about it, if you try to deal with it on a human level, then you are going to fail, because the dog will not understand. If you do not react properly, the dog will be encouraged to continue to press for leadership.

The correct way to respond is exactly the way a canine pack leader would (short of biting the dog in the throat). Put a leash on the dog. Have the dog lie down. Keep him down for at least fifteen minutes. If he tries to get up, put him down again. If he reaches for your hand with his teeth to tell you to knock it off, muzzle the dog. Put him down again. Keep him down until he relaxes. When the dog yields, he will stop struggling. The objective is not to hurt him but to demonstrate that he ranks second on the dominance ladder.

This whole subject is touchy. Most obedience books ignore it in the hope that it will vanish. But the challenge is a perfectly normal occurrence in a dog pack. We emotionalize it into a personal attack on us. The challenge does not mean that the dog does not love you. The dog does indeed love you and will continue to love you whether the dog wins and you become a subordinate pack member or whether you win and the dog settles into number-two rank. The event has nothing to do with love or hate. It is a very simple and direct power play. If you truly love the dog, you will not let the dog win.

The dog is much better off testing leadership with his owner than with another dog. When these tests occur between two dogs, they can easily result in thirty stitches for each participant, generally in the neck and shoulder area. For this reason, if the highest-ranked dog is ever badly injured, he should be separated from the pack lest one of the members decide to displace the leader while he is incapacitated. If all this sounds dreadful, it is because it is being interpreted by human standards. It is perfectly normal for the dogs.

Warning

Maintaining pack leadership in the face of a challenge by a dog that is just testing his strength and yours is something that most people can cope with readily once they understand what is happening. Taking leadership away from a large dog that has been allowed to dominate people and bite them with impunity, however, is a high-risk venture.

This kind of dog is not inhibited when it comes to biting people, and he will energetically defend his leadership privileges. While it is possible to demote such a dog from pack leader to second in command, it usually takes two people and special techniques to do it safely. If you are faced with this problem, get expert assistance. Do not challenge a dominant dog alone, particularly if the dog is larger than you. Even medium-sized dogs have an impressive array of teeth and are physically capable of inflicting a lot of damage on a person.

The difficulty here is that most people are so used to having dogs show restraint that they assume all dogs are harmless. Give a dog the end of a beef shin bone and watch him literally grind the bone into bone meal. Then appreciate just how much restraint the normal dog shows in not using his teeth on us.

Omega Dogs—Not Every Dog Wants to Be Alpha

First the good news. Most dogs do not want to be alpha dogs. Most dogs are low-ranked dogs (called omega dogs) and they will never challenge you for pack leadership. When a litter is growing up, they play-fight themselves into a pack ranking with one alpha dog and one alpha bitch. The others will have learned to be followers.

Taking Back Pack Leadership—Two Examples

Betty Lou owned the most imperious greyhound bitch I ever met. When Sheba was a year and a half old, three-month-old Image was added to her household. Sheba raised Image with an iron paw and very ready teeth. Image grew to be twice Sheba's size, but that didn't matter. Sheba was in charge.

When Image's sire, middle-aged Ikon, needed a home, Betty Lou adopted him. Image and Ikon were both an unusual dirt color and Betty Lou wanted to show them in brace. That is a class where two dogs are judged on how well they match. They matched extremely well and they won many Best Brace in Show awards.

Neither boy messed with Sheba. Betty Lou's pack rank order from top to bottom was Sheba, Betty Lou, Image, Ikon. Ikon had been an alpha dog in his original home and frequently challenged his son for the position of top male. (Nobody dreamed of challenging Sheba.) So Image periodically sliced his sire around the throat to remind him that he was the bottom-ranked dog.

Since Image and Ikon were never together unless Betty Lou was present, they could fight only in her presence and she got considerable practice breaking up their fights. But she observed the same thing I had: Even when she was in the middle of the fight, the dogs were careful not to bite her. In fact, one of her methods to avoid having the old dog torn up was to stuff her arm into the young dog's mouth. He would spit out the arm and back off. Dogs bite what they intend to bite. They don't bite things they don't want to bite.

I don't advise this technique, by the way. If you don't outrank the dogs that are fighting, your arm will get badly bitten. I don't agree that a dog that bites his owner in a fight does it by mistake. After all, wolf packs attack large game, and in the melee of a group attack, they attack only their prey, not each other. Dogs that bite people, bite the people they think they are entitled to bite.

When the pair of Presa Canario dogs killed Diane Whipple in San Francisco, the dogs' owner said that she was lying on top of the victim to keep the dogs from attacking further. But the victim was shredded while the owner was not bitten. Dogs know what they are biting.

When she was nine years old, Sheba died of cancer. That left Betty Lou living with Image and Ikon. It was shortly after that that I received a phone call from Betty Lou. She was crying. She said, "I won't tell you what happened if you are going to say that you told me so." So I promised not to say it, and she told me that she had accidentally bumped Image on the bed and he had bitten her in the face. I was astonished. It had never occurred to me that Image, no matter how unpleasant I found his personality, would bite his mistress. I asked what she had done to him after the bite, and she said that she had put him outside in the yard. That wasn't the answer I had been hoping for.

I drove to her house and took her to the emergency room for a few stitches. The damage was a small-tooth tear through her eyebrow. This is a breed that typically disciplines its pack members with a single well-placed canine tooth driven between the eyes. Image had slightly missed his target on a broader human face. But if it had been more than a single discipline strike, he could have pulled much of her face off.

So what had happened? Why did a dog that she had owned for seven years wake up one morning and bite her? That was easy to figure out. Sheba's death had unsettled the pack structure. As long as Sheba was alive, the most Image could hope to be was the highest-ranked male. He had no chance of taking the pack leadership from Sheba. But with Sheba gone, Betty Lou had become the highest-ranked female. Image thought he could take the leadership from her, so he challenged her. He had disciplined her as if she were an underdog. The difficulty was that Betty Lou was the perfect underdog, a very unassertive woman.

That left the more difficult question of how we were going to reestablish Betty Lou as the pack leader. She was too nonconfrontational to fight Image for the leadership. That was why I had asked what her response to the bite had been. My response would have been immediate discipline to convince the dog that he had made a mistake. But she hadn't and couldn't do that. So we needed a training plan to recover pack leadership in a nonconfrontational way. Fortunately, Betty Lou was also the best dog trainer with incentive methods I have ever met. Convincing Image that she was in charge took months of incentive-based subordination training. Lots of downs, lots of direction, and a month of isolation.

First, Image spent a month living outdoors in his doghouse. That taught him that being in the house was a privilege that he could lose, and it avoided further confrontations. At the same time we enrolled him in an obedience class. For that month, the only contact he had with Betty Lou was when she fed him and when she trained him. In class he could work for treats and do exercises at her request. At the end of the month, he was allowed back into the house, where he got to practice lots of downs. These weren't forced downs, but incentive downs for treats. The down is a subordinate position, and doing a lot of downs on request reinforces the dog's subordinate position in the pack. Then she increased her trick-training routines. In any training, the dog takes direction from the owner, and that helps convince him that the owner is in charge. Image was allowed back on Betty Lou's bed (muzzled for the first three months) and never bit her again.

The second example involves a rottweiler. A friend had been offered a large male rottweiler that was having aggression problems in his home. I can't remember why she wanted to take him, but the question was would she be able to be his pack leader. She was fairly alpha, so we went through the physical means of controlling a big dog, from easy things like never giving him a command unless he had a training collar and lead on, to having him wear a collar at all times so that he could be quickly put on his leash for corrections. It went so far as how to run the lead through a pipe to make it like a "control" stick that animal control folks use. The stick prevents the dog from coming toward you in a retaliatory attack.

She was an accomplished dog trainer and this was the kind of dog the German training methods were invented for. I didn't hear from her for several months. Then she told me the end of the story. For the holidays, she and her brother and the dog stayed the night at their parents'. They were sleeping on the floor. When they woke up in the morning, the dog was standing over his owner, and when she went to push him away, he sank his teeth into her forearm. This was a seriously uninhibited bite and she couldn't get free. Fortunately her brother was a chiropractor, a profession that requires a lot of upperbody strength. He put an arm around the dog's neck and squeezed. That was a brave thing to do since it put the dog's head and teeth right under his own chin. Afraid to let go, he held on until the dog finally released his sister's arm and lay still. He found that the dog was dead. He had strangled him.

The lesson in this story is that some dogs are so dangerous that they cannot be controlled by even a good dog trainer. My friend carries deep scars on her arm to this day. She later told me that she had made a mistake that caused the attack, and she considered herself responsible. I said, "Wait a minute. How could you possibly be responsible for his attacking you?" She thought that if she had not tried to correct the dog from a subordinate position, if she had stood up first and put a leash on him, then she could have prevented the attack. That might be true, but he might just as well have attacked her for trying to get up. (Do not get down on the floor with an aggressive dog.)

Another Word of Caution

Image was a dog that knew what it was to be subordinate. We just had to remind him. He was also a greyhound, a breed known for its amiability. The rottweiler had grown up believing that he was top dog and he was hereditarily aggressive as well. What works to convince a dog with genetic low aggression levels that he is subordinate to his owner is dangerous to try on a genetically dominant, aggressive dog. Depriving a large dog of his established dominance without getting bitten requires a very knowledgeable dog handler. Do not attempt it alone. Get competent help. An uninhibited bite can open up forty stitches' worth of damage in seconds.

WHEN IS COMPULSIVE TRAINING APPROPRIATE?

I spend every Fourth of July judging Utility at the Sacramento Dog Training Club's practice match. As I was loading the jumps back into my van, a mother said to her adult daughter, "She was a judge. She'll know." And then to me, "Can we ask you a question?" I said, "Sure. What is the question?" It turned out that another exhibitor had criticized her for correcting her dog instead of using positive incentive training methods. I looked at the dog. What looked back was a huge male rottweiler with his testicles still attached. He looked quite good-natured, but he was enormous. Far from abusing her dog, this woman could barely have given him a correction that would have attracted his attention. She named the man she trained with, and he is known for training aggressive dogs with German methods.

I wrote *Playtraining Your Dog* back in 1980 because I couldn't find a book that didn't advocate force training. So some people might be shocked to hear me advocating it. I explained to the woman that good trainers adapt their training methods to fit the dog being trained. There were four breeds of dogs that were bred by the Germans specifically to be force-trained: Dobermans, rottweilers, giant schnauzers, and German shepherds. When you meet a very assertive dog of one of these breeds, you are not abusing him to use the methods he was bred to accept. Many of these dogs expect strong leadership from their human pack leader. They actually like it. The rottweiler family left, reassured. In addition to the German four, compulsive methods are also appropriate for the breeds that were created to guard livestock or fight other dogs. It is, however, dog abuse to use compulsive methods on breeds that were not bred to be trained by those methods.

WHEN AN ELECTRONIC COLLAR IS A LIFESAVER

Lately there has been a debate on the use of electronic training collars. The difficulty with banning E-collars is that for some dogs they are the training method of last resort. I don't use E-collars to train sporting dogs or obedience dogs. But I did recommend one a few years ago to an owner whose dog was disciplining human beings. He thought that humans were subordinate to him and that he was entitled to discipline them when they got out of line.

Even if a bite is a discipline strike, strangers do not appreciate it. So when the owner called to say that her dog was pinching people, I knew it was only a matter of time before he would be facing euthanasia. Bites aren't allowed. Well, actually, a lot of bites are allowed among family members, but bites on strangers can end a dog's life quickly. It wasn't that the dog wasn't trained. He could execute the most amazing instantaneous recalls to a whistle from one hundred yards away. So I told his owner about electronic training collars. She ordered a Tri-Tronics collar and used it, and the dog no longer bites people. He also doesn't have outbreaks of barking when she is driving. Is he any less assertive? No, but there are boundaries to his bad behavior that bring it within acceptable levels for him to live in human society. That was six years ago. He hasn't bitten anyone since. An electronic collar saved his life.

When his first E-collar died of old age, the second one came with a warning button. Now he doesn't get zapped anymore. He is a smart dog, and the unelectrified warning buzz is enough to change his mind when he is considering unacceptable behavior. (Well, his owner did call to report that he had killed a goose when a hill cut off the line of sight of the collar. She was horrified, but I wasn't too distressed. Geese are tough and inclined to beat dogs up. Most dogs lose when they take on a healthy and irate goose.)

E-collars are just a training tool, like long lines, or pinch collars, or, for that matter, slip collars. The key to training is what I told the rottweiler family: Use the technique that fits the dog. My dogs are taught with food reinforcement, and their idea of a correction is to have to do the same exercise twice in a row. For dogs with hard temperaments, that blow off their trainers, other methods are needed.

DOGFIGHTS

There are few things more horrifying than two dogs, both of whom we love, trying to rip each other's skin off. And I guarantee that there are better ways to start the morning than to wake at five A.M. to break up a fight between two of the bitches that spent the night sleeping on your bed.

Why do dogs fight? And what can we do about it? Dogs fight because they are dogs. They are willing to fight over food, sex, or pack status. Most fights are between same-sex pairs; dogs fight with dogs, and bitches fight with bitches. Fights between opposite sexes rarely occur over anything but food. The top-ranked dog generally defers to the top-ranked bitch. He accepts discipline from her as he would from his mother.

When we accept dogs into our families, we are often unprepared for the possibility of fights.

So you say that your dogs have lived together for years and will never fight? I had a group of four dogs that lived happily together until they were seven years old. Then the two bitches fought and I could never let them run together again.

There are a few basic rules for fight prevention. The smaller the area in which the dogs are housed, the more likely you are to have a fight. Dogs with a lot of space can get away from an aggressor, or can run off their excess energy. If you are housing dogs in kennel runs and want to have more than one dog in each run, they had better be dog-bitch pairs, since same-sex pairs are far more likely to fight. For the same reason, if you have a single dog and are thinking of getting a second one, choose one of the opposite sex. Bitches that are in season are more likely to fight. Seasons make them snappy.

One of the most extreme forms of pack attack occurs if a member of the pack is down or injured. All one dog has to do is scream in pain, and the dogs that live with him may attack him. The most stitches I ever saw on a greyhound were on a bitch that had gotten her collar hung up on a fence and screamed. While she was hung up, the male whippets she lived with attacked her and sliced up her entire body. Fortunately, her owner was a surgeon.

A dog that loses his coordination may incite an attack. The dog may be thrashing due to a seizure or he may have fallen due to old age. Dogs that are unable to stand often freeze, seeming to know that if they struggle to rise they will be attacked. It is not safe to leave really old dogs housed with young ones. It is not that the young dogs are evil. It is that a struggling dog triggers a prey attack by the young ones.

Dogfights damage not only dogs. They can injure owners as well. At the very first dog-training class that I attended as a teenager, the trainer rolled up his sleeve and showed us long slash marks that ran down his muscular forearm. He said that he had tried to break up a dogfight by grabbing his German shepherd by the ruff from behind to pull it out of the fight. Quick as light, his own dog had turned his head and slashed his owner's arm open. He was suggesting that a fighting dog doesn't know what he is biting and urging us to be careful if we ever had to break up a fight.

Years were to go by before I even saw a dogfight. But, since that time, I have broken up a few fights, and one of the things I have been impressed by is just how careful my dogs are not to bite me when I am elbow deep in fighting dogs. I put this down to my being the unquestioned leader of my pack. Pack leaders have the right to break up fights between subordinates.

In breaking up half a dozen bitch fights over the years, none of the combatants has ever offered to bite me. But when I move in to break up a fight, I make more noise than the dogs, screaming at them to make sure that they know who it is that is joining the fray. I have twice had men come running from considerable distances because of the amount of noise I was making. In both cases, by the time they reached me, the fight had been broken up successfully.

MUZZLES FOR BITE PREVENTION

Racing greyhounds learn to wear muzzles. They are turned out thirty at a time to potty, and each dog wears a kennel muzzle. These allow the dog to drink and pant but not to bite. Kennel muzzles are far superior to conventional muzzles and are available cheaply from the National Greyhound Association of Abilene, Kansas. They used to be made of leather and metal but are now made of colorful plastic. They fit most medium-sized dogs from collies to Dobermans. Muzzles are valuable for preventing disputes among dogs, or preventing a dog from pulling out stitches or from chewing through a leash when the dog is tied. (Goldy likes to convert six-foot leashes into four-foot leashes. Now, when I tie him, I also muzzle him.)

6

Training Basics

If It Eats, You Can Train It

First I would like to introduce Lily, OTCH The Merry Prankster TD, UDX, OA, OAJ, JC, VCD2, and her owner, Julie Hill.

In June of 1996, Lily was the first greyhound to earn the titles of Obedience Trial Champion (OTCH) and Utility Dog Excellent (UDX). The OTCH is a title that rewards precision. It requires that a dog earn 100 points by taking first or second placements in Open B and Utility B classes. The UDX is a title that rewards the consistent performer. It requires that a dog qualify ten times in both Open B and Utility on the same day. Lily was Julie's first obedience dog, and she went from the Novice A class to an OTCH title. She was a red bitch who was rescued from an animal shelter as a puppy and went on to be awarded High in Trial at four all breed trials.

Julie was on her lunch hour in downtown Denver and happened to pass by a corner where a shelter had set up an Adopt-a-Pet booth. She was in the market for a dog and had always wanted a greyhound. When she saw Lily, she immediately fell in love with her confidence and cockiness.

Lily was eight weeks old when she was adopted, and she did not have a racing tattoo. She was the only greyhound puppy up for adoption. Julie asked whether she had litter-mates and was told that she didn't.

Lily was Julie's first dog. Five months after adopting Lily, she bought a show quality bloodhound named Lark, so she actually trained two dogs at the same level from the very beginning. (So did I, training Sunny and Tiger at the same time.)

Julie changed her training methods a great deal over the course of Lily's career, as she learned what she was striving for and how to achieve it. Lily spent the first year of her life in pet classes, where she was allowed to develop a lot of bad habits. When Julie moved from Colorado to Washington, Lily was enrolled in a competition class that was taught by an instructor who emphasized ring preparation and procedure, attention, and proofing as a means of attaining consistency and reliability. After three years with that instructor, Lily was trained for a few short months with an instructor who emphasized attitude, willingness, and enjoyment.

Then Julie moved to Louisiana, where she learned more about dog training from Lily and Lark. Julie says that she was demanding and insisted on correct responses, but keeping the dogs' attitude up was just as important. She learned that if Lily was not happy, she

JULIE'S RECOMMENDATIONS

Julie offers the following advice for owners who are interested in training unusual breeds.

1. Watch the great handlers and dogs (no matter what breed) to get a clear picture of what a perfect performance is and work toward making your dog fit that picture.
2. Don't make excuses for your dogs. They are just as capable of working well as any other breed.
3. Be gentle, respect your dog, and make it fun. If you are not smiling when you train and your dog's tail is not wagging, there is probably a problem with your training relationship.

Lily on top of the Agility A-frame.

would not perform. Julie used a lot of food, play, praise, and random releases to keep them interested and animated. She broke the exercises up into their component parts and worked on the pieces more than she worked on the whole. She reinforced with food every behavior that she wanted and, when possible, ignored unwanted behaviors.

During the week before a show, Julie tried to make sure that Lily made the right decisions. (Lily hated to be wrong.) For example, Julie put dowels out for Lily's go-out spot the first time she was sent so that she would not have a bad go-out that would need to be fixed. If Lily made a mistake, Julie ignored it, but the next time Julie somehow steered Lily to the right choice. Outside the ring at a show, Julie tossed toys for Lily, played tug-of-war, fed her, and did set-ups and releases. Inside the ring, Julie cheerled even more than she felt comfortable doing. Whether Lily was right or wrong, Julie praised her.

At the same time she was training Lily, Julie also trained the bloodhound Lark, who became Ch. Masterpiece Maybe I'm Amazed CDX, TDX, NA, NAJ, MT. Using what she had learned from Lark and Lily, Julie then trained and showed the pointer OTCH MACHS Longtrail Piece of My Heart UDX5. She runs the Dog Finishing School in Louisiana.

Now meet Trip, Ch. Clairidge Light Fantastic CDX, TD.

Are you accustomed to conventional methods and doubt that food and playtraining can work? A series of pictures is worth more than words. The photo sequence shows Trip performing the obedience finish by an optional method called the flip. In obedience, any time that the dog comes and sits in front of the handler, the next thing he will be asked to do is "finish." This means to go to the heel position by the handler's left side. In the Novice class there is only one finish. In the Open class there are four finishes, and in the Utility class there are five finishes. All the obedience finish requires is that, on a single command, the dog move from the position in front of the handler to a position at heel. How the dog manages this is left up to the dog and handler.

In the conventional finish, the dog simply gets up, walks a three-quarter circle clockwise around you, and sits at heel. In the military finish, the dog walks past your left side and then turns around and

sits. In the swing finish, the dog swings its hindquarters in a counter-clockwise half circle while doing a pivot in place with its front feet, to get from a position facing you to one sitting next to you. The flip finish is a swing finish done entirely in the air.

No dog can be made to do a flip finish. Trip had no idea that it was an obedience exercise. She thought it was one of her favorite games. She did at least twenty flips for the photo session, and each one was a little higher and more enthusiastic than the last.

THE OBEDIENCE EXERCISES

Obedience does not have to be like army basic training, where the dog is the recruit and you are the drill instructor. It does not have to be work. It can be play with a few rules to shape the game gently into an obedience exercise. It is possible to show and complete titles on a dog that does not work willingly, but it is not enjoyable. If it is not enjoyable, then why do it? The objective of positive training is to make living, training, and showing fun for both the dog and owner.

GENERAL TRAINING HINTS

Training Time: Train Less, Teach More

In a thirty-minute training session, the dog has plenty of time to think up new ways to entertain himself. The bored dog creates his own versions of the exercises, and his versions will not agree with the AKC's version. This leads to frustrated owners and playful dogs. The owners whimper, "I don't understand why he does that to me in the ring." He does that to you in the ring because he was bored during his training. He would rather show you a new and different version than run through the same old exercises once more. At least if he throws in a new twist, you will react in an entertaining way.

When teaching a new exercise, I rarely train a dog for more than fifteen minutes. Once the dog is trained for the individual exercises of an obedience class, I do run-throughs to practice the class routines and reward the dog. That means the dog is not in the ring any longer than he would be at an obedience trial, which is no more than ten minutes.

The key to interval training is that dogs have excellent memories that are not wiped clean by a few days or weeks of inactivity. A dog remembers indefinitely anything he enjoys. You just have to remember how far your dog has progressed.

What owner can say that he or she does not have time to train a dog for a few minutes twice a week? The only problem with this schedule is that it does not fit in with a weekly obedience class, so I train the dogs individually. Then, if there are not enough matches and practice sessions available to teach the trained dogs to ignore distractions, I enroll an already trained dog in an obedience class for the experience of working in the presence of strange dogs and unexpected events.

A class is not the place to teach a dog a new exercise. Faced with both a new routine and distractions, the dog has too great a chance of making a wrong choice. The dog should have every possible chance of succeeding in a new exercise so that you can reward him.

Training should not be a burden. Work out a routine that fits in with your normal lifestyle. There are owners who have taught heeling in their living rooms. I have taught retrieving in both the living room and the garage. Be inventive.

How do you start training? First you learn to talk to your dog.

Dog Talk—The Universal Incentive

The more a dog is talked to, the more responsive he becomes to verbal cues. The handler's talk helps the dog develop skill in reading people's moods from voice patterns. The dog will learn repeated phrases and sentences. One of the biggest advantages of Rally over the sport of obedience is that in Rally you are allowed to talk to the dog as much as you like. When I started showing my obedience dogs in Rally, I literally talked them through the exercises.

What does all this have to do with training? Talking produces a dog that pays attention to what is said, draws correct conclusions from what he is told, and acts accordingly. The desired goal is a dog that can be talked through life and the exercises. This means the substitution of verbal control, which you always have, for leash control. The leash is an invaluable training aid, but only one exercise (Novice on-lead heeling) is done on leash in competition. And dogs spend most of their lives off leash.

Correcting a dog in the ring, even between exercises, is not permitted in either Rally or obedience. Talking to the dog, between the exercises in obedience, and nonstop in Rally, is allowed, and I highly recommend it. It is not easy to get Novice trainers to talk to their dogs.

Horse fanciers are much better at this kind of talk than are dog folks, because horses require constant verbal reassurance to avoid being startled and to keep their owner safe from a quick kick. The only dog person whom I have ever heard begin talking to a dog at the first suggestion and continue without lapses was a professional show handler. I had never heard show handlers use dog talk and thought that they considered it beneath them, but he had obviously developed the skill for his own training purposes.

Star Traveler being awarded High in Trial at the Western Greyhound Specialty. He loved obedience.

Dogs, like children, friends, and lovers, blossom under steady praise and encouragement. They cannot receive too much appreciation. This kind of praise is called cheerleading and it is vital. Even really rotten working dogs do not get better if they are told how bad they are. If you can bite your tongue and praise the faintest good points in a performance, or if you can praise a performance that really has no good points, you can gradually restore enough self-confidence to the dog to enable him to work better the next time. It goes against the grain to praise a dog that is working poorly, but it is effective. Praise has a much more beneficial effect on the dog's performance than corrections.

When a dog is working exceptionally well, there is a temptation to assume that he does not need to be praised. If you stop the praise, eventually the dog will stop working well. Why should he continue to excel for someone he feels is unappreciative?

Once the dog is trained and close to being ready to show, introduce short breaks in the monologue. Gradually widen them until the dog will forgive a silent performance of each exercise. You still talk to the dog between exercises, and at least one-third of ring time is spent between exercises. You also still talk to the dog during practice sessions.

The Thinking Trainer

Once the dog is verbally responsive, it is time to consider training techniques. One fallacy is that there is one best way to teach a dog a particular exercise. There are as many ways to teach a dog a given exercise as you can find and try. Do not get locked into a method that is not working for your own dog. Class trainers tend to be revered authority figures. Nevertheless, if a class trainer insists that only a particular method will work, he is displaying his own ignorance. Resist the suggestion and find a method that will work for you and your dog. Reject any methods that do not work and keep thinking of new ones to try. The secret here is to keep thinking. Observe the dog's reaction to a technique. If it was a failure, why did the dog not respond to it? If it succeeded, what were its positive qualities? What did the dog think of it? The ability to see the procedure from a dog's-eye view is one of the most valuable abilities a trainer can have.

Many failures are due to a lack of understanding. You try to teach one thing, but the dog, seeing it from a different point of view, learns something quite different. Training of a sort has taken place, but the intended lesson was not taught. The classic examples of this type of failure are the many dogs that are carefully taught not to be housetrained. These dogs usually do not have a great deal of dog-owner contact. The owner goes off to work and the dog feels ignored. One day he learns that by being the reverse of housetrained he can attract attention. It is adverse attention, but that does not matter. To the isolated dog, any attention is desirable. So the dog keeps making intentional mistakes to ask for attention and the owner keeps rewarding him with punishment, another form of attention.

The owner is unable to understand why the punishment does not train the dog, because he or she does not realize that this is what the dog is seeking. What we then have is a dog that has trained his owner to react in a lively manner whenever the dog gives the signal—the signal being little piles and puddles in the house. Training has taken place, but from the owner's point of view, the desired response was not taught. Be careful what you teach.

In training a dog (or person), you see more of any behavior that you reward. I teach most of my dogs to raise their ears for the cue "Ears." Show judges like to see the shape of the ears, and it is cute to have the dog raise his ears when the judge says, "Show me the ears." In teaching "Ears" to Jirel, I inadvertently taught Jirel to raise only her left ear. She had been reluctant to raise her ears at all, so I started rewarding her for raising just her left ear because the left ear was the one the judge could see from his or her side. So she learned to raise just her left ear. When I realized what had happened, I retrained her by not rewarding her when she raised only one ear. I started to whistle to get both ears up and then rewarded that. The retraining took a while, and she still occasionally raised only the left ear in the hopes that would be enough to earn a treat.

In training Ringo to retrieve, he easily learned all the steps leading up to picking the dumbbell off the ground. But when I started to throw the dumbbell short distances, he went to it the first time, picked it up, and then backed up to me. I made the mistake of rewarding him for bringing it back, and then he repeatedly brought it to me by backing up. Be careful what you reward. You will see more of whatever you reward. I then had to teach him to turn toward me after he picked up the dumbbell, so he could walk toward me instead of backing up to me.

Anxiety Faults

A handler related her difficulties with a dog that was a chronic whiner in the long downs. She described every possible form of punishment that could be used for whining and said that none of them had worked. Why had punishment not worked? Because whining is an anxiety fault. The dog starts out being nervous, so he whines. He is then punished for whining, which confirms his initial belief that something awful is about to happen to him. Now, even more nervous, the dog whines some more. If someone put me on a down stay command and did to me the things the lady had tried on her dog, I would do some whining myself! Active punishment of an anxiety fault like whining or sniffing intensifies the problem. The more the dog is punished, the more anxious he becomes.

In starting with one untrained dog that was already a whiner, I varied the exercises to take his mind off the whine. We worked at building his confidence, and aside from occasionally telling him mildly that whining was not polite, I ignored it. He proved to be an eager learner. By the end of three weeks he realized that obedience was fun and he stopped whining, except while waiting impatiently for his turn to work. He could easily have been turned into a chronic whiner with a little punishment.

When Kitty Hawk was ready to show in the Novice class, she had two problems: She was a compulsive sniffer and somewhat insecure. I decided to let her take the possible penalties rather than reduce her already low self-confidence by trying to end the sniffing. The first time shown, she did her expected forty-five-second sniff during the down. At each successive show, her sniff time grew shorter and shorter. Before she was through showing, she was all sniffed out and gave it up as boring.

The opposite of praise is not punishment. Praise and punishment are both forms of attention, and dogs crave attention. The opposite of being praised is being ignored. You praise and reward the good to get more of it. You ignore the bad so that it will disappear. It disappears because it doesn't get any attention.

The Trainer's Goal

With each dog a handler trains, the handler's training skills increase. Her ability to read the dog improves. She becomes able to give increased amounts of positive reinforcement to the dog. Her cheerleading gets better. Her physical coordination improves. (Some training procedures are awkward when they are first attempted.) The trainer becomes more lively and animated with each dog. Her timing improves greatly, and good timing is one of the greatest assets a trainer can have. Making the appropriate response at the proper moment is the goal. And the proper moment is just as important as the appropriate response.

The usual belief is that training is something that is done to the dog, that the ultimate goal is a well-trained dog as a finished product. Actually, the well- or poorly trained dog is an incidental product of the training process. The goal of training is the education and skill development of the trainer, a process that never ends. That is why trainers can stay in the sport for thirty or forty years. The trainer's hope is that each dog she trains will increase her abilities, and that as a result each dog will be better than the one that preceded it. There is a saying that a trainer always ruins her first dog. This is not literally true. Many first dogs are very successful. OTCH The Merry Prankster was a first dog. But the saying is always true from the trainer's point of view. Looking back over her work with that first dog, she can see, with the knowledge gained from that dog, what the mistakes were. She can see what could have been done, no matter how good the dog is, to have made him better. She can then apply that knowledge to the next dog.

This process would quickly lead to perfection, except for the catch: The next dog is a different individual that has his own behavior patterns and characteristics. So the learning process begins again for both dog and handler. The dogs may be learning the same exercises, but the handler should be learning something new each time. The hope is that each dog will have a greater opportunity to work to the top of his ability than his predecessor did. Sometimes there are failures, which can teach even more than the successes. It is as essential to know which methods to avoid as it is to know the helpful ones.

Learning From the Dog

Most training books urge the trainer to be patient. For a lesson in patience, observe the dog's example. Dogs are incredibly patient. They submit to our fumbling first experiments in dog training. While we think that we are teaching them, they will teach us if we only have the eye to watch them and enough humility to learn from them. When we have a clever theory on training, we run it by the dog for testing, and the dog either accepts it or rejects it. Either the theory works or it does not. If it does, then we mentally file it along with other successful methods. If it fails, then it joins the growing collection of abandoned theories.

How does one come up with new theories to submit to the dog test? Trainers swap theories while waiting at ringside, or during the Open B sits and downs. They study training books and books on dog psychology and pack behavior. The chapters on puppy mental development in Clarence Pfaffenberger's *The New Knowledge of Dog Be-*

havior should be essential reading for anyone who is interested either in training dogs or raising puppies. Animal behavior books usually are more interesting than the training books. The behavior books are also useful for the next step, which is to create new theories by studying your own dog. He can teach you more than you can teach him, starting with patience and going on to attention.

Reading the Dog

"Reading" a dog is a process of observing the dog's behavior, body language, and facial expressions and, from these, understanding what the dog is thinking. This is an area where practice makes one increasingly good but never quite perfect.

When you pay attention to the dog to read him better, you become aware of how intensely the dog is observing you. Most handlers have unconscious habits that are beneath notice—except that the dog does notice them. Many dogs have failed in the ring because they correctly responded to their handlers' unconscious cues.

The only way to prevent this kind of failure is to become aware of every action you take while in the ring or practicing. This is as difficult as it sounds. You have to concentrate on both the dog and yourself, to a degree that you are unaccustomed to. It takes extensive practice, and it helps to have another person point out the unconscious cues until you can spot them for yourself.

It is important to analyze failures for their causes. Often, on the way home from a trial, the reason for the dog's behavior suddenly becomes clear. At least it will be perfectly understandable from the dog's point of view.

The better a trainer is, the more observant he becomes of both the dog and himself. The ultimate goal is a team, where both members are under conscious control, responding to clear cues, and totally in contact with each other. Does this sound like drudgery? Actually, it is delightful.

If the training is dull, the result will be a slow-working, bored dog. If the training is overly corrective, the result will be a slow-working or nonworking, flighty dog. Few dogs can be forced into being excellent. All dogs can be invited into a partnership in which they play a game called training and are rewarded for it. The game is made up of friendly instruction with maximum encouragement, a minimum of understanding corrections, a great variety of playful practice, and an endless supply of to-die-for food treats.

Attention

There are classes that teach nothing but attention. I find that training with really good treats automatically gives me the dog's attention. When the dog thinks that his actions control your treat-dispensing hand, the dog's attention is concentrated on you. I used to warm Trip up for competition by simply saying to her, "Tripper, do you want to play the game?" She was so enthusiastic about performing her game that she would start to bounce and fix her attention on me to see what fun thing we were about to do.

Catching for Attention: When Silver moved back home as a five-year-old dog, he arrived knowing how to catch treats. Karen had taught him that. I found catch very useful when showing him. If I asked him to catch, he would stand up alertly and look for the expected flying treat. But it didn't occur to me to teach the rest of my dogs to catch. Sometimes I am a slow learner.

My neighbor raised a rottweiler puppy. Wanting to be on good terms with him, I gave Max cookies every week when I mowed my front lawn. Until they moved away eight years later, Max would be waiting at the corner where our yards met as soon as he heard my lawn mower start in his direction. Max was a sweetie. He had two yard mates, a long-haired Chihuahua and a basenji–border collie cross named Lady. She was given to biting, but we fairly quickly reached the understanding that she had to let me touch her forehead without biting me before I would give her a treat. What I noticed, after years of giving them treats, was that all three of them knew how to catch. That gave me pause. After all, I was the dog trainer and my dogs didn't know how to catch, while hers were just pet dogs and they all caught like professional ball players.

So I set out to teach my dogs to catch. Goldy, Fiver, and Bella learned it quickly. I would close the others out of the area to concentrate on a single dog and toss lightweight treats to the trainee. First I would say "Catch" and move my hand holding a treat toward the dog's mouth. He was allowed to pick the treat out of my hand. That taught him that when the hand moves toward his mouth, he should open his mouth. Then I moved on to tossing treats toward his mouth. Lightweight treats are best because they move more slowly when they are tossed. The dog is not allowed to pick up missed treats. I pick up any treats that reach the floor. Most dogs learn to catch in two days.

Instructors and Training Classes

The handler who is new to dog training may want to look for a good training class. Look for quality instruction and a humane approach to training. Classes are usually run continuously. As soon as one class graduates, another is enrolled. Go and watch the class in progress before you enroll for a later series. Do the class dogs look happy? Are they willing workers? Do the owners look happy? Good. If people are yanking on and disciplining dogs, find another class. If you intend to participate in AKC competition, try to find an instructor who competes. Many instructors direct their efforts toward helping owners combat the large unruly dog population and are not familiar with obedience competition. Only a few of the dogs enrolled in training classes will ever see the inside of an obedience trial ring.

Most training sessions last for an hour, which is long enough to bore most dogs thoroughly. I generally take a pair of dogs and trade off during the session.

Clicker Training

In the obedience ring, I wear an old-fashioned stopwatch. On one occasion it was swinging against a button and giving off a clicking sound. The judge asked me to silence it. I did so, but at the end of the class, I explained to him that, while my dogs are food trained, they are not clicker trained. The inadvertent clicks were not extra signals to the dog. In clicker training, the dog is rewarded with food and the click is used to mark the point at which the dog has earned a treat. Dolphin trainers use whistles to mark the moment of success. Clicker trainers use clickers. I can see using a whistle to mark a behavior on a dolphin. The trainer is not next to the animal and is not going to hand it a treat as it succeeds. I would use a clicker if I had a free hand, but my hands are fully occupied when I train, so I basically clicker train without the clicker. If I had an extra hand, I would use a clicker. Instead, the food delivery or my praise marks success for the dog.

Target Training

This is another item learned from training dolphins. They are taught to put their nose on a target in exchange for treats. The target is a float on the end of a pole that can be moved around to encourage the desired behavior. For the shy dog, it would be useful to use a target stick to teach the dog to touch strangers for a treat. In food training, the hand holding the treat is the target. With it, you can lead a dog around by his nose. If you need a target that is remote from you, it is easy to teach a dog to touch a target stick for a reward. It is done the same way as the food retrieve (see page 212), except that the dog is rewarded simply for touching the target with his nose. He doesn't have to grab it.

This is very easy to teach. First you touch the dog's nose with the end of the target stick and immediately give him a treat. Then you repeat it a dozen or more times. By that time the dog may be reaching for the stick. If not, hold the stick a few inches in front of his nose and tap the end to get him to touch it with his nose in exchange for treats. Touching a target in your hand can be taught in a single session. Some training systems teach the dog simply to use the trainer's hand as a target and to touch it on cue. Once the dog is very good at touching the target in your hand, gradually move the target away from you.

Graduation

Many dogs enrolled in training classes fail their graduation test, which disappoints their handlers. But in a six- or ten-week training class there is time to teach only the basic exercises. The dog comprehends the meaning of the exercises, but he has not had time to develop the habit of responding correctly every time. In addition, most beginning handlers are very tense at graduation. With that combination, it is a wonder that any dog passes. Don't be disappointed.

Pace and Speed

Next to talking to a heeling dog, the best thing a handler can do to help the dog is to walk quickly. The dog should have to move out of a walk and heel at an easy trot in order to keep up with you. A bored dog shows passive resistance by slowing down. If you slow your pace to match the dog's, the dog will slow down further. If, instead of slowing down, you move faster, you make heeling more interesting for the dog. Keeping up becomes a challenge that keeps the dog awake during the heeling.

Friends

If the dog and trainer are friends to begin with, there is no need to sacrifice that friendship just because you think that the dog is working poorly on a given day. Many trainers have unrealistically high expectations, not for the final degree of perfection but for the time it will take to reach that point. As long as the dog is working happily and making progress, you should be pleased instead of impatient. Dogs do have off days. They also go through cycles where they regress and then improve on a given exercise completely independent of your efforts. The best thing you can do when the dog regresses is to relax and take a short vacation.

The Run-Through

There are two kinds of training sessions. In basic training you are teaching individual exercises. In a run-through, the dog already knows the basic exercises. So you practice the exercises as they are performed in competition. Extended training on any exercise before going on to the next one defeats the purpose of the run-through, which is to teach smooth transitions from one exercise to the next. If the dog gets stuck on a particular exercise, repeat it once, if you can think of a way to help the dog perform correctly. If not, then finish the rest of the run-through. The next time you train on individual exercises, work on the one that the dog had trouble with. If he still cannot manage it, but was once able to do it, stop. Do not keep repeating a failure. Repeating a failure merely teaches the dog to fail. You can program failure into a dog as easily as success.

The Sound Dog

In dog show terms, a sound dog is one that is built so that he trots correctly. In obedience, a sound dog is a dog that will perform an exercise reliably even when exposed to distractions like unfamiliar surroundings or strange dogs. A dog at class graduation may know the exercises, but he will not be sound. Another four to eight weeks of practice are needed to produce a sound working dog, especially in the Open and Utility classes. This practice is done in the presence of distractions. Obedience clubs in large urban areas hold practice matches, which provide all the distractions that a trainer could ask for. Trainers in more remote areas have to invent their own distractions. There was once a local trainer who liked to have me run my greyhounds in the park while he was training his Bouvier des Flandres. Two greyhounds playing tag were an excellent distraction.

What can you do if there aren't enough matches? Go to a park. Set up a ring. Practice. There are usually enough people and dogs around to provide distractions. Just being in a new place is a distraction. You can also enroll an already trained dog in class to use the untrained dogs in the class as distractions.

The Ideal Dog

My ideal obedience dog is one that, when presented with a new training situation, starts a search through a variety of possible responses until he is rewarded for one of them. Then he concentrates on the action that brought him the reward. The more confidence the dog has in himself and his trainer, the more behaviors he will try before giving up, and therefore the greater his chance is of finding the desired response. You help by guiding the dog in finding the correct response, by encouraging him to keep trying, and by rewarding him when the goal is reached.

The problem with disciplining unwanted behaviors is that the only way for a dog never to be wrong is for him to do nothing and show no initiative. But you want the dog to show as much initiative as possible. The only force that is beneficial in training is the one defined in George Lucas's *Star Wars,* where "the Force is an energy field created by all living things; it surrounds us and binds this galaxy together." In this sense it is the shared companionship, intelligence, humor, and affection between living creatures, between dog and trainer. In this sense, "May the Force be with you"—and your dog.

Responsibility to the Dog

One of the greatest attractions of obedience training is that it creates a firm bond between the dog and his owner. Once a dog and owner have worked together up to even the companion dog level, that dog has earned pet status. As used here, pet status is not a derogatory term.

Obedience training helps you establish an understanding of and working relationship with your dog. Obedience makes the dog a real living friend. It also makes the dog easier to live with. Dogs with manners and a reasonable command of our language are good companions.

One of the measures of a dog's worth is the amount of time that the owner has invested in him. The more training time that is put into a dog, the more attached the owner becomes to that dog. Breed champions are bought, sold, and occasionally given away free. If you would like to see an interesting human reaction and are prepared to face some incredulous laughter, offer to buy someone's Utility dog.

Even small amounts of training will greatly reduce the turnover in the dog population. So here is a kind word for dogs as pets and companions. No dog is born trained. He is what the handler makes of him, either adversely through neglect or beneficially through work, care, and training. No dog is perfect in the show sense, but every dog can be perfect in the eyes of a loving owner.

Corrections

Let us talk for a moment about correction, force, and punishment. Once a trainer is sufficiently practiced to praise the dog for a good performance, then the alternative is to punish a poor performance, right? Wrong! The alternative is to provide guidance, to use the least possible force, and to give the dog a second chance to perform correctly.

The Worst Correction: Force training tries to make a correction so unforgettable that the dog will never make the same mistake again. If a correction is so strong that the dog never forgets it, there is a good chance that he also will not forget the exercise that led up to the correction, and he will try to avoid that exercise. The dog is not wrong when you correct him. Wrongness is your value judgment. The dog is just not doing what you want him to, and the correction is one way of bringing about the response you desire.

Corrections are guidance. They should not be punishment. The quickest way to make a dog think that even a mild correction is punishment is to add a verbal reproof to it. The collar correction may not tell the dog much about your feelings, but if you say, "Rotten puppy!" along with the correction, the dog knows that he is being punished. Many well-intentioned handlers verbally abuse their dogs in the mistaken belief that this is kinder than a physical correction. Steady verbal abuse is the surest way of destroying a dog's self-confidence.

The Correct Correction: If you give leash corrections at all, give them with or immediately followed by enthusiastic praise. After all, if the correction worked, the dog is doing the right thing and deserves praise for his current correct behavior. The leash correction itself is not a yank on the leash. It is a very quick, moderately firm tug that tightens the collar suddenly and immediately releases it. The idea is to startle the dog. If he gets corrected all the time, it is not going to surprise him. If he is used to being talked through the exercises and working on a loose leash, then the quick, light pop on the neck is all the correction he will need. It wakes him up, gets his attention, and he can then bask in the accompanying praise.

The Second Chance Correction: When an exercise is first taught, the dog will not perform the same way each time he is cued. While still in the learning process, the dog is searching out the possible actions available to him. In the go away, he may go out ten feet, make a sudden turn, and head off in an unexpected direction. In the drop on recall, he will occasionally miss the drop cue and come straight in. He may try heeling on your right side. He may step on the broad jump.

The dog is not committing errors; he is exploring the alternate solutions to each exercise, and this exploration is part of the learning process. Instead of being punished after one of these experiments, take the dog back to the exercise's starting point with a wistful, "Silly, if you are going to do it that way, then you are going to have to try it again." And he gets a second chance, having been neither praised nor punished for the erratic first attempt.

My dogs quickly learned to recognize that an instant replay of an exercise without any reward means the first performance was not a success. Praise and treats are what they are seeking, and if they do not get them, they try another method on the second attempt. When they get it right, they are rewarded with treats, praise, and a change in activities. This can be either the end of the training session, a chance to run and play, or just a change to a different exercise.

The Best Correction: The best correction is no correction at all. This means guiding or even tricking the dog into being right, so that he can be praised and reinforced for his correct behavior.

The Chase as Motivation

Novice obedience can be taught with simple praise and treats as rewards. For the exercises beyond Novice, the dog needs a motivation that can be given at a distance from the handler. The strongest possible incentive for hunting dogs is pursuit. The chase has been bred into them literally right down to their toes. Why shouldn't we use those five thousand years of bred-in instinct to motivate them for the comparatively new sport of obedience? This means getting the dog to play and, in some cases, actually teaching him to play. The objective here is to produce what whippet owners would call a good rag dog, a dog that will fanatically pursue an artificial quarry.

Creating a Good Rag Dog

This is the ultimate training game for any dog except the short-nosed breeds (like pugs or bulldogs) that have trouble breathing

when they exercise. It is used for the retrieve, the broad jump, the go away, and the directed retrieve. The game itself is simple. You need a large supply of expendable but strong rags or rabbit skins (direct from Korea at the local import store, for city dwellers like me). If you can't find rabbit skins, then torn towels, athletic socks, or T-shirts with knots will do. Take the dog out to a safe open area and play keep away, tug-of-war, and catch with him. The dog is always allowed to win and to tear at the rag and kill it.

Some dogs will grab and "kill" a pelt the first time they see it. For those that don't, you get to play with the "bunny," toss it in the air, catch it, shake it, and romp with the dog. Throw the lure short distances ahead of the dog. The first time, you may have to race the dog to the lure and pick it up. Dogs like to play keep away. Even-

TOP: *Lady learning to be a good rag puppy.* MIDDLE: *Chris and Love playing rag games with each other.* BOTTOM: *Trip playing rag games with me.*

tually the dog will win the race. Once a pack has one good rag dog, his enthusiasm is contagious. The others learn from his example.

There is a dog toy that is a grown-up version of the catnip mouse on a string for cats. The canine version is a horse lunge whip with a sheepskin lure on the end of the lash. Any dog with an ounce of chasing instinct loves this toy. It is a great way to play with older puppies and it lure trains them in the process. One distributor at dog shows discovered that Fiver was a fanatic lure dog. So whenever we walked past his booth he would cast the lure out and catch Fiver to demonstrate his toy. Fiver's intensity was a good selling point. I promised Fiver that when he finished his championship I would buy him the lure-on-a-whip toy. I kept my word, and he was thrilled when we finally got to take one home.

I thought that the rag game was an original idea until I spent a dog show dinner in the company of a police officer who trained drug-detection dogs. What motivates a dog to work for long periods of time searching out small concealed amounts of illegal drugs is not the pungent whiff of marijuana or a desire for the handler's approval. The first prerequisite for a drug-detection dog in training is that he learn to be a fanatic rag dog. What the dog is actually hunting is a piece of towel,

TOP: *Sunny liked to chase and catch tennis balls.* MIDDLE: *Squishy soccer balls were fun too.* BOTTOM: *The high-flying tennis balls were a challenge.*

which he is allowed to play with and kill at the end of the search.

After the dog has killed many towels in practice and is sufficiently motivated, his formal training starts. He learns that his beloved towel can be found wherever he smells drugs. Since most drug dealers do not pack a towel in with their shipments, the handler on a real search carries a piece of towel to give the dog at the end of a successful hunt.

Every dog can be taught to play rag games. Some catch on instantly, but some are slow learners. I had almost given up on Kitty Hawk. Her low pack status so inhibited her that she was unable to play with me. She would play only with some of the lower-ranked dogs. When playing the rag games, the other dogs never let her have the bunny. As a last resort, I took her out alone and simply lay down in the park. This often works with insecure dogs. To dogs, height is status. The strongest dog stands tallest. Kitty Hawk had never seen me shorter than she was. Having me flat on the ground removed her inhibitions, and she went wild. She started running and playing with an intensity that I've seen in few other dogs.

It is a rather odd game. Basically the handler just lies down. Your elbows are up to keep the dog clear of your face. (The dog is moving at very high speed and could easily misjudge a foot placement.) The dog does all the playing while you encourage it with peculiar little whines and whimpers. Why do it? It is fun. It shows a new side of the dog's personality. Most important, since we started the game she has gained enough confidence to hang on to her end of the bunny when the other dogs try to take it and to start to behave like a proper rag dog.

My lying flat on the ground inspired low-ranked Kitty Hawk to play. Height is dominance. Do not give up your height advantage with a dog that thinks he outranks you.

Love and Anger

This is the time to deal with one of the seldom mentioned aspects of dog training: the trainer's temper. Some dog-training books contain a contradiction. On the one hand they suggest methods that are basically physical and often hostile. On the other hand they urge the trainer never to lose his or her temper. There is an unfortunate peculiarity in the nature of the human animal that makes it one of the rare pack animals not thoroughly inhibited from harming a pack member that yields in submission. In a wolf pack, when the loser of a dispute turns his head aside to expose his throat or grovels to expose his belly and underside, the winner ends the attack. Among humans, the reverse is often the case, with a display of submission driving the victor to attack harder. It brings to mind the grim old nature movies of baboon packs demolishing downed leopards.

It is not only the dogs that have instincts. We have instincts too, but the dog's instincts are often nobler than ours. The day will come when someone reading this book will lose his or her temper, whether with a dog or a child. What can be done about it? The first step is to recognize the reaction for what it is, an unpleasant but normal human behavior pattern. We may not like our instincts, but we are entitled to them. This is one more area where value judgments on right and wrong get in the way of understanding the phenomenon and of gaining control over it. And controlling it is much more useful than feeling guilty after a tantrum.

With that end in view, let us consider human anger as a behavior pattern that can be understood and modified, just as the dog's reac-

ANYTHING FRIENDLY THAT WORKS IS WORTH TRYING

Anything that does not work for a particular dog—and that includes any suggestions I make—should be rejected. Keep searching for a method that works for your dog.

tions can be. In many cultures, people are far more aggressive than most "wild" animals. Aside from war, people have large numbers of competitive games for the socially acceptable release of aggressions.

A socially unacceptable method for aggression release is the abuse of dogs, children, and other adults. Some obedience books basically recommend a little animal abuse disguised as behavior modification and justified as "for the dog's own good." Well, any contact the owner has with the dog modifies its behavior. I am repelled when amateur authorities on training urge people to overcome their normal reluctance to hurt their dog friends.

Violence is violence. It feeds on itself and multiplies. Ethical considerations aside, the problem with violence or anger in a training program is that it is nonproductive. An angry trainer is no more capable of rational thought than is a frightened dog. The best possible training progress is made when both the dog and trainer are thinking just as hard as they can. The dog has to think actively through a new series of actions before he can commit them to memory and gradually convert them to a habit. So does the owner.

Ways to Eliminate Anger: The habit of reacting to certain situations with a display of anger can be altered. Most references just tell the owner not to get mad at the dog. Here are specific ways to avoid it.

Preprogramming. Memorize a single sentence that is triggered by anger. It is surprising that in the first adrenaline rush of rage, you can key into a calm and cool preprogramming thought. The sentence has to be something that you care about personally. For Trip it was, "If you punish her, you will be destroying the very thing you love most about her" (her utterly fearless confidence). For Sunny it was, "If you punish her, you will find out later that she was right" (and the punishment undeserved). Both statements were simple and true and, with practice, could simply switch off my anger.

Train gently. Train by minimum force methods. Force leads to more force.

Transference. Do not train if there have been difficulties with people at work or at home earlier that day. Even though you may think you have recovered your equanimity, the training situation can reinspire suppressed hostility. Instead, take the dogs for a brisk walk or a run and let the physical activity drain off your tension.

Limit the pack size. When feeling irritable, take along fewer dogs than usual. Three well-trained greyhounds are all I am comfortable with in a small car. In larger numbers, they become selectively deaf to instructions and play the pack's game of "Who, me? She can't mean me," which is irritating to an owner who has been pre-irritated. Actually, it is an amusing game in more lighthearted moments, as each dog tries to appear more innocent than the one next to it.

Population control. Could you manage with fewer dogs to lighten the workload? The dog population should not be allowed to increase to the point where the dogs' care is primarily a burden instead of their company's being a pleasure.

Time off. Take a rest from the dogs. We love them, but they require constant care, and after weeks and years, it can wear us down. Fatigue shortens tempers. The evening after a dog show I am more than ready to feed and settle them in for the night and take the evening off for any fun activity that has nothing to do with dogs. When we become slaves to our dogs, we resent it, and eventually they suffer for it. Some of us get out of the dog game in disgust, while others become overworked and grouchy.

Cool it. An auto air conditioner does more than help dogs arrive at shows without wilting. It also helps their owner keep both his or her cool and his or her temper. Hot owners, like hot hounds, are inclined to be grumpy.

Family time. Take time to be with the dogs for simple companionship, a time when there are no performance requirements for either dog or owner. In this day of rush and hurry, it helps to remember who the individual dogs are and why you love them. For me, this may be five minutes spent with them on the cushions of my kitchen dog corner, or it can be finding out that Tiger has silently disappeared from that corner. He does this by lifting his toenails to avoid clicks on the hardwood floors and slowly drifting into the bedroom. I sit on the corner of the bed with him for a moment and enjoy his company before taking him back to dog territory.

Exercise anger away. A good cry or a run in the park relieves as much tension as having a tantrum at the dog. Any brisk physical activity defuses anger.

Recognize transference. Learn to recognize when you are transferring emotions that have no original connection with the dog into anger at him. After I had spent eighteen months trying to reprogram myself out of the habit of conventional adversary training methods, the turning point came unexpectedly.

I was very worried about a close friend's health. After a late-night hospital visit, I returned to the car distraught, to find that my nine-month-old puppy had been nibbling on the clear plastic welting in the seams of the new seat covers. My dogs are not allowed to eat cars. Here was a perfect justification to punish her. I pounced on her, seizing her by the scruff of the neck, and for the first time in her life she gave a small surprised yelp and collapsed submissively.

I had carefully raised her as a thinking partner, and the shock of seeing her trying to appease me stopped me cold. In a learning moment I recognized that punishing her would be a

A good run on the beach makes everyone happy.

release for worries that had nothing to do with her, and that, after having spent eight months carefully building her temperament into my favorite kind of outgoing self-reliance, I was within a few minutes of destroying her faith in me. Nothing was worth that, so I extracted her from the backseat and, with a lap full of gangly greyhound puppy, had a good cry against the back of her neck until she decided that she couldn't let her owner be untidy and insisted on licking the tears away. We both felt better afterward, and I was never again tempted to break the trust.

Car-oriented readers may ask, "Yes, but what happened to the seat covers?" They never seemed important again, but the clear welting proved irresistible even to my older, trained dogs. The upholstery itself was not touched, but the welting was nibbled away by my greyhounds as cleanly as if it had never been there. By the time the car was traded in, it was completely de-welted. The dogs showed no interest whatever in the new car's upholstery.

When Disobedience Is Not

Contrary to popular belief, the owner is not always right. It is hard enough for the average person to admit that he or she was wrong in dealing with another person. It is still harder for us to admit we were wrong while our dog was right, but dogs are entitled to be right occasionally. Sunny had the annoying tendency of being right whenever I found the two of us at cross-purposes.

She and I were at a lure field trial to pick up the last points for her Lure Courser of Merit title. After one more line break, I called Sunny back from the far end of the field. She ran back along the line while the other two dogs played with the lure. Suddenly she halted and began to spin in a tight circle. This is a danger sign on a lure course; it means that the dog is caught in the line that pulls the lure. The dog spins in an attempt to escape what is hurting him. He continues to spin, wrapping the line tighter and tighter. What is attacking him is the line itself, which can burn like a hot wire, especially with two dogs pulling at the lure. I had seen a Saluki with his leg sliced to the bone in the same situation. It is an infrequent occurrence, but it did not seem fair that Sunny was about to be injured after having run at thirty-five trials without a scratch.

I was running toward her and calling "Down" to immobilize her until I could get there. With each "Down" cue she gave a little dip, but she did not go down. After six tries, it occurred to me that she was not going to obey. So I changed the cue to "Stay." She did respond to that. It broke her spin, and she stood until I panted up to her. A quick check of her showed no marks or cuts, and I gratefully leashed her and started back with a wry comment on my fancy obedience dog's lack of response to the down.

We went back to the car, where she took a drink and cooled out. Then I rolled her over to tape her feet for the next run and discovered the reason for her refusal to drop. On her belly, high in the tuck, was a network of line burns. Every down cue, when she had done her curtsy to start the drop, had brought her in contact with the line, and the pain had bounced her back up. That she would even try to drop after the third or fourth repetition was the remarkable thing. So have faith in your dog. Dogs are right more often than we give them credit for, and they are often right when they do not appear to be.

The Miracle of Habit

It is vital to understand the commonplace but remarkable things we call habits, and also to understand how habits are created and changed. A habit is a time-saving shortcut in the mind. A formed habit is an unconscious mental program that enables us and the dogs to perform routine tasks without conscious mental direction. Often, after a few hours of performing habitual actions and then looking back on the time spent, we may have difficulty recalling what we have done. Established habits don't require thought. When we train, we are forming and rearranging habits in the dog.

All skill learning is habit formation. From skiing to computer operation to retrieving, the world is full of habits. The only thing that is habit free is the intellectual investigation of new information.

A boy watched me type on the computer and asked, "How did you learn to type that fast?" I explained that it was touch typing. That I had taken classes in which I had programmed my brain to know where the alphabet keys were. And that the habit was so ingrained that now I didn't need to think about which keys to strike. I could just think the words and my fingers would strike the right keys. The ability to do that is entirely the result of programmed habits. That is training the brain to react automatically to the stimulus of our thoughts. And that is what we are doing when we train dogs. We are training them to react to our cues with the behaviors that we have taught them.

Forming habits requires a lot of active thought, and changing them requires even more, but executing a habit does not require conscious thought. That is why habits are useful. If each person had to think about all the actions needed to drive a car, the freeways would be more exciting places than they are. Each of us did think of every step when we were forming our driving habits. But now we let those habits handle the routine parts of driving for us.

People often drive home with little recollection of the trip. This lack of recollection is the reason that time seems to pass much more slowly in our memories of childhood than in our recall of recent years. The very first time that an event is experienced, the mind gives it total attention. From the information it receives then, it creates a pattern that will be recalled each time a similar circumstance is met in the future. A child's year is filled with new experiences, and so his or her memory is filled with detailed recollections. However, we hardly remember events experienced through habits, and so, as years go by and our stock of habits increases, we meet fewer and fewer new experiences and therefore store fewer new and intense memories.

Do you remember your very first dog show or obedience trial more clearly than more recent ones? A first occurrence is remembered

7

Forming the Partnership Between Dog and Handler

The Novice Class Exercises and Rally

Training a dog through Novice obedience civilizes him and gives him a foundation of basic manners. All dogs should know Novice.

There are three lists for training: one for equipment, one of training guidelines, and one for troubleshooting.

TRAINING EQUIPMENT LIST

1. One dog, preferably happy and exercised.
2. One baggie full of treats cut into small pieces.
3. One collar (slip or martingale or plain buckle, depending on the dog).
4. Six-foot leather or nylon leash (not chain).
5. Quart-sized plastic bag and paper towels for public cleanup.
6. Water for the dog to drink and a spray bottle of water for cooling the dog.
7. One happy trainer.
8. Long line (twenty to forty feet long with a snap on the end).

9. Light line (two to three feet long with a lightweight snap). Both lines can be made out of thin nylon cord available at any hardware store. It is sometimes called parachute cord.

BASIC TRAINING GUIDELINE LIST

1. Be sure that your dog is hungry when you start training.
2. If you are in a class, keep your dog under control and out of reach of other dogs and handlers.
3. If your dog is too energetic to concentrate, exercise him before training.
4. Pay as much attention to your dog as you expect him to pay to you.
5. Patience is a dog trainer's main virtue. If you feel yourself losing your temper, stop training.
6. Your voice needs to be upbeat, happy, and friendly. It helps to raise your pitch a little for the cues. Speak clearly.
7. Praise, praise, praise, praise—at the moment the dog acts correctly. Don't wait until afterward.
8. It's okay to talk to your dog the whole time that you train. It is better to talk to the dog too much than too little.
9. A dog can be trained without any corrections, but he cannot be trained without praise, rewards, and love.
10. If you don't practice, you can't blame the dog for not learning.
11. Train for brief sessions.
12. Always end your practice session by playing for a few minutes.
13. There is no right or wrong way to train a dog, just lots of different methods.
14. A good trainer is one who can select the correct method for his or her own dog.

TROUBLESHOOTING

1. If your dog is having trouble with the exercise, back up and make the exercise easier.
2. When your dog first learns an exercise, he will do parts of it incorrectly. He needs to be able to try variations without being punished. Variations are part of learning.
3. If you are in a bad mood or irritated at someone, don't train your dog.
4. If you are having trouble with one exercise, move on to something else and come back to the problem area later.
5. Be 100 percent sure that your dog understands what you want before assuming he is choosing not to obey you.
6. Do not assume that the dog is trained when he performs correctly the first few times. Your dog is beginning to understand the cue, but he is not reliable yet. Training consists of first teaching the cue and behavior, and then practicing for reliability.
7. Corrections are not punishment. They help the dog do the behavior correctly so that he can be rewarded for being right.

The lead can be either leather or nylon or cotton webbing; leather is easiest on your hands. Dogs will eat either type of lead. Tiger preferred leather. Sunny would not lay a tooth on leather, but she had a taste for cotton and nylon webbing. Her specialty was expressing impatience when I became involved in dog show conversations. When finally ready to leave, I would find my half of the leash empty while Sunny looked on, impossibly innocent, with six inches of leash hanging from her collar snap. The phantom dog show leash chopper had struck again.

The training collar is the most important single piece of equipment for all classes. Chain collars tend to be thrown off over a dog's head during a jump. A smooth-coated dog can shed a chain collar

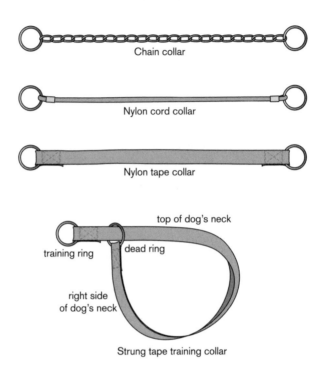

Chain collar

Nylon cord collar

Nylon tape collar

top of dog's neck

training ring   dead ring

right side
of dog's neck

Strung tape training collar

FIGURE 5: *Three types of collar*

simply by lowering his head. I used to see people with metal detectors examining the park where we trained and wondered how many of our vanished chain collars they found while searching for more interesting objects.

For training I used to use homemade collars in which the rings were connected by a nylon tape about an inch wide. The tape collar should be barely large enough to slide over the dog's head. It should rest in midneck and not slide all the way down to the shoulder. These collars are easy to make. My favorite pair, which appear in many of the photos, were made from an army surplus strap and some three-quarter-inch O-rings. The O-rings should be large enough for the trainer to hook a finger through.

All of these collars operate the same way. If a leash is attached to the training ring and pulled, the collar tightens first across the back of the dog's neck (which is why it is important to put the collar on the dog right side up). The strung collar is pictured as if you were looking at the dog head-on. The quick (and it should always be quick) neck pressure is very similar to what a puppy feels when his mom grabs him to discipline him. The idea is to startle, not strangle, the dog. The dead ring is the ring through which the collar slides. If the leash is attached to the dead ring, the collar will not tighten. It then acts the same as a plain buckle collar. Most of my Novice training is done using the dead ring so that the dog can be guided through the routines without tightening the collar.

After years of making my own collars, the Premier collar company sent me some sample nylon martingale collars. When properly adjusted for length, the dog cannot back out of the collar. I fell in love with them and have used them ever since. They work fine on all breeds of dog and are totally nonpunishing. For incentive training you don't need a punishing collar. In fact, a collar is just a convenience; you don't need a collar at all. I have occasionally trained collarless dogs when I wanted to be sure to only use positive incentives.

ACTIVE AND PASSIVE EXERCISES

All but one of the Novice exercises are passive in nature. In passive exercises, the dog works next to the handler (within arm's reach) or is required not to do anything. Heeling and the finish are examples of the dog's working within arm's reach. The stand, sit, and down stays are the exercises in which success means not doing anything. The only action required of the dog for these exercises is that he stand, sit, or lie down on cue.

The Novice exercises are passive because they were originally intended to bring a dog under the owner's control. The only exercise in

	Active	Passive
Novice		
Heeling		✓
Stand for examination		✓
Recall	✓	
Sit stay		✓
Down stay		✓
Open		
Heeling		✓
Drop on recall	✓	
Retrieve on the flat	✓	
Retrieve over the high jump	✓	
Broad jump	✓	
Long sit		✓
Long down		✓
Utility		
Moving stand	✓	
Signal exercise	✓	
Scent discrimination	✓	
Directed retrieve	✓	
Directed jumping	✓	

Novice that requires active obedience is the recall. For this, the dog is thirty feet from the handler and has to get up voluntarily and come to you. As a dog progresses up through the levels of obedience, the exercise types shift from predominantly passive in Novice to almost entirely active in Utility. Trainers going from Novice to the advanced classes for the first time can start to lose control of their dogs because the trainers are unprepared for the shift in the type of exercises. The exercises by class and type are listed in the chart on page 160.

The passive exercises can be taught with a straightforward combination of reward and guidance. The active exercises require ingenuity on the part of the handler. The active exercises use motivations of food, play, and pursuit, and they are the reason that I advocate learning to play with the dog and teaching it rag games.

The key word to the active exercises is *voluntary*. There are two ways of teaching the active exercises. One is to use a variety of tricks and devices like long lines, throw chains, and remote electric collars to convince the dog that you have the power to apply discipline from a distance of thirty feet. This is a difficult fiction to maintain. The dog keeps searching out your limitations.

The other—better—approach is to teach the routines, give the dog an incentive to want to perform them, and practice enough to create the habit of doing them correctly. For this approach, you never discipline the dog when he is working at a distance. The dog is not disciplined while he is working free, for the best of all possible reasons—it does not work. The owner of a simpleminded dog may gallop out and correct his or her dog for a mistake, but a bright dog knows that he is twice as fast as you are. He knows you can't catch him. If an exercise is blown while free working, go out quietly, put the dog back on leash, and do some more practice in close. Changing from working in close to working at a distance is no problem, if the dog is ready for it. Going off leash too soon often creates problems.

THE EXERCISE ORDER

While each new exercise is introduced, earlier ones are still being worked on. Having a number of exercises in different teaching stages

Praise is both vocal and verbal. (Except in Rally where touching your dog is nonqualifying. It took me two zero scores before I learned not to hug my dogs in Rally.)

keeps the dog from being bored. When trouble crops up with a familiar exercise, it can often be cured by teaching a new one. There is no fixed order for introducing the exercises. There is also no reason to teach obedience strictly by class—that is, only Novice, only Open, or only Utility exercises. Mixing routines from the different classes helps provide variety. And many dogs consider jumping to be a reward.

The choice of exercises is guided by the dog's natural aptitudes. A lethargic or insecure dog may do beautiful advanced stays while being unreliable on the more active exercises. The superlively dog needs patient work on the stays while romping through the rest of the lessons. Novice is the only class for which I have a fairly fixed lesson order. The sit and the come are taught first. These are quick to teach and they give you basic control of the dog. A dog that will come when he is called and sit when he is told is not likely to get into too much trouble.

After teaching the sit and recall for a week or two, we add heeling and later the stand and the sit stay. Last comes the stand for examination and the finish. And at the very end comes the down. The down is last for a definite reason: It is too easy. Most dogs would much rather down than sit. It is a good idea to work the dog for as long as possible before he finds out that there is such a thing as a down in obedience. He can still know what "Down" means. Most dogs learn the meaning just by repetition around the house, which is fine. The dog can still believe for the first few months of obedience that the sit and stand are the only positions that will be rewarded.

A QUICK WORD ON PRAISE

Praise is not merely a formal "Good dog!" given at the end of an exercise. Effective praise is contact with the dog whether it is hand, body, or eye contact, or all three, as in the photo on page 162. Praise is small shrieks of glee and wild wrestling matches, depending on the dog. Praise is smiling at the dog. Some dogs have poor eyesight, but many dogs read facial expressions very well. Most of all, praise is ever present.

BASIC FOOD TRAINING
FOR NOVICE

The first step in the training is to teach the dog to bait, which is to hand-feed. Dogs are not born knowing how to do this. They have to learn that anything you hand them to eat will taste better than the food that turns up in their dinner pan each night. If you hand a carrot to a horse that has never been hand-fed, the horse will spit it out and ignore it. The same applies to dogs that have not been taught to bait. In order to teach them to bait properly, the food needs to be special. It has to be something the dog really likes. I have known desperate show dog owners to use flaked smoked trout for a dog that would bait for nothing else. More common baits are liver, roast beef, cheese, and chicken. There are a variety of commercial dried liver products available. My usual training treat is boiled lamb liver. (Or liver muffin treats. See the treat recipe on page 11.)

The second requirement for food training is that the dog be relaxed. If a dog is tense or apprehensive, it ruins his appetite and he is not going to eat. You cannot food-train a dog and severely correct him at the same time, which is one of the things I like about food training. The leash is used for guidance, not snap corrections. If you have been taught to use snap corrections, then train on the dead ring until you are confident that you can resist snap correcting the dog. Corrections are not the point of food training. We are not trying to correct the dog. We are trying to pattern the dog's behavior into the habits we want to create.

All of the food-training methods start with the food concealed in your closed hand with the hand at the dog's nose. When the dog correctly performs the desired move, you open your hand and the dog gets his reward. If the dog tries to reach the reward without making the correct move, you simply keep your hand closed. To get the dog into whatever position you want, lead him by the nose by moving your bait hand.

TEACHING THE NOVICE EXERCISES

The Sit

For the sit, your bait hand starts at the dog's nose and moves up over the dog's head at a 45-degree angle toward his rear. You are trying to raise his head and get him to lean back. A standing dog can raise his head only so far. If he wants to reach something higher than his standing head height, then he can raise his nose farther by sitting, which changes the angle of his back. The leash is snug in this exercise to keep the dog from backing up as your hand moves toward his rear. As soon as he sits, he gets his reward. If sitting does not allow him to raise his head high enough to reach the bait, the dog's next way of raising his head even farther is first to sit up and then stand up. Neither is difficult to teach. Christopher, the male dog in the photos on the next page, had never been taught to sit up; he just volunteered to do it while we were photographing him. His much smaller sister,

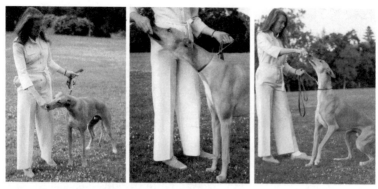

LEFT: *For the sit, start with the dog standing.* MIDDLE: *Raise your bait hand.* RIGHT: *As his nose goes up, his rump will go down.*

LEFT: *When he sits, he gets his treat.* MIDDLE: *If you keep raising your hand, most dogs, like Chris, will sit up.* RIGHT: *Love would sit up and give a high five.*

As the hand moved higher, she would stand up . . . and then stand tall.

Love, had been taught the sit up and stand up, and Chris had grown jealous of her showing off. If you want to teach a dog to sit up, use a cue other than "Sit up," which conflicts with both the obedience "Sit" and "Hup" cues. (Some people use "Hup" as a cue to jump.)

In teaching the sit, avoid pressing down on the dog's rump. If he is going to be shown in either breed or obedience, he had better not sit when a judge presses down on his back. Besides which, pressing down on the back is saved for another purpose. It is one of the cues for the stand.

A former army trainer once wanted to demonstrate a move with Sunny for which he first needed her in the sitting position. He pressed down on her back and told her to sit. She resisted the pressure and stood just as she had been taught. He pushed harder. She won. A dog with braced legs is almost impossible to shove into a sit. I suggested that she would not move until he took his hand off her body, to which he replied incredulously, "Don't tell me that you never pushed her down into a sit!" That was right. She never had been "sat" that way. When he let go of her, she sat on the next order, looking more than a little satisfied with herself.

The Down

For the down, you start with the dog in a sit (see the photos on page 168). Then your hand drops straight down from the dog's nose to his toes. This should pull his head down. Then move the bait hand forward along the ground. And, if his nose follows your hand, he will walk his front feet out into a down position. Some dogs walk out partway but keep their bodies humped up to keep their belly off the ground. Just laying your left hand lightly on their back can cause them to settle down all the way. As soon as the dog is down, open your hand to reward him with the bait.

The Stays

When we teach the sit and down, that is all we teach. All the dog needs to do to be rewarded is to sit or down on cue. The sit stay and down stay are taught separately after the sit and down have been learned.

Passive dogs are often perfectly happy in the sit and down stays. A dog that lacks initiative feels safe in the security of an exercise where no action is required of him, and he may do beautiful, steady, group exercises. On the other hand, an energetic, outgoing dog takes a dim view of anything that restricts his activity and regards the groups as a form of punishment. With a passive dog, there is not much to teaching the group exercises. He is placed on a sit stay, rewarded when he stays, and repositioned whenever he moves. Eventually he figures out that the idea is to do nothing, and he and his owner are both happy. That leaves the owner of the active dog still struggling to teach his or her student that immobility is fun.

There are two keys to teaching the stays to an active dog. The first is not to overdo the correction. When the dog moves, take him back cheerfully and replace him in the sit. The idea is to make the dog understand that he is to remain in place, not to make him afraid to move. The other essential is that the dog have something active to look forward to when he is released from the stay. In this way the stay becomes just a long "wait" interval leading up to treats and a fun game.

Sunny did incredibly elaborate stretches after each group exercise. Trip would do a few leaps and bite my hair after her stays.

The Sit Stay

The key to the sit stay is not to hurry it but to make slow, steady progress with each practice session. Give the "Stay" cue without the dog's name. Most cues are preceded by the dog's name, as in, "Sunny, heel." Dogs often start to move whenever they hear their name, so the stay is given by itself. For an additional visual cue to the dog, we take the first heeling step with the left foot and the first step out from a stay with the right foot. The dogs learn to tell the difference.

With the dog in a sit at the heel position, you give him the stay cue and a hand signal, which is your open left hand moved toward

LEFT: *For the down, start with the dog sitting with your hand at her nose.* RIGHT: *Your hand goes down to the dog's toes.*

his nose and stopped just before touching it. In first teaching the stay, we cheat and touch the nose gently. At the same time we step around to face the dog toe to toe. He will most likely be staying, since in order to move he would have had to push through the hand signal, and once you are in front of him he would have had to push through you. The stay is repeated and the dog is steadied with a hand on the shoulder. Let him see the bait in your right hand, and after a few seconds give it to him. Tell him to stay again and walk around him to come back to heel. Hold the dog still for a moment and then give him several treats while he is still in the sitting position. Then release him.

With each practice, the distance is increased, the handler moving back until the end of the leash is reached. As you move away, you eliminate the treat given as you face your dog, and he has to wait for

LEFT: *Your hand then moves forward along the ground until the dog goes down.* RIGHT: *Saturn is willing to go way down for her treat.*

Once the dog knows sit and down, we can start to practice long sits and long downs. The key to successful sits and downs is getting the dog to succeed so he can be rewarded (not to get the dog to break so he can be corrected).

his treat until you get back to heel position. When the dog is very steady, simply drop the leash on the ground and gradually continue to increase the distance. If there is any chance of his breaking, lay a long line out ahead of time between where he is going to sit and where you are going to stand. Clip it to his collar as you sit him. (If you unreel the long line while walking away from him, he will know exactly what you are doing. Both the long line and the light line should be unnoticed by the dog.)

Your objective in the stays is to reward the dog for holding the stay successfully. I strongly recommend using a stopwatch when teaching the stays. First, it gives you something to stare at instead of the dog. Many dogs don't like being stared at. And it enables you to accurately increase the time intervals.

The Down Stay

This is almost a self-teaching exercise. If the dog is doing good sit stays, he will have little trouble with the stay part of the routine. I want the sit stays to be very steady before I let the dog know that he can lie down. Once dogs discover that they are allowed to lie down in obedience, they start lying down all over the place.

A WORD ON PRESSURE POINTS

Dogs differ from each other in their ability to tolerate hard surfaces. Dogs have a problem that people do not have. When people sit, they are resting on a well-padded posterior. Some heavy-bodied overweight dogs may sit by resting on their rump, but long-legged dogs are not really sitting at all. Their rumps never touch the ground. They actually squat on their hocks (which are the equivalent of our heels). This means that all their weight is resting on their foot from the hock down to the toes. Some dogs have dense fur below the hock, which protects them from the pressure. Dogs with fine skin and short hair have little protection between the prominent hock bones and the pavement. These dogs should not be worked on pavement unless rubber matting or carpet is provided. Ideally these dogs should be shown in grass rings.

The same dogs that are subject to pressure problems in the sitting position have similar problems in the long down unless you have them lie flat on their side. If a prominent-boned, fine-coated dog is placed in a sphinx position on pavement, the pain on his brisket and elbows will force him to move. If you are tempted to punish him for moving, then try a simple exercise instead. Wear shorts and a short-sleeved shirt and take off your shoes and socks. Find some nice rough asphalt and do a one-minute sit; hunker down on your heels for a minute. You may find it a bit uncomfortable. After that, try a sphinx position down. From a kneeling position, reach out in front and rest your forearms on the pavement with the elbows a foot apart.

You probably will not make the time limit. Do your elbows hurt? You bet they do. That is because your weight is concentrated on your poorly padded knees and elbows. This pressure-point problem is the same as that faced by poorly padded dogs. When it comes to ring surfaces, all dogs are not equal. Some dogs are penalized much more heavily by bad surfaces than others.

After you have tried the long down in the sphinx position, roll over on your back and lie out flat. You will find it a great improvement because your weight is distributed over the broadest part of your body. This is the equivalent of having the dog lie flat on his side on a hard surface. If you leave a pressure-point-problem dog on a down in the sphinx position on a paved surface, you should expect him to move. Punishment is not the solution to this. Relieving the pain is the solution.

I sometimes wondered if there was any circumstance under which Sunny would not lie down. At the start of a figure eight, the judge asked routinely if I was ready. I said, "Yes." He said, "No, you are not. Look at your dog." I looked to find that Sunny had silently snuggled down into three inches of soaking wet grass. It is a good idea to check the dog to see if you are both ready. On Sunny's first Open leg, the judge asked that she be stood for measuring. I said, "Sunny, stand." Sunny lay down deliberately. The judge said, "If I measure her that way she will only have to jump eighteen inches instead of thirty-six."

With practice, a dog eventually goes down on the single cue without the handler's needing to lean over or point. If you find yourself at a trial with a dog whose down you are not sure of, there are several things that can help. Drop the dog outside the ring a few times to refresh his memory. Inside the ring, if it is a question of passing or failing, help the dog. Repeat the command if necessary. Go ahead and lean and point. If you can get the dog down without his active resistance, he can still qualify if he holds the stay. The long down is not a test of how well the dog lies down. It is a test of how well he stays down.

THE GROUP PART OF THE GROUP EXERCISES

When the dog is steady on the sit stay for three minutes at a distance of thirty feet, it is time to find other dogs to practice with. Nothing in everyday life prepares a dog for a sit stay as part of a fifteen-dog lineup. Try to avoid practicing with a Novice class that is just starting sit stays. At first you do not need strange dogs bolting past your beginner, nor do you need harried owners leaping back to correct their dogs. Such activity is more distraction than there will be at a normal trial.

The best company to start with is a group of experienced Open B dogs that are practicing the out-of-sight stays. By the time a dog reaches Open B, it may scratch or eat grass or fall asleep in the stays, but it is not likely to get up and leave the ring. The Open B lineup is a peaceful place to practice Novice sits, and the handlers often welcome a Novice dog to help fill out the line. They will be practicing a three-minute sit and a five-minute down, but you can go back and quietly break your dog out of the stays at the one- minute and three-minute marks.

If an Open B lineup is not available, then practice sessions with an experienced Novice class are acceptable, after the rowdier dogs have settled down somewhat. The first time your dog is worked with company, put a long line on him, no matter how reliable he has been in the past. He still has to demonstrate his steadiness in the presence of strange dogs. The end of the line is the least vulnerable position when you are working with a group of green Novice dogs. While the rest of the class does one sit stay and one down stay, do a pair of sits. The down is not introduced until the sits are very stable.

THE STAND FOR EXAMINATION

The Stand

For the stand, you start with the dog in a sit. Then move your hand with the treat forward from the dog's nose on the same level with his nose. He will stand up to let his nose follow your bait hand and you can restrain him with the leash to get him to stop in the standing position, where he is fed and petted. All we are trying to teach here is the stand, not the stand stay. If he stands long enough to reach your bait, that is fine. You are allowed to stack the dog for the stand, which

LEFT: *For the stand, start with the dog in a sit.* RIGHT: *Move your bait hand straight forward on a level with the dog's nose, and the dog will stand up.*

means that you get to position his feet. Leave the dog in a comfortable, balanced position, with the hind feet not extended too far back.

The Stand Stay

Once you have taught the dog to stand up on cue, it is time to teach him to stay and then to be examined. One of the most enduring myths of obedience is that obedience training ruins a breed dog for the show ring because the dog learns to sit and dogs are not allowed to sit in a dog show ring. But the problem with a dog that sits in the show ring is not that he has been taught to sit; it is that he has not been taught to stand properly.

It is an easy mistake to make because the basic sit can be taught in a couple of days while the basic stand takes several weeks. A sitting dog is well settled into position whereas a standing dog is ready to move in any direction. And while the command "Lie down and stay there" makes sense to the dog—he is supposed to get comfortable and wait for his owner—the command "Stand up and stay there" must seem totally irrational to him. An immobilized dog does not stand. He either sits or lies down to relax.

For the stand, start with one sitting dog. With a treat in front of his nose, cue him into standing. If needed, slide your left hand under the dog in front of the stifle, with the palm of your hand down. Once the dog is standing, his rear feet can be placed in a comfortable position. Say "Stay." Help him to hold the stand for a few moments. With each practice, increase the time for the stand even more slowly than you did for the sit stay.

Run your hand down his back and apply pressure to teach the dog to resist it. By this time the dog should be quite secure on the stand and, if he knows the sit stay, he is ready for the final move. You stand the dog, press down along his back, give him a "Stay" cue and a hand signal just as if it were a sit stay, and step in front of the dog. You and he stare at each other for a few minutes and you then walk a counterclockwise circle around him to the heel position. The dog is apt to move as you come to heel, or he may try to sit when he realizes that you are at heel, so at first run a hand down his back and maintain hand contact to keep him standing. Then taper off the hand contact until he will hold the stand without it.

THE EXAMINATION

For the well-socialized dog, the examination is an insignificant part of the routine. Novice exams are limited to the judge running a hand down the dog's back from the top of his head to his rump. First, practice examinations yourself, playing the part of both the handler and the judge. When you can examine the dog successfully, try having someone else do the examination. Very friendly dogs will be steadier when examined by a stranger. If the dog greets the examiner with leaps of joy, stay in close to hold the dog steady until he settles down.

For the shy dog, the examination is more complicated. Start with an examiner known to the dog and practice with the dog in the sitting position. The dog is more likely to hold a sit than a stand. We don't want the dog to have problems with the stand while we are trying to build his confidence for the examination. Stay close to the dog for reassurance. If he will take food, have the examiner bait him. Do not sympathize with the dog's fears. Dogs are sensitive to a slightly disparaging tone of voice, as in, "Hold still, silly. What is this nonsense?" Above all, do not sound worried or irritated. If you are worried, why should the dog be calm?

When the dog can manage an examination at the sit, move him into the stand and keep practicing with you alongside. The last step is for you to move away from the dog. (All of this work is done on leash.) If the shy dog once bolts away from an exam, it will take a great deal of work to steady him again. The examiner should be told to back off quickly if the dog starts to panic.

The most common single fault of Novice handlers in the stand is giving the stay cue while still touching the dog with one hand. The dog is supposed to be standing free when he is told to stay. The second most common error is for the handler to go farther than six feet in front of the dog. Six feet should be easy to judge. It means standing one leash length in front of the dog's nose.

HEELING

There are two basic rules for heeling: (1) food speeds the dog up and (2) leash corrections slow the dog down. Most dogs start out heeling too fast and end up heeling too slowly. Leash corrections can bring an untrained dog under control because you want to slow down that kind of dog. But leash corrections will not make a dog work faster once he is trained and going ring sour, and that is the reason we see slow-heeling dogs in competition. We are so pleased with our initial ability to slow them that we overshoot into excessive slowness. If your dog has been overcorrected into slowness, then you need to eliminate the leash corrections and use food to increase his speed. Better yet, use food training from the beginning of heeling and you will never have a problem with the dog lagging behind you.

Most of us were taught to carry the leash in both hands for maximum control of lunging dogs. I still use that method for rank beginning dogs, but why use it for either sensitive or trained dogs? I have used the hand position shown in the pictures on page 177 for years now. My left hand is behind the dog's line of vision so he cannot watch it for cues. My right hand is free to bait the dog, which encourages him to stay up with me and keep an eye on me. I reward heeling dogs for sitting automatically when I stop. I bait heeling dogs at any point where I want them to hurry. I reward them for keeping up with me in the fast, as they come out of a turn, and as they complete the half of the figure eight where the dog is on the outside of the circle. They learn to connect these parts of the exercise with food and develop the habit of speeding up to move quickly through these maneuvers.

In terms of points earned, heeling is the most important single exercise that a dog can do well. The dog has to heel in all three classes and gets to do it twice in Novice (once on lead and once off lead). One of the best ways of improving heeling scores is to teach him that there are two types of heeling, competition heeling and the less formal heeling that he does just to go for walks with you. The problem here is that 90 percent of a dog's heeling time is spent just heeling around town, while competition heeling is the exception. As an added complication, most of Sunny and Tiger's everyday heeling was done in pairs. As a result, Sunny learned to leave space for Tiger even when heeling alone. Her position remained exact, one dog width out from my knee. Judges found this a little odd, and the habit proved very resistant to change. Now I make sure that a retired or poorer working dog goes on the outside of the pair, with the competition dog staying in close.

Virtually all dogs begin by forging, which is pulling ahead of the handler. After sufficient training in heeling, many dogs end up lagging behind the handler, which is not the goal. The desired result is a dog that moves quickly with his neck alongside your knee and with the dog's head turned to look up at you. Really sharp dogs work as if their necks were wrapped around your left knee. In order to achieve this goal, keep the following rules in mind for the heel training:

1. The leash has to be slack for heeling practice. The dog learns nothing from a tight lead. The lead snap should hang straight down below the collar.
2. The heeling pattern should be short, no more than three minutes long. This enables the dog to work quickly while he is still energetic.
3. You should move briskly enough that the dog really has to stride out or move into a jog to keep up. The slower you move, the slower the dog will move. No matter how slow you walk, the dog can walk slower still. Adapting to the dog's pace makes him worse.

LEFT: *When heeling, food speeds the dog up. Corrections slow the dog down.* MIDDLE: *The leash and food are both used to position the dog at heel.* RIGHT: *Give an occasional treat while you and the dog are moving, not just at halts.*

LEFT: *Off-lead heeling. Saturn wants to know if it will be worth her while.* MIDDLE: *It is worth her while.* RIGHT: *Saturn was Sheila Grant's first Companion Dog greyhound.*

4. Talk to the dog at all times, encouraging him to stay alongside.

5. The correction for a forging dog is not a pull on the collar. It is a verbal caution, "Easy, puppy, back here," and if that does not produce a response, the correction is a change of direction, either a right turn or an about turn with a quick, light tug on the collar and a verbal, "Oops, get up here," to help him catch up.

6. Praise the dog all the time he is heeling, not just at the sits. Pet his head and rumple his ears. Give him a reason to want to stay close to you.

7. In order to heel well, the dog has to want to stay with you. Leash corrections in heeling should go from nonexistent to light and infrequent. From the dog's point of view, he should think he accidentally ran into the end of the leash because he was not concentrating and missed a turn. Particularly, do not continually correct a lagging dog. It makes him worse. Instead encourage and bait him into keeping up.

8. Do not be too eager to take the leash off. The leash is a guide that can be used to help perfect the most experienced dog. If a dog is worked up to a high level of competency on leash, he may not care when it is removed. The first step in going leashless is to leave the leash on the dog and drape the end across your chest and over the right shoulder. This leaves your hands free, but the leash is easy to reach if it is needed. If the leash goes untouched, the next step is adding the light line, two feet of nylon cord with a light snap on one end and a wrist loop on the other.

   To use the light line, attach both leash and line to the collar ring. Do a very short heeling pattern to divert the dog's attention. Conspicuously remove the leash and drop it. Continue heeling. With luck and a well-trained dog, the light line will not be used. If the dog decides to smell the ground or wander off, he receives a single light line tug, which should surprise him considerably. Praise him. Reward him. Do a short heel and stop. Put him back on leash and change to a different exercise. As soon as that first correction is made, the dog is going to watch to see how it was done. The first correction in each session with a light line is the only one that does any good. After that he is only learning to watch for the line. For the dog that is an expert at spotting light lines, clear fishing line can be used with a very small snap.

9. Some dogs that are just learning to heel find themselves on your right side and stay there. From the dog's point of view, he is doing what you want and following beside you. But the AKC is stuffy about insisting that the dog heel on your left side, so if your dog finds himself heeling on your right side, just tell him "Heel" and shoo him around to your left. It is a good idea to teach him to move to your left side on cue in case it happens in the ring.

Dancing With Dogs

Really good heeling is a dance form in which you and the dog are partners. You are leading. Bending very slightly at the knees just before a halt can prepare the dog for it. Turning your left foot in the direction of a turn for a step before the turn is made will warn a dog that carries his head low enough to see your feet. The greatest help you can give a dog is to move smoothly and not go from normal speed to fast in a single step. A military pivot will leave the best dog behind. In right or about turns, the dog has much farther to walk than you do. If you walk with quick little steps through a small radius turn instead of performing a sharp pivot, then the dog has a chance to stay in step.

Good handlers let their normal body language cue the dog. I have seen show handlers who could take a totally untrained dog and in a few minutes have him gaiting like an experienced dog. How do they do it? They do it by being really good dog dancers. What the handler did with the untrained dog was use her body language to cue the dog. In dance language, she "leads well." I used to say of a professional dance instructor that he could "dance with a fence post and make it look good." There is a dance sequence in the movie *Royal Wedding* where Fred Astaire dances with a coatrack and makes it look good.

Heeling Variations for Practice

There are many possible heeling variations you can use to perfect the dog but are never seen in the show ring. They are limited only by your imagination. Here are a few. Many of these are utilized in Rally.

The step off. While heeling in a straight line, take one giant step to the right, away from the dog. This leaves about two feet of space between you, with both still headed in the original direction. Keep walking while praising and calling the dog. The dog will scuttle to cross over and close the gap. He learns to work at staying close and to watch for unusual moves.

The U-turn. This variation is an about-turn done toward the dog.

It can be either two left turns linked or a short semicircle. The latter is the same as the inside turn of the figure eight.

Help for the figure eight. Any variation to practice the figure eight is helpful. The eight is a deadly dull exercise because it is always done the same way. Most judges even call the two required halts at the same place, midway between the posts. In practice matches we do a cloverleaf that includes the judge as part of the pattern. In straight heeling, a serpentine pattern can provide practice for the inside and outside turns of the figure eight. Jogging around the pattern helps keep the dog awake.

We once had a post steward (she was also the judge's wife) who came out in a full-length rabbit-fur coat. Tiger's eyes lit up as this five-foot rabbit approached. On the second time around the figure eight, I ended up on the far end of the figure while my greyhound was still moving leisurely and longingly around the judge's wife. The second halt was called, and I stopped, facing Tiger and his bunny. He gave a last wistful sniff, left her, and completed the other half of the figure eight to come back into heel position.

The pivot. This variation works beautifully in advanced Novice to sharpen up heeling. It is actually the beginning of the directed retrieve exercise in Utility. Starting out at heel, the dog is given the heel cue and you pivot an eighth of a turn to the right. The dog is called, guided with the leash, and told to "Sit straight" to get him into the new heel position.

When he has mastered the pivot to the right, introduce the left pivot, which is more difficult for the dog. Put tension in the leash so he cannot move forward. Give the heel cue and turn toward the dog. Nudge him in the shoulder with your left knee to start him backing around. If his rump swings out from the heel position instead of toward it, guide his hip with your left hand. The first turns to the left should be very small. If he moves and sits crooked at first, praise and reward him, then take a step forward and tell him to sit straight. Eventually he will be able to back into a straight sit, but that is asking too much of a dog that is just learning to pivot. The pivots in both directions teach the dog to adjust his position to stay at heel, and they teach him the difference between crooked sits and straight sits. Incidentally, the command "Sit straight" always applies to a sit at heel. To straighten up a dog that is crooked after a recall, the cue is "Front" or "Come front." It means to sit straight facing the handler. (You may think the dog is sitting crooked in either case, but to the dog these are two different exercises.)

The catch-up heel. The dog is left on a sit stay. You take several steps, and call "Heel," with your back to the dog. The first few times, a great deal of encouragement is in order, as the dog will be confused. He is not accustomed to looking at your back on any exercise except a sit stay. So when you move away from him, he thinks that he should stay put. You can vary the come to heel by adding a turn to either side so that your shoulder is toward the dog when he is called to heel.

In no case are you more than eight feet from the dog, and the move is never done facing the dog or he will confuse it with the recall. The catch-up heel is another way of showing the dog the meaning of the heel position. I've often seen dogs at trials who get out of heel position and then are unable to find the heel position again. This variation is good practice for the ambidextrous dog that at first will heel on either the left or right side. Some novice dogs understand that heel means they should be next to you, before they have figured out which side they should be on. Keep shifting the dog gently to the left side and he will eventually stay there. Do not correct a dog for heeling on the right side. From the dog's viewpoint, he would have been corrected for trying to heel.

THE RECALL

The recall is a four-part exercise. It is composed of a sit stay, the come, the sit in front, and a finish. The parts are all taught separately.

When teaching the come, do not worry about the sit in front. Once the dog knows the finish, do not connect it with the recall—or the dog will quickly learn to do an automatic finish without bothering with the sit in front. A novice trainer once told me proudly that he had taught his dog the automatic finish, and I then had to explain that it is not an obedience exercise. It is a shortcut in the routine that will cost the dog five points.

To avoid this penalty, give most of the praise and rewards for the recall while the dog is sitting in front of you. Once the recall is lengthened beyond fifteen feet, some eager dogs recall as if they were starting after a rabbit. This is beautiful as long as they are able to stop when they reach you. They have a tendency in the early training stages to charge on by and circle around to come back. This type of dog can be helped with a sit cue given when he is still ten feet from you and in full stride. It gives him a cue as to when to slow down. This problem is self-curing. As dogs are worked, they slow down with practice.

I favor the fast-working dogs and humor them. In training, Trip came in at formidable speed and, unable to quite stop, would lift her front, bounce off me, and back down into a sit, having used me as a bumper board to stop with. Does that not sound like normal obedience? We had fun with it. She did lovely recalls and was calm enough to do conventional sits by the time she was shown.

The recall is taught by calling the dog whenever he is walking on leash and by stuffing food in his mouth when he reaches you. I also teach it to litters of puppies by calling them and rewarding them with food when they reach me and sit. To teach them the formal recall later, I first teach them a sit stay and then call them to me, gradually increasing the distance. I have never found the come-when-called to be that much of a problem to teach. It is made up of simple steps, and as long as you don't violate any of the basic rules, it is easy. Recall problems are much easier to avoid than to cure.

Dos and Don'ts of Recalls

DO praise and reward the dog every time he comes when called. Keep a pocket full of treats. Make "Come" synonymous with "Cookies are available."

DO have a separate recall word other than "Come" to call the dog at the end of a romp. Most of mine come nicely to "Cookies." While munching on their cookies, their leashes are attached and they are not unhappy about losing their freedom. They also do not connect the end of playtime with "Come."

DO encourage puppies to come. Puppies have natural recall. It will never be easier to teach them to come on cue. Try to run away from them and call them for play. Carry dog biscuits. To a puppy, "Come" should mean "Come and eat a dog biscuit," or "Come and play with me."

DO use a long line to let the dog range. When he is distracted by something fascinating, call him from behind, tug on the line, and as soon as he turns toward you, welcome him with open arms and treats.

DON'T ever call a dog to you and punish him. If you are absolutely bound to punish him, then run him down and catch him. Even then he will be learning to run from you. If a dog comes, he deserves praise no matter what he did earlier to deserve punishment. And the madder you are, the more praise the dog deserves. He knows perfectly well from your stance and tone of voice just how angry you are. Imagine how hard it is for the dog to come in the face of his pack leader's anger.

DON'T call a dog for unpleasant attention. Use the cookie bait or go and get the dog to grind his toenails or administer medication or put him in his kennel.

DON'T ever chase the dog. Make him chase you. I take youngsters from twelve weeks to twelve months of age to large, safe open spaces at least a few times in their lives and let them run. At first I just release them one or two at a time. As long as I have part of their pack with me, then they will come back to me. If they start to range too far, I turn away from them, call to them, and run away from them. It doesn't take very long before they start keeping an eye on me.

DON'T call a fast dog immediately if you have released him for an exercise run, unless it is an emergency. You don't want to call a dog and have the dog fail to respond. And he is more likely to respond correctly if he is a little tired.

The only problem with the rules for teaching the recall is that two of them fly against our natural instincts. People again and again call a dog to them for punishment, shots, pills, and other unpleasantries. And it is hard not to chase a dog if you have just dropped your end of the leash and he is drifting slowly away from you. It takes a distinct conscious effort to tell yourself, "No. I must not chase him," and turn away so that he can chase you. Even with all the years of dog training behind me, I still have to deliberately arrest that instinct to reach out and move toward a loose dog.

Frosty Paws liked to liven up dog shows. On several occasions when I was changing from her show collar to her regular collar, she managed to duck the collar and take off running. Her idea of fun was to run a few fifty-yard circles around me and then come back, perfectly happy. She was doing her normal exercise run, but in an inappropriate place. On the show grounds, she was not likely to encounter traffic. The challenge was to keep helpful people from trying to catch her, because she considered having people trying to catch her to be an invitation to a game of keep away. I would stand in the center of her running circle calling out, not her name or a "Come" command, because she was not going to respond until she had burned off her early energy, but, "She is okay. Don't try to catch her!" Nobody ever caught her, and after several exciting laps she always came back, which is what she intended to do anyway.

Some Recall Recipes with Distractions

Once the dog has learned to come for treats, we can move on to more challenging recalls. The ingredients are a pocketful of dog treats, a lead between six and twelve feet long, and a number of distractions to divert the dog's interest from you. Parks with ducks or squirrels, strange dogs, or anything new and different are good for recalls.

For untrained adult dogs, take a long walk. It is a bit time-consuming, because nothing can be done while the dog's attention is on you. So put the dog on a slack lead and wander around until he becomes totally engrossed in some outside distraction. Move about six feet behind the dog. Say, "Dog, come!" and, if he doesn't turn, give a quick, firm pull on the leash. The pull should be strong enough to start his head and shoulders turning toward you and quick enough so that by the time he turns far enough to see you there is once more slack in the lead. He sees you bending over, clapping hands, and calling him, so he comes trotting over to receive a great deal of praise and a dog cookie.

The dog learns that when he hears "Come" it is time to stop concentrating on the ducks or squirrels or whatever. This entire method relies on having the dog be so intent on investigating something else that he does not see your action. For this reason, the method does not fit into the routine of a dog-training class. It is something you do alone with the dog. Do not worry if, after having the dog come three or four times, he will not divert his attention or go far enough away from you to practice it again. That means the lesson is over for the day. Try it again in a few days or a week.

For class recalls, the dog goes on a long line. You and the dog start out walking. The dog is not at heel and is allowed to range in front of you. He thinks he is going for a walk. When the dog is out in front about ten feet, call "Come," tug on the light line, and, as the dog turns toward you, back up and bend over, clapping hands and calling the dog so he comes trotting over to receive lots of praise and a dog cookie.

The Problem Recall

All of the suggestions above are intended to prevent creating dogs that recognize "Come" and avoid obeying it whenever possible. While the come is easy to teach either to a puppy or an untrained dog, it becomes much more time-consuming with a dog that has been taught to resist responding to it.

That brings us to the time-consuming conventional methods of first teaching the sit stay and then practicing on-leash recalls until the dog has mastered them. Then longer recalls are practiced on a twenty- to thirty-foot line. The line stays on the dog twice as long as you think it should. The line is inconvenient. Long lines mysteriously tie themselves into intricate knots between training sessions. There is always a temptation to try the dog just once without the line. But if the dog needs to be on a line in the first place, then he needs to stay there until he is sound in the routine. Taking the line off a little too early can undo weeks of work, by teaching him that he has to obey only when he is on the line. There is no element of surprise in this kind of training. You and the dog are eyeball-to-eyeball on either end of the line. If the dog moves before being called, he is taken back. If he does not get up and start in on the first command, a collar tug starts him in. There is not much fun inherent in this situation, so it takes extra praise and rewards to keep the dog lively. The usual dog goody at the end of each recall is essential.

When working with a willing dog, you can increase his pace by practicing recalls that are as much as twice as long as those done in the ring. Having you so far away makes the dog tense and makes him want to come in faster. To increase the speed of a dog that recalls slowly, it also helps to put him on the uphill end of a slight slope so that he will be coming downhill. Do not ask a slow dog to recall uphill.

THE FINISH

Once a dog knows how to sit in front of you for food, he can learn the finish. I like to use a cue other than "Heel" for the finish since to the dog finishing and heeling are different exercises. It is confusing if they have the same cue. For the finish, you simply lead the dog through the maneuver by his nose. To finish by walking around you, the bait is in your right hand and you lead the dog in a clockwise circle around your body to your left side. To finish to the left, the bait is in your left hand and you lead the dog in a counterclockwise circle past your left side so that he ends up at your left side. In either case, once he is in position beside you, you raise your hand to bring his head up and cue him to sit.

There are four types of finishes: flip, swing, left hand, and right hand. (I illustrated the flip in the first chapter.) For the first three finishes, the dog passes you on the left side as he turns and sits at heel. What distinguishes the three from each other is the way the dog makes the turn. For the flip, the turn is done in the air. For the swing, the turn is a pivot with all his feet on the ground. For the left-hand finish, the dog walks past your left side, turns, and comes forward to heel. For the right-hand finish, the dog walks a clockwise circle around you and sits at heel.

The Flip Recipe

Since I used the flip as a pictured example, it is only fair to explain how it is taught. To begin with, the flip is not an appropriate exercise for all dogs. The first necessary ingredient is an outgoing dog that is a rather eager bouncer. At about the age of four months, most of my

THE FINISH:
1. *Tony starts in a front sit and gets a pet.*
2. *He is guided in a counterclockwise circle to my left.*
3. *He winds up at heel.*
4. *He sits at heel and gets a treat and another pet.*
5. *He is watching for the next treat.*

dogs are taught to keep all four feet on the ground. The prospective flip dog is taught instead that he can leap up and down all he wants, but if he reaches out to tap a person on the chest, the response will be a disgusted "Ick" and a "No feet" cue. Dogs learn quite quickly to keep their front feet tucked in and just bounce on their back feet.

Unfortunately, this is not absolutely reliable. Every once in a while a quick foot will reach you. If you are not able to tolerate an occasional tap, then forget the flip and teach a conventional finish. If the occasional muddy foot does not discourage you, as soon as the dog knows the sit command, he can start on the flip. Trip started the game at five months of age.

First you roughhouse with the dog for a few moments so that he wants to jump up. Bring him on leash into the sit position. Step around in front so that you are facing him. He does not have to know "Stay" for this, as you can steady him with a hand on his neck or shoulder while you move in front. Talk to him. The monologue at this point goes something like this, "Waaait. Eeasy, dog. All right, are you ready?"

He is watching you, because you have just been playing with him and he wants to play again. What follows may be hard for dignified trainers—but it's just the two of you, and the dog won't tell anyone. You give the cue with a small squeal of glee and a little bound in the air. You can flap your arms or clap your hands, whatever the dog thinks is fun. If he accepts your game, he will give a small leap in place, for which you praise him enormously, and you wrestle with him for a few seconds so he does really get to play. Do it twice more and quit for the day. The dog should always want to do more leaps than he has the chance to do.

Three or four days later, try it again. When he is well into the game after a few weeks, and you have both his attention and a consistent bound in place, add the second part. After the bound in place, praise him verbally while taking a couple of steps backward and calling him, if necessary, to get him moving briskly toward you. Guide him with the leash so he will pass by your left side. When his head is close to your knee, change direction; that is, stop backing up and step forward. As his head comes past your knee, call him and guide him with the leash to turn toward you. At this point you are walking forward past his tail and he is turning and trying to catch up to you, coming up on your left side to heel position. Do not make him sit at that position. Praise him when he gets there. Then tell him to sit. Now he gets his main praise, body and eye contact, and another chance to play with you.

*Trip demonstrates
the flip finish
where she pivots
in the air.*

The leash guidance is not a snap or a correction. It gently shows him which way to move. What he is doing is a leap in place followed by a swing finish. After he plays the game for a month or two, you will see him gradually start to swing while airborne. At first he will swing just a little bit to your left and finish the rest of it on the ground, but as the habit grows stronger and he gets both the range and the feel of it, the whole exercise will be done above the ground. You may think that six months is a long time to teach an obedience exercise. It is. But it is not a long time to play a fun game. At the time the photos were taken, Trip had been doing the flip for nine months, and the total elapsed training time on it was about six hours done in three-minute sessions.

One word of caution: Keep your chin up! Once the dog is doing the leap, resist the temptation to lean over, look down at him, and give the command. The dog does not check to be sure that everything above him is clear before he leaps. He tucks his nose down and leads with the top of his head. He is rising fast and the top of his head is very hard. Try to avoid it. I have had to have a few teeth capped.

The cue word should be something other than "Heel," as the dog will bounce a little whenever he hears the finish cue. Trip was taught to finish to "Heel," and as a result she now does regular heeling on hand signals to avoid little extra leaps in the ring.

HAND SIGNALS

Although you have not been trying to teach the dog hand signals, the fact that he is following your bait hand through the exercises will have taught him the basics of hand signals. The rising hand means "Sit." The hand going down to the ground means "Down." The hand moving away from his nose at nose level means "Stand." Your hand spread out in front of his face means "Stay." The circle to your left with your left hand means finish to the left, and the circle with your right hand means do a right-hand finish. When the time comes to teach him formal hand signals, you can build on what he already knows.

THREE MORE EXERCISES TO GET READY FOR RALLY

Rally is a sport in which the handler and dog walk from station to station in the ring and perform the obedience move shown on the Rally signs. Novice Rally is done on-leash. Rally Advanced and Rally Excellent are done off-lead. You are allowed to talk to your dog throughout the class and give repeated cues. You are not allowed to touch your dog. Any dog trained through his obedience Novice level can pass Novice Rally by learning a few extra items. You need to teach the moving down, where you are heeling with the dog and down him as you stop. And you need to teach the inverted U-turn where you turn counterclockwise while the dog turns clockwise in an about-turn. The dog does a regular about-turn; you are the one who turns the opposite way. There is also a reverse U-turn, where you and the dog both turn 180 degrees to the left. You won't see any of these turns in obedience, but they are not difficult. Rally has a much higher passing rate than obedience. As a result, most exhibitors enjoy it and it has become very popular. As Rally and Agility entries have gone up, obedience entries have fallen off. Passing Rally is much more fun than failing obedience, and the number of ways to fail is much smaller in Rally than it is in obedience. About the only ways to fail the Novice Rally class are to get lost on the course or to touch your dog. In the advanced classes, you can also fail if your dog leaves the ring or just runs out of control. (Sometimes the dogs get excited by the jumping in the advanced classes.)

8

Jackpot: The Final Step in Food Training

Food Training for Competition

So your dog is nicely food trained and now you want to show off how well trained he is at an American Kennel Club obedience trial. Here, a lot of good food trainers hit a snag. AKC rules forbid carrying or offering food in the obedience ring or in a tracking field. The ban on food in tracking is new enough so that I had titled tracking dogs both prior to the ban and after it was in place. And it was tracking that showed me how to train a dog that would complete an AKC obedience class without food.

The problem was simple. Handlers with a good-working food-trained dog would enter the Novice obedience class and find that their dog would stop working before the end of the off-lead heeling. They would start the class well but, by the time the first two halts had been called in the heeling pattern, the dog would look uncertain. During the off-lead heeling, the dog would fall farther and farther behind. When he was six feet back, he would halt and let the handler walk away. Why did he stop heeling?

Look at what happened from the dog's point of view. In training and in practice matches, he had been rewarded every time he performed part of an exercise correctly. He had been rewarded for every straight sit in the heeling pattern

The jackpot system is borrowed from tracking training. Sunny loved to track.

and for every about-turn. He had come to rely on the food to tell him when he was right. He had come to expect a reward for every correct response.

What happens when you take him into competition thinking like this? The two of you heel, do a couple of turns and a halt. He sits beside you, but you neither praise nor reward him. Instead you say "Heel" and start off again. From the dog's point of view, by not rewarding him, you have just told him he was wrong. Every time that he expects to be rewarded and isn't, that is another indication that he is continuing to make mistakes. By the time he gets to the off-lead heeling, you have told him that he is doing it all wrong at least a half dozen times. And so, somewhere during the off-lead heeling, he decides that he can't do anything that will please you and he stops.

This is not a spiteful plot that food-trained dogs spring on their trainers. It is the predictable result of showing a dog that expects to be rewarded for every correct action. And the solution is simple.

The solution is to teach the dog the joy of working for intermittent rewards. I start out by rewarding every second correct response. Most dogs can skip every other reward with no problem. Then we go to every third response. Gradually we reach the point where the dog is rewarded only at the end of the off-lead heeling, and the long down.

You need to realize that our reward-every-correct-response reflex is just as much a habit as the dog's routines. And it is our own response that we have to modify in order to teach the dog intermittent rewards. To do that we have to pay attention to what we are rewarding. That takes more thought than rewarding every correct move. If we are going to reward only one-third of the correct responses, then we want to reward the ones that were the hardest to perform, or the ones that were done exceptionally well, or the ones where failure would be nonqualifying instead of points off. Now offering rewards takes a judgment call by the trainer about whether to reward this move or the next.

When the intermittent rewards have reached the point where there are rewards only at the end of the off-lead heeling and the long down, what the dog receives at that point is a jackpot—all the rewards he would have received up till that time if he had been getting rewarded for every response.

This jackpot system is a training trick from tracking. When you start teaching a dog to track human scent, there is food every ten feet along the track. During the training, the spacing between treats is gradually increased, and all the food that isn't left along the track is lumped together in a jackpot at the end. Most dogs learn to pass up the small food rewards in their rush to get to the jackpot.

I want a dog to come into the ring with me and, when he doesn't get rewarded at the first sit, say to himself, "Wow, this must be one of those jackpot training sessions. I can hardly wait to get to the end of the off-lead heeling."

Why do I reward the off-lead heeling instead of the recall, which is actually the last exercise? Because most dogs that I have seen fail the individual exercises, fail on the off-lead heeling. I want

All dogs love to track. Tracking training is food-based, incentive training. Does Love look like she is having fun? Obedience should be this much fun.

the dog with me at the end of the off-lead heeling pattern, so that is where he gets the jackpot reward.

By the time you reach the end of the off-lead heeling, the class is so close to over that if, on three occasions, you "forget" to reward him and go straight to the recall, he will forgive you the oversight. I have never shown a dog that failed to recall because I didn't reward him for the heeling.

In competition, the dog is rewarded with a jackpot whenever he leaves the ring. He is rewarded for both the individual exercises and the group exercises. I have stuffed baggies of treats in trees at shows all over California. Lacking a tree, you can have a friend hold the treats away from the ring.

So you have your first qualifying score. What is next? Take another lesson from tracking and intersperse the trial performances with both heavily rewarded and intermittently rewarded practice sessions. In tracking, a short, heavily baited track is called a motivational track. It builds the dog's speed and confidence. The same applies to a reward-every-correct-response obedience practice. Don't ever make everything the dog does difficult. The idea is for the dog never to know whether this will be a heavily rewarded, an intermittently rewarded, or an outside-the-ring rewarded performance, and for him to be familiar with all three types of routine.

9

Happiness Is a Well-Trained Dog

The Open Class Exercises

OPEN A: THE DISASTER CLASS

Some of the dogs that breezed easily through Novice will also succeed in Open A. Most dog-handler teams, however, have a problem with Open A. At an average obedience trial, over 60 percent of the Novice dogs will qualify, while a passing rate of 25 percent is considered normal for the Open A class. This percentage is not due to any impossibility in the class exercises. Once the dogs are experienced in Open A, the success rate in Open B rises above 50 percent. What makes Open A the disaster class is that many inexperienced handlers assume it is simply an extension of Novice. It isn't. The Open exercises are different in kind from the Novice exercises.

The Novice exercises are designed to display control of the dog; they are passive exercises requiring simply that the dog obey. The Open and Utility classes introduce exercises in which the dog has to act on his own initiative at a distance from his handler. It is at this point that the willingness of the dog to participate in the sport is going to show up. It is also at this point that your ingenuity is called upon to provide the dog with both more inventive instruction and positive incentives to perform.

Sunny retrieving over the high jump.

I have a special affection for the Open class. If your dog learned Novice by positive reinforcement methods, then just continue that system for the next two classes. The higher you train in the class levels, the more important it becomes to have the dog's goodwill and willing cooperation. It helps to turn our dogs into praise and treat junkies.

JUMPING

With the exception of physically challenged dogs, most dogs like jumping, and it can be used as a reward for other exercises.

Equipment

Obedience Jumps: The first major piece of equipment needed for Open obedience is a set of portable jumps, which consists of one high jump and one broad jump and one bar jump for Utility. Standard-sized jumps used in obedience trials are five feet wide. No one needs jumps this size unless the jumps are going to take up permanent residence in the backyard or be transported by van. You need lightweight jumps between 42 and 48 inches wide that can be transported to a variety of training locations. Portable jumps are commercially available from mail order companies.

Dumbbells for Pointy-Nosed Dogs: The AKC specifies that the dumbbell be a single piece and be in proportion to the dog's size. Most wooden dumbbells are not made in a single piece. They are made from a center dowel with the ends set on and glued. Many of the wooden dumbbells are not hardwood. I was surprised to find that some of the larger ones weigh as little as if they were made of balsa. These have a tendency to break when thrown. The light weight is sought because the average dog is more willing to lift a light object than a heavy one. Plastic dumbbells are popular and durable, but there is little choice about their shape and they tend to be heavy.

Dogs with pointy noses have some special requirements when it comes to dumbbell selection. If the ends of the dumbbell are close together, with a short dowel, a dog with a narrow jaw has a better chance of grasping the dowel in the center, instead of draping it unbalanced out of the corner of his mouth. If the dumbbell ends are tall and narrow, their height will raise the dowel, making it easier for the dog to grasp without needing to scrape his chin on the ground. This is also a good idea for dogs with flat faces, like pugs and bulldogs. The narrowness of the ends decreases the total weight of the dumbbell, making the dog more willing to carry it. The dowel should be half the diameter of those on conventional shepherd-style dumbbells. In the photo, the dog in front is holding a dumbbell proportioned for sight hounds. The dog

behind is holding a conventional dumbbell, and he is unable to close his mouth comfortably because of the large size of the dowel.

Tiger and Sunny with conventional and sight hound style dumbbells.

Dumbbells made to this pattern must be made of hardwood for strength, due to the thinness of the parts. I have never broken a hardwood dumbbell. It is utterly dismaying to see

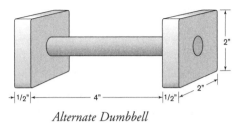

Alternate Dumbbell

someone blow a leg on his dog's CDX because of a broken dumbbell.

Dogs seldom bring back a strange dumbbell. I train with a pair of dumbbells interchangeably and carry the extra one along to shows, having learned the hard way. Just as we went into Open B, we were blithely informed by the lady with the country's top German shepherd that she had borrowed our dumbbell, having left hers in the car. Her dog had performed fine with the strange dumbbell, but was Tiger about to bring me a dumbbell covered with strange German shepherd spit? Not likely. He kept looking for his own. If you do find yourself in the difficult situation of having to use a strange dumbbell, get some of your dog's saliva on the dowel so he has a chance of claiming it as his own.

Jump Training

Owners with confirmed fence leapers will find this section amusing, but many dogs need to be taught how to jump. Dogs that have been raised running in broken terrain will know how to jump; yard-raised dogs may not. I once obtained a kennel-raised greyhound that actually had to be taught how to run. Faced with a pair of reluctant jumpers, I thought about the early training for jumping horses. They are usually started slowly, over short, solid obstacles, to develop timing, balance, and confidence, and to teach them to pick up their feet.

So I set a plywood sheet four feet wide by sixteen inches high across the bottom of one of our gate openings. When the gate is open, the dogs can pass through it only by jumping the plywood, while I have to step over it. The pack runs back and forth over it in stride. After jumping it on his own a half dozen times a day for several months, even the least coordinated dog will have learned to jump competently. (By the way, it is a gate that only I use. The jump would be a hazard to unsuspecting visitors, most of whom are not prepared to run short hurdles.) Once the dog knows how to jump on his own, we can start the training with the obedience jumps.

Health Concerns for Jumping: Dogs of some breeds, like greyhounds, Dobermans, and poodles, are built for jumping and love to do it. This is one exercise where they have a decided advantage over breeds like basset hounds and bulldogs that may have difficulty jumping the required heights. A dog with hip problems that cause him pain when jumping will start to refuse the jump. Or he will jump half-height hurdles while refusing to jump full-height ones. This kind of behavior can indicate the presence of a chronic or recurrent injury, which is not apparent in the dog's normal gait.

Fast-growing puppies of large breeds are subject to both injuries and osteochondrosis, which can cause recurrent lameness and joint tenderness. For these reasons I no longer ask dogs under eighteen months of age to jump hurdles at their full competition height. When a dog has superior jumping ability, there is a temptation to

display it early. But a dog can learn just as much over a half-height fence as he can over a full-height one. For training purposes, the obstacle has to be high

Greyhounds were used in the creation of Doberman pinschers, and you can see the similarity in Willie's jumping style.

Sandi Schneider's Lottie was the first Ch.-UDX Great Dane.

enough only to ensure a jump on the dog's part.

Jump Height and Jumping on Lead: The high jump boards come in two-, four-, and eight-inch sizes. For the average dog, start with the eight-inch jump. For smaller dogs, start with the two- or four-inch jump height. The first jump should be a height that the dog doesn't really need to jump. He could step over it. So can you. He is going to jump because you are going to run alongside of him. You say "Over" and jump, and he jumps with you. The foot fall pattern of the gallop will make him jump instead of simply stepping over the obstacle.

The dog is on leash to keep him alongside you, but it is a loose leash. This is a good place to use the dead ring on the collar to avoid accidentally correcting the dog if he jumps enthusiastically enough to take up all of the leash slack.

Teach All Three Jumps: There isn't any reason to teach only one jump at a time. When you are running a dog over the jumps, set up all three jumps in a row, at minimum heights and about fifteen feet apart. The idea is to jump the whole series, one right after the other. This arrangement has the advantage of giving the dog something to look forward to beyond the immediate jump and of keeping him moving in a straight line after each jump.

Many dogs land off center or cut jump corners because throughout their training they have always been turned or stopped on the far side of a jump. When working with a single jump instead of a series,

Trip running the broad jump.

you and the dog should keep running for ten to fifteen feet on the far side of a jump before the dog is allowed to turn to the side. It is as important to run out of a jump landing as it is to run into the takeoff. The aim is for your dog to run straight at his jumps and jump squarely without twisting into an off-balance landing. A dog that always lands with a twist to the right is not distributing the landing impact evenly and is putting extra stress on the leg he lands on first.

Some of the heavily campaigned senior obedience dogs eventually develop landing-impact-related leg and back ailments. I have a particular aversion to jumping a dog over any greater than half-height jumps when practicing on a cement floor. No one would ever expect either a horse or a human athlete to display jumping abilities on a cement floor. Dogs have no special immunity to the structural wear caused by repeated landings on an unyielding surface.

Each type of jump presents a different problem to the dog. The high jump is the easiest jump for most dogs. It is simple for the dog to judge the height of the plain white jump. The broad jump is more difficult than the high jump. While a dog has either to climb or jump over the high jump, there is no reason he can see for not stepping on or between the sections of the broad jump. This is why the broad-jump training is started with a single board and, when more boards are added, they are first placed so close together that the dog cannot step between them. One or two of the sections are turned on edge to give the surface an uneven height and make the dog reluctant to step on it.

Most dogs seem clumsy when first introduced to the broad jump. I suspect this is because it resembles nothing they meet in normal life, and they have difficulty evaluating its size and shape. The dog in the photo on the facing page is jumping much higher than she needs to. This kind of jump is typical of an animal jumping an obstacle whose location she is aware of but whose actual size and shape she is not sure of. The dog simply jumps on cue, giving extra clearance. With practice and familiarity, the dogs acquire the flat jumping trajectory needed to clear the broad jump with minimum effort.

The Utility bar jump is a most difficult jump for the dog to evaluate accurately. It is marked in flashy black and white stripes, which make it stand out clearly to human eyes. But dogs do not see the way we do. The stripes that make it so visible to us simply break up the bar's outline and camouflage it in a dog's color-blind sight. When set low, the bar is relatively easy for the dog to see against the plain grass or ground. The difficulties show up when the bar is raised higher than the dog's head and he is trying to spot it against a broken background of buildings, fences, awnings, and campers.

I have seen experienced Utility dogs jump blindly at the bar when they were looking at it with the sun behind it. The more cautious dogs simply balked, peering at the jump, trying to figure out the bar's height and location. Because the bar jump is visually difficult, I like to include it with the rest of the early jump training so the dog will be comfortable with it by the time he reaches Utility.

Running over the jumps can be used as a reward at the end of a training session or done entirely separately. When the dog is jumping eagerly, you can run alongside the jumps instead of over them, holding the leash with an outstretched arm to be sure that the dog is still centered over the jumps. Since setting up the jumps is time-consuming, there is a temptation to get the maximum use out of them and overdo the jumping. The dog should never have to jump more than twelve obstacles at a session. Stopping early saves his interest for the next jumping practice.

The High Jump

The only jump that a dog has to jump in two directions is the high jump. To teach him to go over and back, I put him on lead, sit him in front of the single-board high jump, and toss a treat to the far side, sending him with an "Over." If this doesn't work, you toss the treat, say "Over," jump the jump yourself, let him get the treat, and then guide him back over the jump. For most dogs, the treat on the far side of the jump is enough encouragement to jump. Then you back up, call him back to you with another "Over" cue, have him sit in front, and give him another treat. Next you move to jumping over and back off lead.

Increasing Jump Height: When the dog is jumping willingly in both directions, you start to increase the jump heights very slowly. Do not be deceived by a good jumper's natural ability. Some dogs can jump nearly any reasonable height that they believe they can clear, but they need self-confidence to do it. The jumps in these photos are higher than the same dogs would be required to jump under the present rules. (The jump heights have been lowered since these photos were taken,

Sunny would not have to jump this high under today's jump height requirements.

so that now only a really tall dog would have to jump thirty-six inches.) Any able-bodied dog should be able to jump the heights required by the current rules.

Sunny was pressed to jump too high, too young, and under poor lighting conditions. Not surprisingly, it shook her confidence. For months she would readily clear thirty-four inches but occasionally lost her nerve at thirty-six inches. This impasse was not a discipline problem, and a rest followed by practice at lower levels helped her overcome her bad beginning. Don't go too high too fast.

The Broad Jump

All of the exercises prior to the broad jump require that the dog move either toward you or away from you. The broad jump is the only Open exercise where the dog has to move at a right angle to the direction in which you are facing. The directed jumping in Utility is the only other exercise with a similar crosswise direction.

Recall Over the Broad Jump: The jump and the turn after the jump are taught separately. By now the dog knows how to jump the broad jump because he and you have been running the jumps together. The dog also knows how to do a recall from a sit. The next step is to combine the two and teach the recall over the broad jump. The dog is ready when he is jumping willingly at your side, either off leash or on a loose leash, without trying to run out around the jump. Set the

jump at half the length he has been jumping to make it look easy. Put the dog on a sit stay several strides

Tiger recalling over the broad jump.

back from the jump. Then recall him from the far side of the jump using the "Over" cue in place of the "Come."

The key to the broad jump is to place the dog far enough from the jump to allow adequate takeoff room, and to stand far enough back so that he will not have to land on you. Crowding the dog in either direction can make him balk or run out. Don't chastise the dog for stepping on the jump. Simply set him up to try it again and cue him with more enthusiasm. A fast-moving dog does not have time or room to step on a jump. Turning a few sections of the jump on edge will make it look less inviting to step on.

The reason for halving the length of the jump is to reduce the chance of the dog's trying to run out to the side. Some insurance against early runouts is to have an obstruction on each side of the jump so that leaping the broad jump is the easiest way through. The local municipal rose garden was a great place to practice the broad jump, as the rosebushes on the side of the grass walks did not give a dog a chance to run out. When working in the open, a dog that runs out is met by the trainer at the side of the jump, put back on leash, and taken back to running the jump until his grasp of "Over" is firmer.

When the dog is recalling over the jump reliably and enthusiastically, gradually increase the length of the jump. When he is readily jumping three-quarters of his required show distance, introduce the final step.

Moving to Beside the Jump: Once again set the jump at half length. Place the dog as if for another recall. Instead of walking on past the right side of the jump to your recall position, stop next to the jump, face the jump (not the dog), point at the jump, and say "Dog, over" while tossing a treat to a spot ten feet past the jump. If the dog's habits, acquired from the broad-jump recall, are sufficiently strong, he will very likely jump it just as he did for the recall. After he gets the treat, a quick cue of "Come" should turn him back to you and to sit in

The finished broad jump

front for another treat. If the dog has the habit of jumping straight, which he learned from the re-calls over the jump, then he will continue to jump without cutting the cor-ner, even after you move next to the jump.

One of the problems for a large dog with a long wheelbase is his large turning radius. In the turn toward the handler after the jump, a wide turn will bring the dog back to the handler at an angle, resulting in a crooked sit. It takes a special effort for the dog to remember to swing his rump around to a straight sit in front. When he sits crooked, take a step back and call him. If he still sits crooked, and you slide your right foot forward, it will encounter the dog. If you tell him to "Front" and run your foot over his left foot, tickling him with your toes, he will most likely hitch his rump out of the way and into a straight sit, where he is rewarded. Eventually he will straighten up prior to sitting. For dogs that didn't turn far enough, tickle their right foot with your left foot.

THE RETRIEVE

The Erratic Dumbbell

The dumbbell is a sly and devious beast. Go to any obedience trial and watch for its tricks. See the middle-aged lady heave it clear out of the ring twice in a row as if she were practicing for the Olympic javelin team. See the polite gentleman judge bring it back

The throw for grass

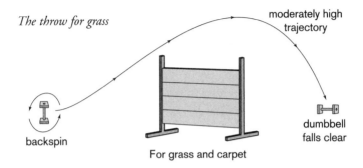

For grass and carpet

The throw for concrete

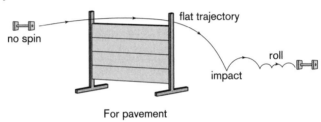

For pavement

to her each time, while the dog looks on in some confusion and decides that if the judge will bring the darn thing back there is no point in having a mere dog retrieve it. See the dumbbell thrown neatly in good position only to have it bounce fifteen feet to the side. The path of a bouncing dumbbell is about as predictable as that of a fumbled football in a Super Bowl game.

At the same time that we are teaching the dog to retrieve, we should be teaching ourselves how to control dumbbell throws. We do this by practicing without the dog. It is easier to concentrate on one thing at a time.

The throw for grass. In order to keep a dumbbell from rolling from its landing position, throw it with a moderately high trajectory so that it is falling almost vertically when it lands. The addition of a backspin will keep it from rolling away from the jump. In order to apply a backspin, hold the dumbbell by its upper end with your hand down at your side. With your arm staying down, flex your wrist forward ninety degrees so the dumbbell comes to the horizontal position. Do it again and release the dumbbell. It should have a backspin. This same flip of the wrist, while using the arm to throw the dumbbell, will release it with a backspin.

The throw for floors and pavement. When faced with a very smooth, hard surface on which the dumbbell is going to roll no matter how it is thrown, all you can do is to try to control the roll. This is achieved by using a throw that you know will roll after impact, a throw with a flat trajectory and no spin—this is the kind of throw that causes nervous exhibitors to throw the dumbbell clear out of the ring. Under the pressure of competition they forget their own strength. In order to make use of this throw, you should aim for a point short of where you want the dumbbell to come to rest, leaving space for the roll to take it to the desired place.

Pretraining Games for the Retrieve

The dumbbell as a play toy. There is no reason that a dog's first sight of a wooden dumbbell should come at a training session. Recently a trainer asked why his dog refused to pick up a dumbbell although he willingly carried rubber chew toys. That gave me a sudden mental image of the puppy pen at home with its litter of hard rubber toys and two well-chewed wooden dumbbells. I suggested leaving a spare dumbbell in the run for the dog to play with. Three weeks later the report came back that the dog now would not only pick up the dumbbell but would defend it in tug-of-war games with its kennel mates. There is no reason for a dog to think dumbbells are for obedience only. They make fine toys. Their main drawback is that they are a little noisy when played with on cement at two in the morning, but you can go back to sleep reciting, "CDX, here we come."

The rag game. From the rag game (see page 143) the dog has learned to run to a target, pick up an object from the ground, and follow something white that his owner throws. He learned that all of

Retrieving on the flat.

this is fun. In the meantime, at home he has learned that dumbbells are just hard play toys. Once the dog has mastered the pretraining play, teaching the retrieve is fairly simple. When the dog is a keen rag dog and voluntarily plays with a dumbbell, he is ready to start on the formal training.

The Food Retrieve: Formal Training

How do you go about using food to teach the retrieve? I teach the dog that the dumbbell is the trigger that makes me give him food. He hands me the dumbbell and I give him a treat. This is just like B. F. Skinner teaching pigeons to peck at a lever to receive corn. I break the retrieve down into extremely small steps and teach each step, rewarding successes with treats. And those treats have to be something that the dog is very fond of. Since there are a lot of rewards to be earned in each training session, the treats need to be in tiny pieces. I generally use liver or roast beef. Each step is followed by a treat when the dumbbell is removed from the dog's mouth. Each step is performed until it is performed correctly, and then performed five more times before moving on to the next step.

FOURTEEN STEPS TO A HAPPY RETRIEVE

1. The dog allows you to open his mouth, place the dumbbell in it, and then remove it immediately.
2. The dog voluntarily opens his mouth when you rub the bar of the dumbbell up and down against his front teeth, lets you place the dumbbell in his mouth, and then remove it immediately.
3. The dog voluntarily opens his mouth to accept the dumbbell without the tooth rub.
4. The dog reaches for a dumbbell held just in front of his nose.
5. The dog reaches for a dumbbell held at first one and then two and then three inches in front of his nose. And then held a few inches to his left and right. The objective is that he look for and seize the dumbbell without having to move his body.

   By this time the dog will generally hold the dumbbell very briefly while you let go of the end and then quickly take it again to remove it. It is normal for the dog to want to grab the dumbbell and then spit it out quickly to get his treat.

   I usually do steps 1 through 5 with the dog sitting. For the next step we go to the down. With the dog lying down:
6. Hold the dumbbell in front of the dog and below his nose, getting him to reach down for it.
7. Place the dumbbell between his front legs on the ground within easy reach. The dog has to reach down, grasp the dumbbell, and then release it to get his treat.

   At this point some dogs will raise their head with the dumbbell still in their mouth, which enables you to take the dumbbell from them and reward them like crazy.

   Some dogs need more encouragement. Sunny at this

point would reach down and grab and then release the dumbbell where it lay on the ground without moving it. To encourage her to pick it up, I tried two moves. The first was to run my fingers under her chin and raise her head with the dumbbell still in her mouth. Then I would take it and praise her.

The second maneuver was to place the dumbbell fairly close to her chest instead of near her pasterns. When it was close to her chest, she would have to bend her neck and reach for it and would then straighten her head and move the dumbbell to a more comfortable position out toward her front feet. At this point I was just trying to get her to move the dumbbell, instead of grasping and releasing it in the same position. After two days of each of these maneuvers, she suddenly picked it up, was rewarded lavishly, and after that she handed it to me regularly.

The objective is to get the dog to grab the dumbbell and raise his head, enabling you to take it from him quickly. When he finally picks it up and hands it to you, he gets praised and rewarded to the skies. Once he hands it to you and is rewarded enthusiastically, it is like seeing a lightbulb go on in his brain. You can almost see him suddenly say, "Oh, that is what she wanted!" You have to be quick on your toes here to get a hand under the dumbbell, enabling him to hand it to you as he spits it out.

8. When he has the snatch off the ground perfected, place the dumbbell outside of his front legs to the right and left where he can still reach it easily without moving out of the down.

9. When he has mastered the grab and lift, start to tell him to hold it or to "Wait" after he has lifted the dumbbell. Slow down reaching for it to get him to hold on until you take it. If he spits it out too soon, just ask him to pick it

up again. Now he doesn't get the treat unless he holds the dumbbell long enough for you to remove it. Gradually build up the time for the hold.

10. When he is doing a good grab and present in the down position, release him from the down, and with him standing next to you, drop the dumbbell in front of him and ask him to bring it. Most dogs will simply reach down and lift the dumbbell to your hand at this point. Remove the dumbbell immediately. You are not asking him to hold it for any length of time.

11. At this point, since I am usually teaching multiple dogs, I often drop a dumbbell or two on the ground with two or three dogs present, say "Bring it," and whoever hands the dumbbell to me first gets the treat. A little competition really sharpens up the kids. But if, as usually happens, one dog gets very good at getting the dumbbell first, you need to let the slower or less dominant dogs have a chance to perform as well.

The first eleven steps can be easily taught in ten days or two weeks with one short training session a day. It is a great thing to teach indoors during the winter. I teach this much of the retrieve to my tracking dogs, where I don't need them to retrieve but I need them to indicate articles on a track by either touching them with their nose or by picking them up and dropping them.

Sometimes you meet a dog that is creative. When I was teaching this to Sheena, Traveler, and Star, two of them had mastered the snatch off the ground and hold, while Star wouldn't open her mouth. She would put her nose on the dumbbell and push it, no matter where I put it, but she wasn't picking it up. A week into the training I realized that I was rewarding Star for placing her nose on the dumbbell bar. And since that is what I was rewarding, that is what she had learned. I had inadvertently taught her to place her nose on a target. There was nothing wrong with Star. She had learned what I had taught.

That night I resolved not to reward her for anything less than opening her mouth for the dumbbell, and I helped her a few times by going back to an earlier step and placing it in her mouth (and rubbing the treat over the dumbbell dowel). That night she not only learned to grab the dumbbell, but she quickly caught up with Sheena and Traveler. You could see the lightbulb go on in her head as she said, "Hmm, I don't get treats for putting my nose on it anymore, but I do get treats for putting my mouth around the dowel."

If you are getting an unexpected response, look at what behavior you are actually rewarding. You are almost certain to be rewarding the odd response. The dog learns to do whatever you reward him for.

You might think at this point that you have finished teaching the retrieve. Not so. If you are interested in a formal competition retrieve, you still need to teach the dog to retrieve a thrown dumbbell at a distance; wait until you send him to retrieve; present the dumbbell while sitting in front of you; hold it for increasing time intervals until you take it. All of these are taught separately.

12. To retrieve from a distance, I usually wrestle with the dog and toss the dumbbell increasing distances, letting the dog run after it as it is thrown and building up the distance slowly: three feet, six feet, nine feet, twelve feet, which is about all the distance I can get in my living room. If he runs out and comes back without the dumbbell, he does not receive his treat and is sent immediately again, with cheerful enthusiasm. If he didn't see where the dumbbell landed I will point it out, or rethrow it. But he

receives his treat only when he brings it back to me. At this point I am not asking for a presentation or a sit in front. He just has to get it close enough to me for me to grab it and reward him.

13. When he is retrieving happily from twelve feet, I ask him to sit when he gets back to me. Most dogs will absent-mindedly hang onto the dumbbell while they sit, and that gives you a chance to take it and reward them. If your dog drops it, you just ask him to pick it up and hand it to you by repeating the "Bring it" cue.

14. The last thing I teach is the wait at heel until the dog receives the cue to retrieve. The dog knows a sit stay from Novice. Ask the dog to sit beside you. Give him a "Stay" cue, slide your left index finger through his collar ring to hold him in place, and throw the dumbbell with your right hand. Then release and send him. Quite often when you first ask a dog to retrieve from the stay, he won't move. In that case, you release him and race him to the dumbbell, encourage him to pick it up, and run back to your starting point, where you take it and reward him.

There are two transitions that can take some time to make.

Changing From a Training to a Competition Dumbbell

I usually start with a lightweight dumbbell that has a dowel that is only ¼" in diameter so the dog can easily hook his canine teeth under it. After he is retrieving well, I go to a standard wooden dumbbell that is slightly wider than the dog's jaw. To make the change, I go back to first handing it to the dog and rewarding him, and then to dropping it at my feet and having him pick it up and hand it to me. I also rub a little liver on the dowel of the new dumbbell. Each dog gets his own dumbbell. They don't like to share each other's spit.

Changing From Indoor Retrieving to Retrieving on Grass

I also usually teach retrieving indoors during the winter. Once a dog is retrieving willingly indoors you might think that you simply walk outside and ask him to retrieve from the lawn. The first time I tried this after a winter of inside retrieving, I was amazed at how long it took to get him retrieving well off of grass. Again you start by dropping the dumbbell at your feet and rewarding your dog for picking it up. It helps to keep the grass cut short and scrupulously clean. A dog will not retrieve if it means putting his nose close to an old pile of feces, even a very small one.

Warming Up

To warm up a dog for the retrieve, I hand a seated dog the dumbbell just to check to be sure that he still remembers to do a take on cue and to give me a chance to praise him for it.

Teaching Variations

Once the basic retrieve is mastered, most dogs work faster if the dumbbell is thrown far enough for them to have a chance to run to it. In order to teach the dog to actually look for the dumbbell, you should throw it different distances and occasionally off-center in a crooked throw. If the dog is used to retrieving after a crooked throw, then having one occur in the ring will not be a disaster. Practice retrieving from three- or four-inch-tall grass, or close to a tree, or from under a bush. The idea is to teach the dog to watch where the dumbbell is thrown and to exert a little effort in locating it. It is not sporting to hide the dumbbell completely. We are not teaching the dog search and rescue. The dumbbell should be in view, just not as exposed as on a close-mowed lawn.

The Rest of the Retrieve

The rest of the retrieve is the hold for presentation. The retrieve is taught without bothering about the presentation. As long as the dog brings the dumbbell and holds onto it long enough for the owner to reach it, the dog is rewarded. We do not want to introduce a delay in the reward until the dog is retrieving willingly. Once the dog is retrieving well, the hold for presentation is introduced. The presentation is of little use to most dogs. It is a relic from sporting dog training, where the dog is taught to retrieve live birds to the hand, and a bird dropped at your feet was likely to fly away. My dogs have yet to bring me anything that, if dropped at my feet, would not just lie there until I could decide what to do with it. However, on to the presentation.

Presenting the Dumbbell

As the dog comes back from a happy retrieve, greet his return with a "Sit" cue given when he is still several strides away. Since the dog already knows the front sit from the recall exercise, it takes little effort to transfer the sit to the retrieve. What many dogs like to do, however, is sit, look up at you, and spit the dumbbell on your foot. For one of these dogs, the sit is quickly followed by a "Hold it" cue. A hand under the dog's chin to tilt his head back and keep his mouth closed will keep him from dropping the dumbbell. Do not pinch his mouth closed on the dumbbell. That hurts his jaws and makes him try to get rid of the dumbbell even harder. Instead, praise

---

RETRIEVING PROBLEM SOLVERS

1. If the dog knows how to retrieve, throw the dumbbell at least twelve feet (better yet, twenty-five feet). A pickup from the ground immediately in front of the handler is one of the hardest for a tall dog to make. He is probably looking out over the dumbbell and does not even see it.
2. Give the cue cheerfully. Why should he retrieve for a grouch?
3. Greet any retrieve with glee and congratulations.
4. Simple bribery is a great help in speeding up of the retrieve. Dogs quickly understand the principle of exchanging a dumbbell for a treat.

*Trip retrieving happily . . .
over the low jump.*

him for holding it, then tell him to "Give," and take it from him.

Retrieve Over the Not-So-High Jump

Before starting this exercise, the dog should be willing to do a ten-foot retrieve and be familiar with jumping on leash. There is a trade-off in benefits in adding the jump to the retrieve. Dogs that carry the dumbbell loosely (many barely hook their lower canines under it) tend to drop the dumbbell when they first try to jump with it. On the other hand, dogs with no great enthusiasm for retrieving often find the jump exciting, and its use may speed up their retrieve.

The first jump should be knee-high to the dog. Do two retrieves on the flat and run over the jump with the dog on leash a few times. Move in close to the jump, no more than a stride back, and toss the dumbbell between the uprights so that it stops a little beyond where the dog will land. This is the same retrieve the dog has been doing with a couple of extra "Over" cues. There are two reasons for starting with a very low jump. The dog should be able to see the dumbbell lying on the far side of the jump, and it should be easier for the dog to return over the center of the jump than for him to detour around the sides.

At first, talk him through the parts of the routine. A "Sit, stay" holds him for the dumbbell throw. A "Dog, fetch" (or "Bring it") cue gets him up and moving. An "Over" helps him take the jump. It may be followed by another "Fetch" if he needs help at the far side. When he picks up the dumbbell, he gets praise, a "Come," and another "Over" for the return jump.

Dogs usually go over and take the dumbbell readily. But the beginning dog often has difficulty remembering that he has to jump on the way back too. When a large dog turns back toward the handler, he may no longer be in line with the jump, and it is then just as easy to bypass it as to detour to jump it. To help the dog make the detour he needs to jump again, move toward the jump and tap the middle of it with an "Over." Then back quickly out of the way. If he detours around the outside of the jump, meet him and guide him back over the jump.

Most dogs will hurry back to a kneeling handler. Kneeling is an invitation to playtime and hugs that few dogs can resist.

Once a dog is at the point shown in the photos on p. 220, he knows all the basic parts of the retrieve over the not-so-high jump. The only difference between this dog and the ones shown jumping full height earlier in this chapter is time and practice. Gradually the talk is shortened to a single "Fetch" or "Bring it" cue as the dog's habits strengthen. Slowly the jump is raised, but no faster than the dog will jump willingly. Jumping a dog within his skill level builds his confidence.

The jump heights for the retrieve should be lower than those the dog is practice jumping, so that the retrieve jump always looks easy to the dog. The main work of increasing the jump height is done in the free jumping. The dog should be sure that he can jump a given height before he is asked to do it while carrying a dumbbell.

Waiting out Anticipation

Once an eager dog learns the cue for an exercise, he often anticipates the cue and volunteers to start the exercise on his own. If the dog is disciplined for anticipation, as far as he can tell he is being punished for performing the exercise. That will discourage him. If he anticipates the cue, steady him with a hand on his shoulder or his collar until the cue is given. We want dogs that eagerly anticipate the exercises and look forward to performing them.

But we also want dogs that wait for the cue to start. The way to achieve both objectives is by teaching the dog the meaning of "Wait." To the dog, "Wait" introduces a time delay between his desire to act and his moving into action. It means that yes, he can do what he intends, in just a moment. This may seem like a rather generalized concept for a dog to understand, but do not underestimate the dog. "Wait" is easy to teach, just by using it in varied situations. The word is always followed by a brief delay, then rather calm praise, and finally by permission for the dog to do whatever the "Wait" postponed.

Steadiness

The wait cue teaches steadiness. To you, the dog seems to acquire steadiness very slowly. While the wait seems simple and is easy to teach, it does take time to make it completely reliable. What you are doing is instilling deeply seated habits through patient repetition. The result is a dog that performs because the habits are so ingrained that it does not occur to him to do anything except respond to the cues. Such a dog is very reassuring to show. I prefer him to the dog that has to evaluate for each exercise the chances of getting away with not performing correctly.

Anticipated Finishes

The dog sits in front of you and, before he can anticipate the finish, you say, "Wait, wait there." This usually distracts the dog from his intended finish and causes him to look at you for further information. This causes a small delay, and he is then told that he is a good dog and gets his ears rubbed. Dogs were not given soft, seductive ears for nothing. This is one situation where the praise is calm and heartfelt instead of enthusiastic. You are trying to restrain the dog, and whoops of glee would encourage him to anticipate. If he tries to break under the praise, you can gently hold him still by the collar. Then tell him to wait again. Reward the dog in the front position, and, after a brief hesitation, cue the finish and then reward that.

Anticipating the Retrieve

Now that you have taken the time to develop your dog into an enthusiastic retriever, he is going to want to chase the dumbbell as it is thrown, in spite of being on a sit stay. However, you do not want to discourage his retrieving. For a few months I hooked a finger through Trip's collar to hold her in place as the dumbbell was thrown. After the stay cue and the throw, she was told "Wait," and I gradually released the collar until she was sitting free for an instant before she heard the fetch cue. This same method can be used for all the exercises in which the dog is required to leave the handler's side but tends to leave a little early.

THE DROP ON RECALL—THE INCENTIVE DROP

Trip recalled at a full gallop. My obedience club folk with their trotting shelties and setters said optimistically, "That is a beautiful recall, but you will never be able to teach her the drop." I considered their point. In training it always helps to be sure of what you really want from the exercise. In this case I wanted a dog that would drop with the same enthusiasm she showed on the recall. She should think that the drop was part of a game. Achieving this meant inventing games that contained the drop. A little bribery again proved useful.

Cookie in the Kitchen

This is easy to teach. Instead of just handing out crackers at random, first put the dog on sit in the dog corner. "Dog, down." After a few down cues and perhaps going to him to move the treat along the floor the same way the down was taught, he learns to go down before you go to him. The moment his elbows touch the rug, a treat drops on the floor in front of him. Then you gradually move away from the dog when you give the cue, and toss him the treat when he drops. Eventually you can drop him from twenty feet away.

This is one of the games in which the dog thinks he controls the owner. The dog is full of energy and wants to bounce up and lick your nose. He learns that he is free to do so but that a lick does not trigger your treat handout response. Only a drop activates that response. Dogs pick this up quickly.

Usually a half dozen guided downs that result in food are enough to give the dog the idea that having his chest on the ground moves your hand to his mouth. This is taught away from the training area. Dogs that are good at it will start to drop whenever you walk past the refrigerator in the hopes of activating the response. Once the dog has learned the game, remember to play it with him occasionally to keep him in practice. He may do a lot of volunteer drops that you do not notice and do not reward with food. He will become discouraged unless you make the effort to reward him from time to time.

The Down Cue

"Daaaoouwn!" is not the way the down cue is given in order to get a quick reaction from the dog. *Down* is a one-syllable word. It is one of the mushier cues, since it lacks crisp consonants. However, by stressing the *d* and contracting the rest of the word, it is possible to make the down cue into a brisk one-syllable word. Brisk cues produce quicker responses than drawn-out ones.

The Recall From the Drop

The first training for the drop is taught separately from the recall to avoid slowing the recall. You don't want to slow a dog down on the recall because the dog's response in the recall will be carried over into his performance of all the related exercises where he approaches you.

Once a dog's recall has been slowed, that same slowness will be reflected in the retrieves, the signal exercises, scent discrimination, and the glove exercise. We try to preserve his speed by not recalling him into a drop. Instead we practice remote drops and recalls from drops.

The Remote Drop and Recall: Once the dog has Cookie in the Kitchen mastered, practice dropping him everywhere: in the park, on street corners, out in the yard—and don't forget his bait. Try giving him a "Down" when he is five or six feet away with his side to you. He will likely turn and come. Take him gently back to where he was and repeat the "Down." Give him his cookie and add "Stay," which he already knows.

If he dropped without help, run out to him to reward him and tell him to stay. You run to the dog to reward him before he breaks the down, but he does not know that is the reason for the hurry. He just knows that if he holds his position while you run to him, he will be rewarded. Then tell him to wait, hurry away from him, turn, and after a moment's hesitation, give an enthusiastic "Come." You are trying to teach the dog that immediately after the drop he will have a chance to run to you, which is fun. And it is your job to make it fun with praise, play, and treats. Leap up and down and whoop a little. Back away from him. Talk to him. Do whatever you have to do to bring the dog out of the down at a run.

Putting It All Together

What we have been doing is teaching the dog to drop on cue, both close to and at a distance from the handler. When the dog is doing a reliable drop, we try it during a recall.

First take the dog to the spot where you want him to drop. Put several treats on the ground and let the dog see and smell them. Take the dog past the treats and put him on a sit stay facing them. Then stand next to the treats, call the dog, and down him at your feet with his nose on the treats. He gets treats and praise and is told to stay down.

Then back away from the dog, wait a moment, and call him to come, where he gets another treat. When the dog is reliably coming to the treats at the drop zone and dropping to eat them, start backing up. If he still goes to the treats and downs on cue, run to him and give him extra treats. Then back up again and call him to finish the recall.

If he drops on cue, fine. If not, take him back to where he should have dropped and tell him to down and stay. Give him a treat. Then back away from him, praise him, and call him out of the drop. This shows him that he should have gone down and that, if he does drop, he gets to finish the recall in a few moments.

The first time the dog does drop, run out to the dog to treat and play with him, then release him from the exercise as part of his reward. Later on, when he is dropping regularly, every time he does so on cue you run to the dog to reward him, and then back off again to do the rest of the recall. Still later you alternate recalls with no drops, recalls with drops where you reward the dog and release him just for dropping, and formal drop on recalls where the dog does the entire exercise. If you neglect going out to the dog some of the time, his performance will deteriorate.

Once the dog knows the drop on recall, he will start to anticipate the drop. I then practice three straight recalls for every recall with a drop in it. The dog quickly learns that the Open ring means he will have to do a drop, so at practice matches I do only straight recalls.

The faster the dog does the recall, the farther out he should be told to drop. If a dog is close to you by the time he hears the drop cue, it is too easy for him to come on in and either not drop or drop at your feet. So start by giving a drop cue with a lot of emphasis and a hand signal for good measure.

The incentive drop worked so well on Trip that her recall became not slower, but faster. When showing her, I had to warn the judges to tell me to call her and tell me to drop her without any hesitation between the two commands or she would reach me before I could tell her to drop. Most of them then said to drop her next to the high jump. That worked, but in order to do it, I had to give the come and drop cues without any hesitation between them. She could cover half the ring length while I was saying, "Tripper, Down."

The Long Sit and Long Down—Group Games

Dogs respond to the group exercises according to their temperaments. From Novice, the dog knows how to do a thirty-foot sit stay and down stay with the handler in view. What remains is to increase the duration of the stays and to hide the handler.

We spend 80 percent of our time on the sit stay. Once a dog is steady on the sit stay, the down stay is easy. Here are two games for the stay.

The freaked-out handler. Leave the dog on a sit stay. At a distance of thirty feet, you turn to face the dog and lie down. The dog remains sitting. A prone handler is a great temptation to the dog, because a dog will drop on his belly and hold eye contact to invite another dog to play. At this point the dog may come over to see if you are still alive and want to play. If he does break, take him back, replace him cheerfully in the sit, and repeat the exercise. When the dog will tolerate a flat handler, you can add as many variations as your dignity will

Tiger, Trip, Kitty Hawk, and Sunny practicing sits and downs.

allow. Stalking the dog on all fours will rivet any dog's attention. The objective is to create uncertainty in the dog's mind as to what is about to happen, or, rather, to create the certainty that some kind of fun is going to happen when he is on a stay, if he just remains awake and watches for it. For some dogs, the most entertaining thing they can think of is food, so we bait them at intervals during the stay.

The vanishing handler. The key to having the handler vanish is to vanish slowly. Go from hiding behind trees, to hiding behind cars, to hiding behind buildings. The dog practices the sit stay while you play peekaboo with the dog, keeping him in view. Before you try it, the dog's stays should be good enough so that you can be sure that the worst he will do is get up. If he is likely to leave, then he goes back on a long line, or gets inconspicuously tethered to a tie stake.

10

The Superclass for Almost Every Dog

The Utility Class Exercises

THE REAL SUPERCLASS

If any reader has reached this point without noticing, Utility is by far my favorite class. Novice, with its repetition, is a bit dull, and Open, while more varied than Novice, is still too predictable. But the mere contemplation of Utility quickens my heartbeat and breathing. Utility is the class where the dog is working on his own volition, where communication between owner and dog is crucial, and where an owner has as good a chance of blowing a performance as the dog does. To a great extent, it is this aspect of having the owner on trial that makes Utility exciting. A large percentage of the nonqualifications in Utility are caused by handler error. Fully 40 percent of my dogs' Utility nonqualifications were handler-error caused. The challenge is to minimize the errors.

UNDERSTANDING UTILITY

The Utility exercises require that the dog make choices: whether to bring back one scent article or a different one,

Tiger does directed jumping.

whether to take the glove in front of him or one off to the side, etc. Each time the dog is faced with a choice, the possibility exists that he will choose the nonqualifying alternative. The fact that the choice may be nonqualifying does not make it wrong; wrongness is the owner's value judgment. If a dog is punished for being wrong, he can become unable to make choices for fear of being wrong again. A good Utility dog must have the confidence to make choices. Confidence is created by teaching the dog that some choices will receive enthusiastic rewards while other choices produce no response.

The number of alternatives available in each Utility class makes passing it a less than even bet. A Utility B class with a majority of UD dogs has a good day if one-third of the dogs qualify. A Utility A class, for nontitled dogs, has a spectacular day if 20 percent of the dogs qualify. The average show time for earning a UD is ten to fifteen trials, but it does not have to take that many for a properly prepared dog. Tiger finished in seven trials, while Sunny took eight.

THE UTILITY HIGH

The life of a dog exhibitor has many kinds of high points. Later championships may seem less important, but no dog owner forgets the moment his or her first Champion finishes. In lure coursing, there is the fun of finishing a Field Champion or Lure Courser of Merit and the excitement of winning an Invitational Best in Field. There is the maternal pleasure of watching your dog's puppies winning in the show ring as the next generation matures to provide one more link in the breed's history. Each of these moments is special in itself, but none of them quite matches the end of a successful Utility routine.

There is nothing to do except think of the months of training extending back to Novice, to think of the traveling and the shows, and your thoughts turn to gratitude to the dog that is your partner, and you know that he has done his best. What happens then? Well, even experienced handlers have been known to shed a few tears of sheer delight. Suddenly there is a catch in your throat, and the dog's outline becomes a bit blurred to your misty eyes. It is absolutely delightful, and I hope every reader has a chance to experience it at least once.

Before teaching Utility, check the Utility exercises with the AKC to see that they haven't changed. The AKC loves to fiddle with the Utility exercises. In the last thirty-five years, they have made no changes to the Novice or Open exercises (except to permit variety in the order in which the Open B exercises are performed). In the same time, they have made two changes to the Utility exercises. First the seek back exercise was replaced with the directed retrieve. (This was unfortunate because having a dog that knows how to backtrack you and find dropped items is useful in real life. It is worth teaching even if it is no longer a competition exercise.) Then the group stand for examination exercise was replaced by the moving stand for examination. This was a good change. Some judges took a long time to examine a whole ring full of dogs. It was tedious for the dogs to stand for that long. In the moving stand, the dogs have to stand only long enough to be examined individually.

YOUR DOG CAN SCENT

The hounds that hunt by sight are supposed to have the best vision and poorest sense of smell among dogs. However, all dogs can smell well enough to do scent discrimination. A nose keen enough to find bitches in season and disgusting things to roll in is good enough to identify human scent. While people have a self-image molded by deodorant ads, dogs consider people to be one of the stronger-scented animal species. For a demonstration of this theory, visit the primate section of any zoo.

All this knowledge didn't prevent me from wondering about the truth of the saying that sight hounds can't work scent discrimination. But at the Santa Barbara KC Obedience Trial many years ago, the puppies with their shiny new CD titles and I watched Utility until a whippet worked scent discrimination. He did not qualify that day, but he showed us that we could do Utility. After all, if a whippet can scent, so can a greyhound, and we went home with a set of scent articles as a promise for the future. A year later at the same trial, we showed in Utility.

The first step in teaching a dog anything is for the trainer to decide that it is possible. Given a thinking trainer and a willing dog, a great deal more is possible than is usually attempted. Do not limit yourself unnecessarily. Most things are attainable if you believe in them.

THE MYSTERY OF SCENT

Scent discrimination is mysterious to us because it uses the dog's ability to detect a scent that is below the threshold of our perception. It is easier to understand if we consider using our own scenting abilities to distinguish one gardenia-scented article from among eleven rose-scented articles, something that is well within our abilities. The entire perfume industry is founded on our ability to distinguish large-scale, enhanced odors. Or to put it another way, a blindfolded man in a room with eleven ladies who are chewing garlic and one who is wearing Chanel No. 5 can identify the latter individual and retrieve her. Or, just to give equal time, a woman could easily locate one freshly showered Brut user in a locker room full of postgame soccer players.

The mystery in scent discrimination is purely a matter of degree. It may be a mystery to us, but it is not to the dog. While this exercise is the one that the handler is usually the most worried about, it is one of the easiest for the dog to learn. It is taught in small steps, however, so the total elapsed training period is somewhat lengthy.

THE BEST WAY

The key to good training is resourcefulness and adaptability, the ability to find a successful approach, to discard methods that do not work, and to keep trying new ones. The methods given so far in this book are not the only ways to teach an exercise. They are just methods for other trainers' consideration that I have had success with. With that disclaimer, we can go on to the one exception to the rule: There is one best method of teaching scent discrimination, and that is through the use of immovable articles.

Watch experienced dogs work. Often, as they give each article a quick sniff, they linger over the scented article and then leave it and check out the rest of the collection again. That extralong sniff indicates the correct article. It is known as "marking down" an article. Since the dog knows which article is scented, why does he not retrieve it immediately? He is not trying to give his owner heart failure. He is trying to decide if he is sure enough of the scent to pick it up.

In training we make sure that the dog cannot be wrong. For the initial training, the clean articles are fastened down. The only article the dog can retrieve is the scented article. Since all he can bring back is the correct article, he is praised every time he attempts the exercise and quickly learns to enjoy it. At first he may try to pick up every item, but he gradually learns to save time by using his nose to locate the free article.

The tie-down method of scent discrimination requires a lot of miscellaneous equipment, but it produces reliable, happy workers.

- Twelve pieces of hardwood doweling
    Large dogs: 6" long by 1" diameter
    Medium dogs: 5" long by ¾" diameter
    Small dogs: 4" long by ½" diameter
    Doweling comes in thirty-six-inch lengths, which we saw into short pieces and sand smooth. Then we boil and air-dry them to kill the scent of the owner. These clean dowels touch nothing living until practice time. If you think a bitch defending her pups is fierce, you should see a trainer defending his or her clean dowels.
- One pair of rubber gloves for handling the clean dowels without scenting them.
- A scent tie-down board or tie-downs for grass, depending on the stage of training. The easiest beginning scent board is a standard 2'-by-4' sheet of Peg-Board. The easiest way of attaching the articles for large- to medium-size dogs is to use the Peg-Board fittings that are designed to hold broom handles. The fittings hook easily into the board, and the dowels snap into the fittings.
- For later practice on grass, you will need some clear fishing line, fifteen-pound test or stronger, and some hooks that can be anchored in the ground. Some people use gutter spikes, the 8" nails that are used to hold roof gutters to a house. They bend the tops over to form a hook. I cut the ends off a lot of wire clothes hangers instead. Each hanger can provide two U-shaped lengths of wire that can be used to hold an article in soft ground.

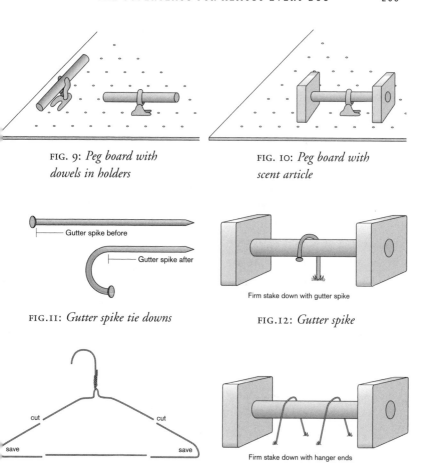

FIG. 9: *Peg board with dowels in holders*

FIG. 10: *Peg board with scent article*

FIG.11: *Gutter spike tie downs*

FIG.12: *Gutter spike*

FIG.13: *Wire hanger tie downs*

FIG.14: *Article with firm tie downs*

Scent Discrimination Indoors

This is a perfect exercise to teach in the house, where you will be out of the rain during the winter and close to the air conditioner during the summer. With the gloves on, assemble the scent board, clean dowels, and holders. Clip one clean dowel to the board. Wearing just one rubber glove makes it easy to use that hand exclusively for clean articles and for touching the board itself, while dirty articles, the scented article, and the dog are all managed with the bare hand. Take one article and write an initial on the end of it. If you are training more than one dog, mark one article for each dog. This will be the scented article for that dog for all the initial training. Keep this dowel separate from the others. Don't boil it to kill the scent. It is intentionally as smelly as possible. Do a little yard work with it tucked under an arm or into a bra.

Then bring the dog on a leash to where the scent board has been laid out with its lone clean article. Sit the dog and let him watch while you put the scented article on the board in a holder that is clipped to the article but is not clipped to the board. Snap on the holder so that both articles will look the same to the dog. Otherwise he will quickly learn to go to the one without a holder. The holder on the scented article is a dummy. It is never fastened to the board.

Take a deep breath and send the dog. He most likely will try to pick up whichever article he reaches first. If he tries for the tied-down article, let him struggle in silence. If he then goes to the scented article, great. If, however, he quits working when the first one won't come loose, cheerfully lead him to the other and have him retrieve it.

The articles should be about a foot apart. Whether he succeeds at first or needs your help, praise, praise, and reward when he brings it back. At this point it is a game for the dog, not a formal exercise. All he has to go on is your enthusiasm. Do not work more than three articles in a row. Frequent, very short training sessions work best for this game. Having a scent board tilted up against a wall makes it easy to play whenever you have a spare moment and the inclination. My dogs were quite happy to try it twice a day, briefly, with a little liver for bribery after each retrieve.

If the dog touches an article, he puts his scent on it, so discard that article as unclean and replace it with a fresh one before you send the dog out again. At first the dog will touch the articles often, which is why you need the supply of clean dowels. With practice, the num-

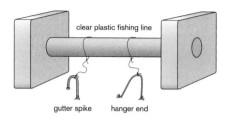

FIG.15: *Article with tie downs that allow the article to move*

ber of clean articles on the board is increased slowly to five. There is always only one scented article. Putting out more than one would confuse the dog. Since he cannot bring them both back at once, he would have to decide between the two.

Teaching scent discrimination is based on gradually increasing the amount of choice a dog has. Developing the complete exercise extends over a four-month period. When the dog is working well with five dowels on the scent board, I switch to actual articles with the clean articles still fastened to the board. When he is working the articles well, we move outside and off the board. Each article has a six-inch leash made of clear plastic fishing line with a loop in each end. The article fits in one loop while either the bent gutter spikes or the hanger ends go through the other loop and into the ground. When first working outside, pin down the clean articles securely. With time, give them more slack until the dog can pick up one before he finds that he still cannot retrieve clean articles, only the smelly ones. The two worst things you can do are correct the dog near the articles and overpractice.

What flusters owners most is when the dog manages to get a clean article loose from its anchor and retrieve it. If a dog gets an article loose, greet him calmly, take the article, and then send him again. Make the tie-down system more secure so that it will not happen again. The Peg-Board holders work fine for the majority of dogs. However, if your dog is a really eager, determined retriever, you may need a more secure tie-down system. The first time I sent Trip to the Peg-Board, she braced her feet, tore all the articles out of the clips, and brought all the liberated articles to me in sequence.

Clean Article

A clean article is one that has been given good air circulation (aired out) for at least two days and has not been touched recently by you or the dog. Teaching dowels are used at first in place of competition articles, because initially the dog will touch many of the articles. Every article the dog mouths has to be replaced. The hardwood doweling can be boiled briefly and air-dried to remove scent for the next day's practice. A learning dog uses up a lot of clean articles, and leather scent articles cannot be boiled.

Secondary Scent

Scent is not a mysterious quality. The body constantly sheds small skin and oil particles, which the dog is able to detect by smell. When you put scent on an article by holding it, the article bar is coated with skin oils and these skin particles. This scent is transmitted to anything you touch. When a scented object is touched to a clean article or to the grass, some of the particles are rubbed off and transferred to the new objects. These now carry your scent even though you never touched them. The dog then may retrieve a supposedly clean article that has been secondarily scented, or he may retrieve a supposedly clean article that was placed on the ground in the same spot where a scented article lay in earlier practice. In both cases the dog is correct. He is identifying the owner's scent with no way of knowing that it is a secondhand scent. Many dogs have been failed for correctly retrieving articles that were secondarily scented.

Dirty Article

This is not a magazine item. It is an article that has been accidentally scented and so must be removed from the layout, as it will attract the dog. Your scent can be applied either by your accidental touch or by contact with a scented article. As I have noted, scent rubs off secondhand. The usual dirty article, however, is one that the dog has mouthed, leaving his saliva on it.

Consider this for a moment. Through all the months of Open, the dog has been retrieving his own personal dumbbell. How does he know it is his? He identifies the scent of his own saliva on the mouthpiece. The dog has been extensively trained to retrieve objects with that scent. If he finds the familiar scent in a pile of discrimination articles, he will retrieve the familiar one. This is why we cannot leave an article on the scent board once he has touched it. It goes in the dirty article pile along with the ones that have accidentally been touched or stepped on. Keep these articles out of the dog's reach.

Air Scenting

The conventional dog does scent discrimination by working the pile, moving from one article to the next, head down, checking each item for scent. He may inspect every single item several times before making a choice. He looks industrious. The air-scenting dog looks as if he is not even working, and he may be occasionally failed for the appearance of not working. He goes to the pile and stands in the midst of it with his head up. His head may move a little and his nostrils may flare, but he looks for all the world as if he is either defying the owner, watching the bitch in the next ring, or going to sleep. After a few minutes he will suddenly drop his head, sniff three articles, and bring the scented one without ever having checked the others.

How did he do it? He was air scenting. Scent rises to him as he stands over the articles, and it enables him to determine the approximate location of the desired one. When he knows its general location, he drops his head and has to make a final check of only a few articles to find the right one.

There are drawbacks to having an air-scenting dog. The most serious one is that many judges don't recognize when a dog is air scenting and may fail the dog for not working, when he is air scenting. The rules require the dog to work continuously. It is desirable to have a dog that "works" the articles persistently. However, if a dog's clear preference is to air-scent, and he is consistent in locating the right article, I would accept an occasional judge's failure rather than refuse to allow the dog to air-scent. There is no profit in interfering with a dog that is consistently passing any Utility exercise. Tiger air-scented and Sunny worked nose to the articles. There was no noticeable difference in their qualification rate on this exercise. If something works, leave it alone.

Leather and Metal Articles

Store leather scent articles in a dry place. They mildew in damp surroundings.

Metal scent articles sometimes come with metal slivers still attached from the manufacturing process, so smooth them off. Dogs can usually find scent on a metal article more easily than on a leather one, which has its own conflicting leather scent. Once they have identified the metal article, however, many dogs are reluctant to retrieve it. Try it yourself and you will understand why. Metal feels uncomfortable against your teeth. It does not taste great either. To compensate, it is a good idea to do plain old-fashioned retrieves with the metal article before introducing it in scent work.

Articles do not have to be dumbbell shaped. One successful competitor used empty miniature fruit juice cans for his metal articles.

Step-by-Step Learning

In scent discrimination, things get progressively harder. First the dog learns to choose between articles with no scent and one with your scent. Then he learns to choose between articles with other people's scent and one with your scent. The final step is to teach him to distinguish between your fresh scent and your old scent. Old scents may be hours or days old.

When the dog is performing scent discrimination well, deliberately touch all the articles at the *end* of each training session so they will have your day-old scent on them for the next practice session. Then for the next practice a few days later, the dog will be se-

Scent is first taught on a tie-down board. In this photo, the board is being exchanged for staked-down articles on grass.

lecting from nine articles with old scent and the desired one that you have just touched. That lets the dog learn to select the article with your freshest scent. Why bother with this last step? You do not want him retrieving at a trial an article that you touched in practice days before, or an article that you used in the previous day's show.

Panting and Hot Weather

Dogs scent beautifully in wet conditions and moderate rain. The weather to worry about is heat. A dog that is panting through his mouth is not scenting through his nose. He may wander around a pile of articles for a long time but, until he actually uses his nose, he will be no closer to finding the object than when he started.

LEFT: *Tiger is air scenting.* MIDDLE: *He checks a couple of articles . . .*
RIGHT: *. . . . and selects the correct one.*

Scenting the Articles

When you are showing with real scent articles, there is a trick to scenting the article. When I judge a match, I am intrigued at the various ways the exhibitors scent the articles. Some barely touch them. Others massage them briskly. Some rub the outside of the article ends. What they hardly ever do, and what I recommend, is place their hands on the insides of the ends of the articles. Especially with a dumbbell with narrow bars, the insides of the ends of the article are the largest areas that you can scent. And you want most of the scent between the ends of the dumbbell, not on the outside where it could be transferred to another article by accidental contact. Yes, do scent the dumbbell bar, but don't forget to rub your hands on the insides of the dumbbell ends.

Giving the Dog the Scent

The rules allow you to hold a hand in front of the dog's nose briefly to give him the scent. Unless the dog is going to be shown by a variety of handlers, this move is unnecessary and distracting. By the time a dog reaches Utility, he knows what you smell like. From the dog's viewpoint, your scent is very strong. Often dogs that have had the hand-to-muzzle cue will sneeze as they start for the articles. They are clearing their nose of the hand's overpowering scent, so that they can sort out the milder odors on the articles.

Adapt to the Dog

Sunny had her own peculiarity. In practice she very reliably retrieved the first two articles, but if she was sent out again, she consistently failed on the third article. It is easy to think that if a little practice is good, then more practice must be great. In this case a little practice was good, but more was a disaster. The solution was realizing that all she needed for qualification was to bring two articles, and she was doing that. There was no point practicing her with a third article since it led only to failure and hard feelings. So I quit pushing her. She was happy, and our scent discrimination "problem" disappeared. Many training problems are created by the handler, not the dog.

THE SIGNAL EXERCISE

This exercise is flashy and impressive to onlookers while still being easy to teach. The hardest part is making up your own signals. The AKC allows each handler to make up his or her own signals. The only restriction is that the signal hand start and finish at the handler's side and that the signal in between be one continuous motion. Hesitating in midsignal is known as "holding the signal" and technically is not allowed though often done. The best way to study sample signals is to watch the handlers during the signal part of their Utility routines. In making up your signals, be sure that none of them conflicts with the signals used to point out the desired jump in directed jumping. Also be sure that the start of one signal doesn't resemble the start of another signal.

General Hints on Signals

Use bait to teach the dog to wait for cues and to keep his attention. Give brisk signals. The slower the signal is, the slower the dog's response will be. Be consistent. Once you find out which signals work well for your dog, do not vary them. Be aware of and in control of your habitual hand motions. A nervous owner can drive a good signal dog up the wall with meaningless gestures.

The Signal Order

In competition, the signals are always given in the same order. First, the dog is heeled on signal. Second, the dog is cued to do a standing stop at heel. On the "Stay" signal, the handler walks to the far end of the ring and turns. He or she then signals in order, and with pauses in between, the down, the sit, the come, and the finish. So there are six signals: heel, stand, down, sit, come, and finish. In the ring, the signals are always given in this order. The dogs learn the order rather quickly and sometimes go on to the next move before that signal is given.

The conventional way of counteracting this anticipation is to give the signals in a random order in practice to try to keep the dog from guessing which comes next. I tried it and ended up with a confused dog that guessed anyway, only she guessed wrong. It resulted in an unnecessarily low percentage of qualifications. Unhappy with that, I taught the next dog the routine in consecutive order, giving him a "Wait" cue with a pause and a cookie between each set of cues. With a single exception, he qualified on the signals every time he showed. As long as the class requires them in order, I will teach them in order. Why make things difficult?

Teaching the Signals—When Anticipation Is Good

With the exception of the stand at heel and the move from the down to the sit, the dog already knows a verbal cue for each hand signal. A great deal of time in obedience is expended in efforts to offset the dog's tendency to anticipate cues. The anticipating dog is only volunteering to do whatever is next as soon as he can figure out what it is. The gentlest way to teach signals is by encouraging the dog to anticipate. At first, run through the routines with the use of both verbal and signal cues given at the same time. They teach the dog the routine order and familiarize him with your chosen signals.

Gradually, delay the verbal cue a bit so that it comes near the end of the signal. If the dog is getting sufficient praise and rewards to make him want to do the exercise, he will start to move as soon as he recognizes the signal and before he hears the following word. While eventually the "Down," "Sit," and "Come" signals will be given from a distance of thirty feet, they are taught within leash reach. The leash is not used for corrections. It is wiggled to get the dog's attention if he stargazes, and is used a little for guidance.

LEFT: *The first step in the signal exercise is heeling.* MIDDLE: *Heeling from the front . . .* RIGHT: *. . . followed by the stop on stand.*

The Correction for a Blown Signal

The correction for a misread or ignored signal is the verbal cue that follows the signal. The secret to the signal exercise is its inevitability. Every time the dog sees a signal, he will perform the exercise. If he does not do so in response to the signal, then he will respond to the following spoken cue. Reward the dog after every single signal, not at the end of the whole sequence. For the down and sit, this means walking out to the dog for praise and goodies between each signal. It teaches the dog to wait for his rewards before going on to the next response. If the dog is rewarded only for the final step—the come and finish—he will start omitting the middle steps to reach the reward sooner.

The Stop on Stand

This is usually taught by signaling the dog with one hand and running the free hand under his flank to hold him in the stand as he stops. What has to be overcome is the dog's well-taught reflex to sit whenever he is heeling and you halt.

Getting the dog to stop in a stand is fairly simple. The difficulty is that the dog tends to walk forward and stop hip to hip with you instead of stopping in heel position with his neck alongside your knee. Faced with a dog that was a confirmed drifter, I struggled along for several months trying to think of a solution. Finally I thought, "Why does she drift in obedience, when she does a perfect stop on stand for breed shows?" It can take months just to ask the right question.

Her show stops were good because I had taught them to her by an entirely different method. The show technique was simple and relied on positive reinforcement. Every show dog is taught a free stack for the moment when he is halted in front of the judge. At this point a sloppy stop is a disaster, so we practice good stops.

Conformation classes teach three things: judge's exams, gaiting patterns, and the square stop. Trot the dog out on leash and, as he is stopped, wave a piece of dried or cooked liver in front of his nose just out of his reach. Tell him to stand. His head comes up and his attention rivets on the food. It takes a few days to teach and a few weeks or months to perfect the stand. The dog learns that the only way to activate the owner-liver-feeder mechanism is to stand alertly. He learns that standing still and posing gets him more liver than reaching for it does.

Once he has learned to stand, wave additional liver under his nose to coax him to make small shifts in his position, to place his front feet

LEFT: *The down is next.* RIGHT: *All the way down, Trip is not looking at me.*

evenly and straight beneath him. Then bait him a little to get him to raise his head and ears and display an alert (hungry and gluttonous) expression. Through all of this he sees a piece of liver between your fingers and his attention is drawn by a quick flick of the wrist, offering and withdrawing the food. The ritual flick of the baiting hand is the basis of a perfectly good hand signal that any hand-fed dog is familiar with. Why not use it for the obedience stand? So I pocketed some bait and tried it with my drifter. On the third try she did a perfect heel position, head high, stand.

The Down

The down signal was taught back in Open when I taught the remote drop and used hand signals for extra emphasis on the drop on recall. Now it is just a matter of practicing to delay and eventually eliminate the verbal cue. The signal down is just a drop on recall from a stand.

The Tickle Sit

To move to a sit from the down, a dog has two choices of strategy: Either he stands up and then sits, or else he keeps his rump on the ground and backs up his front feet to lift his body into the sit. This second method is preferred because his fanny stays in one place. The

LEFT: *A wiggle of the leash gets her attention.* RIGHT: *A toe tickle moves her into a sit, followed by a recall.*

dog that stands and then sits often moves forward a step or two (or six) while he is standing, which can cost points in the scoring.

To teach a dog to do the walk-up type of sit, place him in the down position and face him. Give the signal and the verbal "Sit" cue. Reach out with your right toe and tickle the ends of his toes, pushing his paw slightly toward him. Most dogs respond by pulling the paw back. In order to have room to do this, the dog has to rise into a sit position. If he leaps up to leave, it means you are using too much pressure.

The idea is to tickle the tips of his toes, not stomp on his foot. We tried for a photo of dog and handler toe to toe but were unable to persuade the dog to stay lying down while her toes were tickled. The dog learns to keep an eye on the handler's knee for this exercise, and as soon as that knee flexes, the dog moves.

THE RECALL AND FINISH

These are both exercises that the dog already knows, so like the down they are just practiced with combined hand and spoken signals. The verbal cues are gradually delayed until they are omitted entirely.

The most common signal evasion is for the dog deliberately to avoid looking at the handler. Looking away so he cannot see us is the dog's equivalent of a person's turning down a hearing aid so he cannot hear us. At a trial, if the dog glances away, wait for him to look back at you before giving the next signal. At eight A.M. on a December trial morning, Sunny dropped onto the frozen ground (for which I was grateful). On cue, she moved back up into the sit. She then turned her head ninety degrees to watch, with apparent fascination, the ring to her left. The judge waited a moment and signaled the recall. I waited for her head to turn back, and waited, and waited. She never looked at me. The judge finally said to call her in. We were up against it. If I called her, it was nonqualifying. If I gave her the signal and she did not see it, that also was nonqualifying, but at least that way there was a chance she might respond. I signaled the oblivious dog. Having watched me out of the corner of her eye for the entire time, her head turned back to me and she did her recall. She has excellent peripheral vision. Never despair. There is always hope, even when the dog has a peculiar sense of humor.

THE MOVING STAND

In the moving stand you heel the dog, tell him to stop and stand, walk away from him for twenty feet, turn and face him. Then the judge goes to the dog and does a more thorough exam than the Novice class exam. After the judge leaves the dog, he or she will tell you to call your dog to heel. The dog is supposed to come to you and go straight to heel without sitting in front of you first. Mind you, you have spent all of Novice and Open trying to keep your dog from doing automatic finishes, and to keep him from stopping while he is heeling. So now the AKC has added an exercise that makes you teach him to stop while heeling and do an automatic finish.

The dog knows all but one of the parts of this exercise, which makes it possible to talk him through it. The overly thorough exam is the only thing that will be new to the dog. To teach the stop on stand, heel the dog, then give him a stop on stand signal while gently touching his nose and keep walking. He should stop at the touch. Then walk back to him to reward him. For the come to heel (automatic finish), pick a cue that is different from either come or finish. Give the cue, bounce up and down to get him coming to you, and when he gets ready to sit in front, lead him around behind you with a treat. You have spent so much time trying not to let the dog learn the automatic finish that it is easy to teach. Practice stand stays where you are twenty feet in front of the dog. Then practice the Utility exam with you doing the examination. Then recruit strangers to do the exam.

THE DIRECTED RETRIEVE

The heart of the directed retrieve is the dog's ability to do a good pivot at heel. When the gloves are set out by the ring clerk, they are positioned behind the dog and handler. In theory this is done to keep the dog from watching them laid out, but, since all the dog has to do is look back over his shoulder, some dogs peek. The judge indicates a particular glove by number, and the first thing you have to do is remember which glove goes with which number. When you are facing the gloves, they are numbered 1, 2, 3 from left to right. But when the judge tells you the number, your back is to the gloves. More than one handler has ended up facing the wrong glove. However, once you figure out which glove you are supposed to turn to, you do a pivot in place and the dog turns with you.

This is where the quality of the pivot matters. If the dog has been taught to go straight out and to retrieve whatever is in front of him, he will do just that. If dog and owner are both facing glove number one, the dog will retrieve glove number one. If the pivot was sloppy so that you are facing glove one but the dog is sitting crooked facing glove two, then the dog will go straight out and retrieve glove two. We need good pivots that end in straight sits. We get them by practicing pivots and by calling on the dog to straighten up if he needs to. This is done without bothering with the retrieve. Since the dog and handler are not going anywhere in a pivot, it is possible to practice quite a few pivots in less than two minutes. It also does not take any space and is the ideal exercise when you have neither time, space, nor equipment to practice anything else. Perfect pivots pay off. They are also very helpful in Rally. Many of the Rally exercises consist of obedience practice routines like this.

Sunny would eventually straighten her sit for a quizzical look and a lifted eyebrow. She also had the endearing habit of picking a glove to stare at. If she was sent out, she would retrieve the glove her nose was

THE DIRECTED RETRIEVE SEQUENCE: *1. We start with our back to the gloves. 2. We pivot to face the left-hand glove. 3. I am facing the left glove but Sunny is looking at the right glove. If I send her now, she will retrieve what she is looking at. 4. When she isn't sent, she looks at the left glove. 5. I send her to retrieve it. 6. You can't hold the signal. 7. Sunny retrieves the correct glove. . . 8. . . . brings it back. . . 9. . . . and delivers it.*

pointing at. If she was not sent out promptly, then she would pick another glove to stare at and would retrieve that one if sent. She just cy-
cled through the gloves until told to retrieve and would bring
whatever she was looking at when she heard the cue. It was reassuring.

All dogs are different. Tiger had his own system. He performed
clean pivots and had the desirable high percentage of straight sits,
which was fortunate because once he had his rump on the ground
and his attention on a glove, there was no chance of distracting him
to a different one. He had to get it right the first time because he
would sit endlessly targeted on the wrong glove.

As long as the handler is allowed to face the desired glove, the dog
is perfectly capable of taking his direction from you. All that is
needed is a good pivot and a straight go away. Sometimes the hand
signal distracts the dog. He turns his head to watch your hand and
starts out without concentrating on a particular glove. So I add the
signal after the dog is steady on the directed retrieve and will not be
distracted by the signal. The signal would really be of use only if you
had to stand in a fixed position and had to send the dog in a variety
of directions. That way, the dog would not be able to take direction
from your position.

DIRECTED JUMPING

All directed jumping is divided into three parts. While it is called one
exercise, it is really three separate exercises, and the parts are rarely
combined except in the show ring. The parts are the go away, the remote sit, and the directed jump. On the first cue and signal, the dog
leaves you and crosses the ring in the go away. On the second cue, the
dog turns and sits in the remote sit. On the third cue and signal,
the dog returns to you by detouring over the indicated jump. After
the finish, the whole procedure is repeated for the second jump.

The Go Away

The dog in the photo below is in the first stride of a gallop and is accelerating. She started when she heard the first syllable of the cue, and I had not had time to drop my hand through the rest of the signal. In order to get a dog to move like this, she has to be moving toward something she wants keenly. For the dog that will play, that object is a target toy; it can be a rag or bunny skin. If I am slow in providing a toy, my dogs will retrieve all the litter on the field. The play target go away is the fastest of all the go aways. If, however, the dog is indifferent to toys and rag games but will eat, a perfectly acceptable target is a saucer with a treat on it.

There are two basic things to remember for the go away. The first is that the longer the go away is, the more speed the dog will use. After the initial learning stages, our practice go aways are normally forty to fifty yards long, as compared to a ring go away of forty feet. The second consideration is that the basic purpose of this training is to build such a strong habit in the dog that when he hears the cue "Go," he will have run forty feet before he has time to think about what he is doing. A lot of repetition slows the dog down. If you did three fifty-yard sprints, you would start to slow down on the fourth one too. So we do not do more than three go aways in a session. They are either worked separately from routine training, or else they are the very last thing done after a practice. They are the dog's release. (If you are using food instead of a target toy, then

The go away. Trip hauling out into a run.

you get to do more repetitions. Dogs are more quickly bored with toys than food.)

The go away was introduced when you played your first rag games, but here is the formal part of it. Tease the dog with the rag, or give him a cookie sample, depending on what you are going to use for bait. I was once caught between a class trainer who insisted that everyone use gloves for bait and a dog that insisted on food. The resulting compromise was gloves with dog crackers inside. If you use food, it should be on or under an object that is more visible to the dog than a small dog cracker. We do not want the dog doing a search routine to locate a cracker in the grass. Do not, incidentally, use a glove. Doing so interferes with the glove exercise. (The bitch trained with the cracker-filled glove acquired a tendency to check out all the gloves on the glove exercise to see if any of them contained dessert.)

When the dog is interested in the bait, put him in a sit stay. Walk out twenty feet and put the target down. Sometimes the dog will break the sit stay, especially if you are teaching this early in the dog's training career, which is when I start it. If he breaks the sit stay, take him back to his original spot (leave the target behind on the ground) and tell him to sit and wait. (If you are using food instead of a target toy, then start out with the food five feet away, do a lot of repetitions, and gradually move the food out to twenty feet.)

At first, give him whatever your command release word is, for instance, "Okay," along with the "Go." If he does not move, push on his shoulder to get him on his feet and race him to the toy or bait with whoops and encouragement. After a few tries he will outrace you to the target and, once he beats you to it, you will never outrun him to the target again. By the way, he gets to play with or eat treats from the target every time. He does not have to win to earn it.

This is not a retrieve. He does not have to bring the target back. He should grab it and run with it. Teach this exercise in a large, safe area. His reward for doing the go away is the chance to play with the target. This is why the exercise should be something that he wants to do much more often than you give him the chance to do it. Infrequent practice will keep his attention high. Once he has the idea and is doing twenty-foot go aways, gradually increase the distance to two or three times the length of an obedience ring. This is not difficult. As long as the dog sees the target dropped, he will not be too concerned about its distance.

A good rag dog already knows this much of the game. However, in competition we cannot drop a target outside the ring, so now we have to teach the subtle part. We begin to conceal the target so that the dog cannot see it until he has covered the first forty feet of the run. Dogs are built close to the ground. We can see an object on the ground at a much greater distance than they can because of our greater height. In order to conceal the target from the dog, all that is needed, when it is fifty feet away, is to place it in a slight depression in the ground. I use the holes around sprinkler heads in the park.

It is not fair to keep changing your target location. Pick one and stick to it. Don't worry about not being able to send the dog in any direction. Right now all you want is to send him reliably in one direction.

I practice go aways in two different park areas. In each one we have a standard go away direction, and there are two target concealing sprinklers in line with each other. If the dog reaches the first sprinkler and does not find the target, he knows that if he keeps going straight, the second sprinkler will have it. It is interesting to see just how much faith a dog can have.

We once had a judge from out of state set the scent articles in the center of the ring between the jumps. That requires sending the dog out in the same direction as if he were doing a go away. Tiger went out to the articles, through the articles, past the articles, and continued under the far ring rope, on a very nice go away. There was an athletic field beyond the ring. It was a miserably hot day. He had just taken the points in breed and I was feeling rather mellow. Curious to see just how far he would go, I didn't interfere. He was trotting along fifty yards out when the judge suggested that perhaps I had better call him or we might never see him again. He would just disappear into the west, like the hero at the finish of a western movie. I called. He returned along the same line and picked out the correct scent article on his way back.

Tiger was not generally noted for his sense of humor, but every dog has his day and this was his. On the long stand, he sat. On the long sit, he lay down. And on the long down, which he always passed (except for this day), he stood up. He had made his point. That was the last time we entered obedience in temperatures above 100°. (Actually, our first 100°+ Trial should have been enough. He retrieved the correct scent article and, with an eloquent expression, spat it out on my foot.) Some owners are a little slower to train than others. It took two tries for him to teach me that we would rather spend summer days at home than suffer through the heat of an inland dog show. After that I started the tradition of giving the dogs a month's vacation from training every August.

Hiding the Target: The next step in the go away is to progressively conceal the target. At first it is on the ground next to the depression. One run at a time, it gradually sneaks farther and farther into the depression until, after a few weeks, it is entirely out of sight from the dog's starting position. The important part is that the dog has faith that it is indeed there, whether or not he can see it from the start. You are building his habits. Do not send him out unless the target is there. Do not break the faith at this point. If he overruns the target or has trouble finding it, run out and show him where it is; don't let him start to circle and hunt.

In the beginning, I let the dog watch me hide the day's first target. Later on, I hid the first target before the dog was brought out on the field. Eventually he came to believe that when I tell him to go out, there will be a concealed target in position, even when he has not seen me go near the place.

Do not be concerned that the dog is always being sent to a specific location. You will transfer this orientation to the Utility ring, where he goes down the center of the ring between the high and bar jumps. As long as the dog is used to going straight for thirty yards, he will go straight between those jumps to the far ring rope. Start setting the target along the line you want him to take, and the dog starts to use your direction and the jump location to orient himself in the ring.

The target is often set outside the ring to teach him not to stop at the ring ropes. Even when the dog is showing, most practice go aways are still done in the open with the sprinkler heads and the long go away. If you neglect this, the dog will lose speed and distance.

The Remote Sit for Food or Play

In the ring, after the dog has done his go away, he is supposed to turn around and sit facing the handler to await the cue to jump. It does not always work that way. On a warm afternoon I watched a heavily coated dog do a nice go away only to ignore the "Sit" cue. He ducked under the ring rope and went directly to his owner's canopy where he lay down in the shade. In theory, though, the dog is supposed to sit inside the ring rope.

Back in the Open class, the dog was taught the remote down until he dropped any place within forty feet of the handler. You can also use

food to teach the remote sit. You just have to wait out the initial confusion period when the dog remembers the down training and does volunteer drops instead of the requested sits. Keep picking

The go away: Back to the rag game. First tug-of-war.

Then a remote sit.

up the dog before giving him the food. The dog will eventually realize that you want sits now instead of drops.

Or, to avoid the confusion, teach a play sit. First romp with and tease the dog with the fur piece. Then suddenly conceal it behind your back and give the sit cue. If the dog sits, it hears a quick "Stay." Back away until you are fifteen feet from the dog. The distance reinforces the stay and builds the dog's anticipation when the fur is brought back into view. A few more "Stays" may be needed at that point to keep the dog where he is. When he is waiting for the next move, throw the fur to the dog and he gets to take off and play with it. The dog is being taught that whenever he hears the words "Dog, sit," if he sits quickly and looks expectant, he will be on the receiving end of a furry toy. This is one of those exercises where the dogs think they are training us, teaching us to throw them bunny skins or old white athletic socks.

The dog may not sit on the first cue. He may stand, or drop, or recall instead. The correction is to put the dog gently in a sit stay, which he already knows, and to back off to establish the fifteen-foot separation distance. This teaches the dog to respect the distance, and that he won't be thrown his toy until there is at least that much distance between him and you.

The sit is rewarded with a catch.

The Comic Strip Method of Directed Jumping

The go away is not used to place dogs for most directed jumping practice. The dog is heeled out and placed in the desired location.

Given enough pictures of this exercise, I could omit the written explanation entirely. The directed jump is a crooked recall done over a jump. In order to achieve it, start with a straight recall. The next step is to do straight recalls over the bar jump. On page 260, the handler is kneeling in the first photo to give the dog confidence and to increase his speed. Kneeling reduces the handler's dominance and is an invitation to play.

The bar jump is used as the teaching jump in order to give the dog the maximum possible practice with it. At first the bar is so low that the dog barely needs to jump. For a twenty-six-inch-tall dog, an initial six-inch jump is fine. The dog shown in the first five bar jump photos on the next page is using an intermediate height jump. Her intense facial expressions are the result of her concentration. She is still learning to evaluate the bar's position properly.

To move off center, place the dog on a sit stay squarely in front of the jump, then start to edge to the left, moving a little farther with each practice session. For each jump, start with your feet together and hands at your sides. As you give the "Dog, over" cue, take one

TOP: *Directed jumping. First the dog is recalled over the jump with the trainer in line with the dog and the jump.* MIDDLE: *Then the handler moves sideways with the dog still in line with the jump.* BOTTOM: *The handler leans and the dog still jumps straight.*

large step toward the center line of the jump and hold the signal. A beginning dog concentrates on your face and hands. The dog does not care where your feet are. If he can see your face and hand framed between the jump uprights, he is going to jump, instead of coming straight to you and bypassing the jump.

Once the dog will take the jump with you five feet off center, repeat the procedure for the other side of the jump. If you first moved off to the left, now work your way out to the right. The exercise has to be taught in both directions. This is like ice-skating, where knowing a certain turn to the right does not help at all if you want to try the corresponding turn to the left. Each direction has to be learned separately.

The result is a dog that will respond to either right- or left-hand signals and will jump even though you are off to one side or the other. At this stage, the dog is still centered in front of the jump. Once that is learned, go on to the third step. Here the jump and handler are lined up, but each time the dog is heeled into his starting position, that position is farther off to the side. He is still twenty feet away from the jump to give him takeoff space, but he is placed so that he has to detour to the jump deliberately. This is fairly easy for the dog that has had to retrieve a lot of crookedly thrown dumbbells. Whether you were practicing off-center throws as I recommend or you just have naturally poor aim, the dog that is used to coming back over the jump from a lot of strange locations already knows how to detour to a jump. If not, then you get to teach him.

The Last Step

In the final step, everybody lines up with the jump again, and then both you and the dog gradually move to the side. The goal is for you and the dog to face each other with the jump off to the side and have the dog detour over it on his way to you. After one side is going well, practice in the other direction to keep the dog from acquiring a preference for the right- or left-hand jump.

SOLVING PROBLEMS

Run Outs

If the dog does run around the jump, it means one of four things. Usually the jump has been raised too fast or you or the dog has moved too far off center too quickly. In those cases, you lower the bar and move back toward the center line and proceed more slowly. The third possibility is bad footing for the takeoff. The dog will have more confidence if the jumps are set at half their normal height. The last possibility is low-grade lameness, which can cause a reluctance to jump. One of the most common causes for the early retirement of dogs from obedience and agility is the discovery of hip dysplasia when the dog is X-rayed to see why he is having trouble clearing the jumps.

Run Outs and Run Unders

The best solution to run outs is not to press the dog too hard. Dogs run out when they are worried about their position or the jump height, or are getting sore or tired. However, even a good dog may occasionally be confused and miss the jump. You can usually read this in the dog's approach while he is still ten feet on the far side of the jump. The correction is for you to run forward and meet him next to the jump. Then take his collar, lead him back to his side, and lead him over the jump. This is what was happening in the photos on page 261, except that the dog got flustered at being led and knocked the bar off.

A quick word about setting up the jump: If the dog is jumping from the same side each time, then the bar goes on the side of the up-rights away from the dog's approach. This is so that he can knock the bar off its balance pins without having also to knock down the uprights. When you are working a dog back and forth over the jump, place one upright on each side of the bar so that at least one end of

TOP: *If the dog runs out, she is taken back to her spot . . .* MIDDLE: *. . . and run over the jump.* BOTTOM: *The bar is set to fall if the dog hits it.*

the bar will drop, no matter which side it is hit from. Even when only one end of the bar falls, it will give the dog space to clear the middle.

If a dog regularly hits a jump, then lower it. Time and experience will give a dog the confidence he needs to clear the required height. Pressing for too much height early can make the dog jump shy and teach him to run out around the edge of the jump. To the dog, the jump should always look easy.

PRACTICING WORST POSSIBLES

It is a great help to practice worst possibles. For Open, this means practicing retrieves after unfortunate dumbbell throws. For directed jumping, it means practicing jumping from the position the dog would be in after a very poor go away. These photos show this sequence. First Sunny is heeled out and placed in a sit position in the worst position she could assume in the ring. This is where she would be had she done a crooked off-center go away to the ring corner farthest from the jump she is supposed to take, and then sat with her back to the jump. It is a position quite commonly seen at a Trial. It is usually the result of the dog's having previously retrieved a glove from that corner in the directed retrieve. If a dog sits with his back to a jump, some judges out of pity will call for the jump that the dog is facing. Others delight in requiring the jump that is the farthest away.

To be ready for these, my dogs spent so much practice on crooked positioning that, if I set them up in front of one jump with their back to the other one, they wouldn't even look at the jump in front of them. They knew that they were going to have to turn around, run across the ring, and clear the far jump. It is easily taught. You just keep moving the dog gradually across the ring the same way that he was first moved out of line with the jump. By the time the training is finished, you should be able to send the dog over either jump from any position along the back ring rope.

This was especially useful with Sunny. I taught her the go away before finding the proper way to do it. We went through three methods, and the result was so much mistraining that she ended up with intermittent crooked go aways that kept turning up at inconvenient times. We would be at a Trial and she would end up in the far ring corner with her back to a jump. The judge would sympathize with us and mentally write her off as failed. I loved the judge's surprise when she would race the full width of the ring to take the indicated jump.

TOP: *Worst possibles. The dog is gradually moved sidewise until she will ...*
BOTTOM: *...eventually jump from anywhere along the back of the ring.*

THE SIGNAL

Before you actually show in Utility, the signal is gradually made briefer and the step toward the jump omitted until the dog takes direction from a single wave of the arm and a verbal "Dog, over" cue.

THE LAST STEP

When the dog is ready to show, then the go away, the remote sit, and the directed jump are combined in the practice run-throughs, but only for the first two jumps of the day. To practice additional jumping, you go back to placing the dog in position.

AN OBJECT LESSON

In my first Trial for Utility, both Tiger and Sunny were entered, although I really had little hope for Tiger's readiness. Sunny was about a month ahead of him in her training at that time, but as long as we were making the trip it seemed pointless not to enter them both. (Besides, I did not want to admit to Tiger that I did not think he was ready yet.) Sunny added an extra drop to the first exercise (Signals) and nonqualified. That took the pressure off.

I traded her for Tiger and went back into the ring with no particular hopes. I was watching Tiger's back as he went out in the go away when I realized that he was working smoothly and passing very nicely. I almost stopped breathing. Go aways were his specialty. He pivoted to face me and sat precisely centered with his shoulders against the ring rope.

The judge said, "The high jump on your right." I have always had difficulty telling right from left in moments of stress, so I took a

GAIL'S HELPFUL HINTS FOR UTILITY

1. Never give up.
2. Proof the dog at matches before starting to show in this class.
3. Remember that the dog has to make choices in Utility and discipline reduces his ability to make good choices. Don't be disturbed when the dog offers some variations on the exercises. It proves he is thinking and making choices. Just don't reward his nonqualifying choices.
4. If the dog is reliably doing two correct scent articles, or one glove retrieve, or two go outs and failing on the next one, don't ask him to do that next one. He could be telling you he is bored with repetition.
5. Once the dog is trained, alternate practices where every exercise is rewarded with practices where only the last exercise is rewarded with a jackpot.

quick glance to my right to be sure that the jump there really was the high jump. Most of my dogs learn to recognize this slight turn of the head as I check to be sure that I'll be sending them to the correct jump, and they prepare to head for the jump that I've looked to. Tiger took the high jump with enthusiasm and did his final go away.

He sat waiting for the signal to send him to the bar jump, and I grew overconfident. Pride still goes before a fall. He was working like an experienced dog and making the whole class look easy on a day when the UD dogs were having a miserable time qualifying. My class trainer was outside the ring just behind me, and he cared if his students passed. The crowd was packed to see the greyhound's first try at Utility. And I blew it.

There are several aids that can be given in the cue for the directed jump. Things like my normal glance to the left to be sure that the bar jump is really on that side. The cue does not have to be a flat "Over." It can be "Tiger, Over." The dog will be on his feet at his name, taking his direction from the arm signal. This delays the "Over" a bit, to where it can reinforce his inclination to jump as he is headed toward the jump, or at least looking at it. I ran through the available aids that

I could give Tiger, and, because he was working well, and to show off, I gave him a flat "Over" and the hand signal, with none of the aids that he was used to in training.

Taken by surprise by the change in my cue, he ran for the bar jump but was off to one side and stopped, perplexed, on the outside of the upright, looking for a bar to jump. He had been carrying a 196 score. Never refuse to help your dog, particularly if he is inexperienced in the class. Having him qualify with a second place the following weekend emphasized the fact that I was the one who had failed him the first time. I had allowed the opinions of the spectators to divert me from what I should have been concentrating on—Tiger and our communication. When in the ring, the dog is the only one that matters. Do not change your cues in the ring.

11

The Inner Winner in the Ring

How to Be a Winner No Matter What Happens

It is also essential that the dog demonstrate willingness and enjoyment of its work, and
that smoothness and naturalness on the part of the handler be given precedence over a
performance based on military precision and peremptory commands.

—AKC OBEDIENCE REGULATIONS, "PURPOSE"

RING WISDOM

Many strange and wondrous things happen when a handler decides
that his or her dog is ready to be shown. There is a fey and unreal
quality to some performances at an obedience trial. It is as if the
two hundred feet of ring rope create a magic circle within which
anything is possible. How can a well-trained dog and a hopeful
owner achieve a state of total disaster so quickly? Basically, because
the owner's time and effort have been spent in learning about dogs
and dog training. Meanwhile, he or she has not been studying what
happens in the ring. Show techniques and ring procedures are seldom taught in obedience classes. They often are not even mentioned.

I was introduced to them at my first obedience trial. Totally inexperienced, I arrived at the ring with six-month-old Sunny
and Tiger to encounter a kindly Novice A judge. He
asked if we had shown before.

"No."

"But you have been to practice matches?" he asked hopefully.

"No."

Still optimistic, he persevered. "But you have been to your class graduation?"

"Not yet."

The judge looked a bit wistful and cheerfully invited us into the ring. It occurred to me that there was still more to learn.

PASSING OR FAILING?

Exhibitors are often harsher judges of their own performances than the licensed judge is. Most trial judges want to see the exhibitor qualify, and they know considerably more about the rules than the beginning exhibitor. The exhibitor may think that any errors in performance on the dog's part will mean failure. The judge knows

For dogs like Sasha, jumping is a reward.

Which doesn't mean that they don't also get food and play rewards. Riot and Pat White.

that only certain errors require a nonqualifying score. The majority are "points off" errors, for which a minor or substantial deduction will be made from the score, but the dog may still qualify.

It is fun to be able to tell a suffering owner that the failure he or she has just described is only points off and that the dog is still passing. When trying for her first CD leg, Sunny sat up in the last seconds of the long down as the handlers were returning to their dogs. My Novice heart fell, but some instinct (at that point it certainly was not knowledge) told me to wait until the scores were handed out. It was a very hot show and a long wait, but worth it to find out she had qualified, minus a few points for her premature sit.

When in doubt, wait for the final scores to be handed out. As long as the judge has not told you that a specific exercise was failed, there is still hope. There is also an area covered by the judge's discretion, where he or she may choose to rejudge a dog on a specific exercise if it was interfered with because of unusual circumstances. This can be anything from being run over by an Old English sheepdog to being barked at by an irate bitch.

THE OBEDIENCE REGULATIONS

A surprising number of exhibitors don't read the obedience regulations. Every exhibitor needs a copy, and the American Kennel Club is happy to send a copy to anyone who requests it. They are available on the Internet, but paper copies are easier to use. The regulations aren't cast in stone, and they are updated periodically. Hot and heavy arguments take place each time they are revised, over the meaning of individual sentences. Obedience regulations are as subject to interpretation as breed standards.

The easiest way to get the regulations under control is to color-code a copy. I underline the principal features of each exercise in green. These are always found in the first paragraph of the exercise description. The section on scoring the exercise gets coded red for the things that require a zero score or more than half of the points off, yellow for substantial deduction faults, and blue for minor faults. This way it is possible to get the major, minor, and disastrous types of infractions sorted out.

It is also useful to request a copy of the *Guidelines for Judges* from the AKC.

Beware of Secondhand Rules

There is no substitute for studying the rules yourself. At any obedience trial or dog-training class there is no shortage of folks who will tell you things about the rules that are not true. The following are samples of things I have been told are part of the rules:

If a dog does an automatic finish, he is failed.
You cannot dampen a dog down on a hot day.
You can't show a dog in a leather collar.
If a dog drops a dumbbell and picks it up again, he will fail.

All of the above statements are wrong. Beware of secondhand advice, no matter how well intentioned it is. Take a copy of the rules along when you show.

HOW TO ENTER A DOG SHOW OR OBEDIENCE TRIAL

Obedience Trials are open to any purebred dog that is not blind or lame. Neutered dogs, monorchid and cryptorchid dogs, and dogs that have lost their pedigrees can be shown in obedience Trials, Agility, Rally and tracking tests. The only thing they can't be shown in is dog show breed classes.

How do you enter a dog that has no registration papers? You obtain from the AKC what is called an Indefinite Listing Privilege (ILP) number. All the dog has to do is look like a member of some breed. Ask the AKC (www.akc.org) for an application for an ILP number. Return the application with the filing fee and two photos of the dog. When they send you the ILP number, the dog can compete at AKC events. The AKC is even talking about opening their Trials to all dogs.

In order to enter a show or obedience Trial, you need to locate the show superintendent or the Trial secretary at least a month before the show date. Entries close several weeks prior to the show to allow time to have the catalog printed. Kennel clubs that put on dog shows and obedience Trials usually hire a professional show superintendent to handle all the paperwork. The superintendent mails out premium lists that announce the show, list the awards, and contain entry blanks. The entries are sent back to the superintendent, who then has the catalogs printed, assembles the judges' books for recording the results, and is present at the show to administer it.

Obedience clubs put on independent obedience Trials that have a smaller number of entries. Often a club member will be Trial secretary and handle the entries. If you want to be notified of such Trials, you need to drop a postcard to each club in your area, requesting that it put you on the mailing list for future Trials.

The quickest way to start receiving premium lists is to send an e-mail to the dog show superintendent requesting them. An Internet search for dog show superintendents will provide a list and links to their sites. Also search for a dog show calendar. Show people schedule their lives by these calendars.

After you have mailed your entry to the superintendent, he will send you a schedule of the event and a printout giving your dog's catalog number. You take that to the show, arriving at least an hour before your estimated show time. You also take treats, water, a spray bottle, a chair for you to sit on, and something for the dog to lie on. Portable shades are a good idea at most shows.

THE DAY OF THE SHOW

Check Out the Ring

Some distractions in the ring can be prevented with a little observation and effort. It is possible to suggest to a family enjoying a smorgasbord lunch on the lawn at ringside that they might like to cover a few of the more tempting appetizers for the next few minutes or risk losing them.

Double-roped rings are best. They hold the spectators several feet back from the dog and prevent them from dribbling popcorn on the dog's back. Sunny was mad for peanuts, which she would happily retrieve for me to shell out for her. Showing on a football field after a game, she tended to work from peanut to peanut.

If there are skateboarders playing just outside where the long-sit line is going to be, and the ring stewards do not remove them, you can do it. Just rush over before the group moves into the ring and ask that the skateboards go elsewhere for the ten minutes.

Many dogs in this day of plastic-wrapped dog food are attracted by the crinkle of cellophane. A few kind words to a ringside crinkler will usually get him or her to put it away for a little while.

Check the heights of the jumps. Check the ring surface. Grass rings may have holes, sprinkler heads, bare spots, dirt clods, or puddles, depending on the weather. Asphalt-surfaced rings may have eroded paving, cracks, and bumps. Concrete rings can be wet and slick. Whatever the surface, try your best to help the dog. In a grass ring it is not necessary to have the dog sit in the holes. If need be, you stand in the hole and give the advantage to the dog. If the ring is paved with runners or carpet strips for the dogs, then give the dog the center of the runner to walk on. He needs it more than you do.

You can help a dog pass the long sits and downs just by being a little careful about what you are making him lie on. As the line of dogs walks into the ring, check the ground. As you prepare to stop, it is nearly always possible to shift at least a dog's width in one direction or another. Pick a spot that you would like to lie on. If there is carpeting with wide tape fastening the seams together and you are in the sun, do not put a dog down with its belly on the tape. Tape gets hot in direct sunlight.

At one show, the lawn had been aerated, which left the ring covered with small dirt clods. It was easy to reach down and brush a small clear space in front of Sunny. Then, instead of dropping into her usual sphinx position, she stretched out flat on her side. She realized that her shoulder was on a collection of lumpy clods. During the three minutes of the down, she rolled her front upright, inch by inch. She was still not comfortable, and I was waiting for her to stand up to shift position and then lie down again. She fooled me. She gave a little hitch and moved from the hip lying position to a sphinx position without having risen. Finding herself safe in her little clod-free patch, she settled in to wait out the exercise.

Warm up your dog briefly before showing. Once the dog is alert and ready at the ring entrance, you can only hope that he will be allowed to show at once. If the order is changed, and the dog has to sit around idle for another twenty minutes, he will go back to sleep. Even worse, if he is brought up to a ring-ready state repeatedly and the showing is postponed each time, he will become too bored to care about getting ready to show when it finally counts.

Many large dogs refuse to jump full height on poor footing. On bare cement, the problem is usually slickness, and you can help by treating the bottom of the dog's feet with one of the commercial non-slip substances like Tacky Paw. If this is not available, an emergency substitute is to dip the bottom of the dog's feet in Coca-Cola and let it partially dry.

The only solution to really bad ring conditions is to protest to the host club and to the AKC. Showing should not be painful for the dog.

WHEN IN DOUBT, SMILE

We showed in Open for a judge who had the jump in the center of the ring with the broad jump next to it. They are usually on opposite sides of the ring. Sunny cleared the broad jump, turned to come back to me, and froze as she saw the judge and me standing on opposite edges of the high jump. I could see her trying to sort out what was happening. Was she supposed to come to me to finish the broad jump exercise, or was she in trouble for not jumping the high jump? She looked from it to me. I smiled until my face felt stiff, then re-laxed, because a fixed smile loses its effect, and smiled once again. Sunny was reassured and came in to sit in front. The judge said jok-ingly, "I should penalize you for facial signals." She was kidding, but had she chosen to, it would have been fine with me.

The job of the handler is to get the dog to perform the exercises correctly. It is the responsibility of the judge to make whatever de-ductions from a perfect score he or she feels are justified.

WHAT TO DO WHILE FAILING

"He has failed at three straight Trials, and he is such a good working dog," sniffled the handsome young man with the handsome Belgian shepherd.

"What does he do?" I asked.

"He only comes halfway in on the recall and then he sits."

"Every time?"

"At three straight shows."

"What do you do when he sits? Do you call him again right away?"

"I wait until the judge tells me to call him."

The young man had three separate problems: (1) finding out what caused the dog to make its first mistake; (2) the fact that the mistake was fast becoming a habit; and (3) not knowing how to help the dog once he had failed.

What should you do as the dog fails an exercise? If the dog is still in position to perform the exercise, give him an immediate verbal second command, which is usually all that is needed to have him complete the exercise. A second command is not training in the ring; it is just an extra command. It will lead to a zero score on

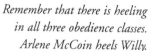

Remember that there is heeling in all three obedience classes. Arlene McCoin heels Willy.

most exercises but it is used only if the dog has zeroed anyway. It ensures that the dog successfully completes the exercise and prevents the formation of the habit of failure. (Failures in the group exercises are accepted as indicating a need for more practice, more exposure to distractions, or a need for more practice matches.)

NEVER FAIL HEELING

There are two main ways to fail an off-leash heeling exercise. The first is to have the dog say, "The heck with this," and leave the ring. The more common way is for the dog to stop in his tracks and stare wistfully after the departing owner. Once you are several feet from the dog, the dog decides that it must be a stay exercise and he stays in place and fails. What never seems to happen is for the owner to realize that he or she is losing the dog and to say once again, "Dog, heel." One additional heeling cue is points off. It is not nonqualifying. Not knowing this, most owners just walk away from their dog. I did it myself once and know how it feels, which may be why I hate to see anyone else in the same situation. When you walk away from a dog in the ring, you are teaching him to freeze during the heeling pattern when he is shown. This can set up a pattern that is difficult to break.

HOT DOGS

People and horses can remain active in hot weather because both have the ability to sweat. The evaporation of sweat is one of the most efficient ways of getting rid of excess body heat. But dogs can't sweat, and this leads them to dig holes in the ground, both to reach cool earth levels and to create shade. They also sleep out the warm part of the day in the shade. When we take them to an obedience trial in warm weather, it becomes our responsibility to keep them cool. This means providing shade, drinking water, and artificial sweat in the form of a spray bottle full of water. The dog is kept damp, like a load of laundry waiting to be ironed. The idea is to wet down the parts of the body that have large blood supplies: the top of the head, the ears, the throat, the underbelly, and, on a male dog, the testicles. The best way to keep a dog comfortable is to avoid those shows that are usually hot.

LOVE AND DISAPPOINTMENT

No dog works spectacularly all the time. To all dogs there eventually comes an off day. When this happens in the ring, it is not uncommon to see an owner showing disappointment in the ring. The owner's rejection of the dog can reach a point where it seems that they are a pair of strangers that somehow ended up in the ring together by accident. The owner is punishing the dog for working poorly by rejecting him.

The problem here is that the more the dog is rejected, the worse he is going to work, both for the rest of the day and in the future. A dog that is having problems needs help, not rejection. He needs additional cues. He needs intensified praise and encouragement at the very time when it is the hardest to give. At this point we find out if the owner is worthy of the dog. It is easy to love a dog that is performing well. But the goal is to make love unconditional, to be able to say, "I love the dog," independently from, "The dog is working poorly [or well] today." The two statements have nothing to do with each other, and once the owner truly believes this or she will never be disappointed again in a ring performance, the resulting sense of optimism and freedom it gives is amazing. If you love the dog before you take him into the ring, you can love him just as much when you leave the ring.

OBEDIENCE FLAWS

Nothing is perfect, neither dogs nor dog sports. They all have some faults. Three problems in obedience are the boredom of most Trials, the attitude of some exhibitors, and the zeal of a few judges.

Time at the Trial

I vividly recall my very first Trial. It took four hours to show two dogs. I watched the rings, read most of a paperback, and went home thinking, "How can all those people do that for fun? What an incredible bore!" As it turned out, what the regular obedience exhibitors do during the waiting time is to renew old acquaintances, catch up on the grapevine news, and just plain visit and socialize. By the next Trial I was no longer a stranger, and I never did manage to read another book while waiting. So the tedium of the Trial is a problem that solves itself as one's circle of friends expands. The time-consuming routine of an obedience Trial is just a bit of an initial shock to the breed exhibitor who is used to bouncing into the ring at the scheduled time and then being through and ready to go home a half hour later.

Hyperexhibitors

The problem with the minority of exhibitors who become hyper-competitors is that they lose sight of the purpose of obedience Trials. Many of these fanatic obedience addicts believe that the purpose of obedience Trials is to give the contestants an opportunity to earn obedience titles, obedience championships, and places in the year's top-ten dog standings. Competition is not the purpose of obedience. The actual purpose is stated in the *AKC Obedience Regulations:* "The purpose of obedience Trials is to demonstrate the usefulness of the pure-bred dog as a companion of man." There is no mention of two hundred-point scores, or High in Trial winners, or even competition.

A demonstration is a "display" of the dog's abilities. The definition of competition is "a contest between two rivals." Unfortunately, for a number of entrants, obedience seems to have become more a contest than a demonstration.

So what is the matter with having obedience become a contest? The basic drawback is that in any contest there are a few winners and many losers, and both suffer in the long run. The winners develop an addiction to winning. The losers are disappointed in themselves and their dogs. And both reactions damage the relationship between the dog and his owner.

Awards are singularly cold, hard objects. They will not snuggle up to you on a chill day or lick your hand when you sweat. The hope is to bring the emphasis off the trophy table and back to the dog, where it belongs.

Judging the Judges

What many obedience judges have in common is that they are well-intentioned, hardworking, and underpaid when compared to breed judges. They also have firm opinions on the sport of obedience.

An interesting thing happens when a hypercompetitor becomes a judge. The sport of obedience has a different meaning to the hypercompetitor than it does to the average exhibitor. Average exhibitors seem to make stable, pleasant judges. The hypercompetitors, on the other hand, move into judging with an agenda. They believe that there are too many high-scoring dogs and they set out to remedy that. They look for ways to maximize the deductions from a dog's score. This can lead to some interesting interpretations of the rules.

I was told by a competitor who would soon be a licensed judge that not enough points were deducted during the long down. He thought that points should be taken off for any movement by the dog. In order to receive full points, the dog should lie at attention in the sphinx position. All I could ask was, "Why? What would be accomplished except to make the dog less comfortable during the exercise?" His reply was that there were too many high-scoring dogs showing and not enough points deducted. This left too many of them at the top of their classes.

Is it possible to have too many good dogs at the top of a class? And what would the totally immobile down do for either the sport or the dog and owner? There is already a move toward this in the hyper-judges, who deduct points from a dog that sleeps on the long down. They maintain that the dog should remain alert.

There is a huge problem with this contention. Nowhere in the regulations for this exercise does it say that the dog should remain alert. All that the rules say is that the dog has to remain down in the same place and refrain from barking or whining. The rules do not say that the dog cannot move at all. They say only that the dog is not to move from the place where it was left. Judges who score off for things not cited in the regulations are violating Chapter 2, Section 5 of the regulations on "No Added Requirements." Judges are not allowed to add their own requirements to those of the AKC.

What is needed in judging is not increased precision or additional items for which to deduct points but an understanding of the purpose of each exercise and of the sport as a whole. Such understanding should be combined with a knowledge of the rules as they are written and the common sense to interpret those rules in the light of the purpose of obedience.

A hazard in any kind of judging is that the judge may be so caught up in looking for minor faults that he or she misses the overall quality and balance of a dog in breed or the overall willingness and cooperation shown in an obedience performance. What does the whole dog look like in the ring? Is he a dog you would like to have? Would you like to see more like him? If he wins a lot, then you will see more like him in future years. Are we going to have more obedience dogs that are precise but dull and methodical plodders, or do we want dogs that make the sport look fun? That choice depends first on the trainers who take happy dogs into the ring and then on the judges for their evaluations of those dogs.

THE PRESENT

In wanting to win, we become so entrapped in hopes for the future and recollections of past triumphs and disasters that we lose the ability to do what dogs and children are good at—to live in and feel the present, to experience wonder and curiosity and feel what is happening right now.

Most sports focus on a moment that requires such immediate concentration that we are forced to live in present time. Whether the sport is powder skiing or jumping horses, river running or acrobatic flying, the attraction of these high-speed activities is not, as is commonly thought, their element of risk. The attraction is that the speed and degree of risk force total concentration on the activity and this compels the participant to live in the present. It frees us of the baggage of past memories and future fantasies that litter our everyday minds.

It is only when we are thinking in the present that we can learn anything, since learning can only be experienced in the present. A good golf swing, target shot, sprint, artwork, or seduction are all done in present time. More important, good dog training is done in present time. Nothing exists for the trainer except himself or herself, the dog, and their communication. Training becomes play and an end in itself instead of homework to be done as a means to show wins. As long as the trainer keeps his or her priorities in order and remembers that he or she and the dog come first and that the trial is a subordinate activity, the results of a show performance will not be allowed to affect the friendship between the dog and owner.

MAGICAL TRIAL MORNINGS

The morning of a dog show, obedience or Rally Trial, or lure course is a magical time. It is also a bit difficult to explain to nonexhibitors. The cold facts of the activities—that you are getting up at five A.M. in order to drive two hundred miles to a dog show—can elicit sympathy from even the sternest listener. Sympathy is always welcome, so why should we tell them that we do not deserve it, that those early mornings are fun?

First there is the satisfaction of rising early enough to wake up the dogs for a change. A call brings them, sleepy-eyed, out to yawn and stretch in disbelief at the surrounding darkness. Then a transformation takes place as they realize from the early hour that it must be a dog event day, and they change from reluctant risers to a wildly excited pack. No one wants to be left behind, as they each entreat, "Take me." "Take ME!" "TAKE ME." "TAKE US ALL."

So the traveling dogs are selected and the stay-at-home dogs are fed in consolation. Fresh water containers and ice are loaded into the car, which was packed the previous night. Finally, the dogs are tucked in and we are off. After the excitement of the departure, the dogs promptly go to sleep. Sunny slept in the backseat. Tiger rode in the passenger seat with his head in my lap. He had logged sixty thousand miles, and on each trip he would still rouse intermittently from his dozing to check on our progress, nuzzle under my hair, and give my right ear a kiss. Then he would drop his head back onto my knee where it rested through a thousand hours of similar drives. While Tiger napped and watched for our destination, Sunny snored contentedly behind us.

It is the start of a new day when anything is possible, and dreams of Best in Shows, or High in Trials, or Best in Fields rest gently with us. We can entertain them for what they are, fantasies and hopes for the future, with the acknowledgment that, although the odds may be long against us, there is always the possibility of the ultimate win. Puppies do win Best in Show, and Novice A dogs do win High in Trial. When we have cherished and played with our fantasies, we can move on to the more attainable hopes of qualifying in obedience or taking the points in breed.

The outcome of the day's activities does not matter to the dog. Only you and your opinion of him matter to the dog. When we first began to show, we started a little ritual that went with the morning drive. It consisted of pats for each dog and a single sentence: "For any weird and wonderful thing that you choose to do to me in the ring today, I forgive you now." The ritual may not have helped the dogs, but it did wonders for relieving my tensions and keeping my goals in perspective. Just one thing—for it to work you have to truly mean it.

GOALS AND ASPIRATIONS

It is a fact that every dog except one is eventually a loser at a show. Because of the pyramidal nature of the competition, dogs are eliminated until finally only the Best in Show or High in Trial dog remains undefeated (for that day). This is a depressing way of looking at the structure, and it ignores one vital point.

Within a show or Trial, there are many levels of accomplishment available to each dog and owner. It is the owner who selects the goal for that day's competition: Two hundred points is a perfect obedience score; 170 points is a barely passing score. I have seen an owner bitterly disappointed with a 194.5 score, and owners who were thrilled with scores of 172. The first owner had missed her self-set goals, while the happy owners had achieved their goals.

How can we each avoid the winning-losing trap? It can be done only by coming to an understanding of what our individual goals are. We must know what we want in a relationship before we can deliberately create it. We seldom make the effort to recognize our desires and act on them. Without that recognition we go through life reacting to outside influences instead of creating what we seek.

What do you want of your relationship with your dog and what price are you willing to pay for it? Place ranking numerical priorities (1–12) on each of the following questions:

———— Do you want a High in Trial Dog?

———— Do you want an Obedience Trial Champion?

———— Do you want titles, whether CD, CDX, UD, or OTCH?

———— Do you crave someday to win a runoff with a sheltie?

———— Do you prefer a methodical, precise worker?

———— Do you want a dog with high average scores?

———— Do you want a dog with a high percentage of qualifications? (the last two questions often do not go together.)

———— Do you want to improve your communication with and understanding of the dog?

———— Do you want to be pleased with your effect on the development of the dog's personality?

———— Do you want a dog that enters the ring bouncing and leaves it smiling?

———— Do you want a dog with obedience, show, and field trial titles?

———— Do you want an outgoing, enthusiastic, self-confident dog?

You would probably like to have all of the above. The purpose of ranking them is to find out which ones you want the most and the least. Writing down the goals is easy. Assigning numerical values is revealing. They help us to communicate with ourselves. In looking at the completed ranking, highly competitive people are likely to find the first six items high on their standings.

I want to make space in obedience for those people whose primary interest is in the development and performance of the well-adjusted, exuberant, confident, willing companion dog, and who attend Trials to exhibit the results of this type of training. These folks will prefer the last six items. Good training teaches the trainer more than it teaches the dog, until, for many trainers, the competition aspects become minor.

THE IMPOSSIBLE DOG

In the Old West it was possible to make a modest living from the efforts of one really good bucking horse. A man would ride into town with a led horse alongside. He would pass the word around that the horse had never been ridden and he was willing to back the horse against anyone who thought he could break it. The suckers would be drawn in like moths to a flame by the challenge of the horse that no one could ride. Well, Old West cowboys are not the only suckers.

When Tiger and Sunny were showing in Novice, a komondor was showing in Utility. Jago (pronounced yaw-go) was not qualifying in Utility. When we showed in Open, he was still in Utility, now being shown by a substitute handler, a young man who had responded to

the challenge of getting the dog to pass. He had bet the owner that he could succeed where the owner had failed. The young man lost the bet. It was the

Sunny flying over the bar jump.

Jago in the same position over the same jump.

only time I ever saw a dog urinate on both the scent articles and the jump.

When Tiger and Sunny went to their first Utility match, there was Jago with his owner, dismayed but still practicing. He introduced himself since he felt that people with unusual breeds in Utility should stick together. And he had spent so much time in Utility that he already knew everyone else. We were just roughing out the form of the exercises and ring procedures at that first match, and from our performance he would have been justified in assuming that we would be in Utility for a good long time. Eight weeks and seven practice matches later we were at our first Trial. Four trials later we had three UD legs between the two dogs.

At this point, Jago's owner offered to bet that he could earn three UD legs with Jago before I could finish both Sunny and Tiger. I hate to take a sucker bet, but he insisted. We won, but in a way he won also. Sunny finished at a foggy Pacific Coast Saturday show. The next day we were showing only in breed since it was a hot, inland show. Jago, as always, was in Utility. His owner left his scent articles in the car and went back for them, leaving Jago with a group that contained some of the top trainers in the nation. They had occasionally been intrigued enough by the great hairy problem of Jago to try their hand with him.

There was a newcomer in the group who had moved out from the East. For his benefit, talk turned to Jago and his endless nonqualifications. The largest man in the group, a strapping six-foot-three two-hundred-pounder, took the dog and the new man with him to the underpass of the adjacent football field. Curious, I followed to watch and had my entire opinion of the dog revised. I had always seen him as a huge, hairy clown playing to the audience for laughs and frustrating his long-suffering owner by never failing the same way twice.

Until the moment he stepped into the underpass, that is what he was. The handler placed the newcomer in a corner and said with a smile of anticipation, "Watch this!" He then heeled Jago and gave him one firm collar correction. Jago was transformed from a slouchy, surly worker to the epitome of the obedience dog—fast, precise, happy. I was astonished. That single correction on any of my dogs would have totally killed his enthusiasm for the day, but Jago loved it. And then the answer came. As the song puts it, "Different strokes for different folks." Jago was a big, strong, barely domesticated guard dog that admired and respected nothing so much as a demonstration of strength. He had been allowed to become a slob, but if given the strength to bring it out, hidden beneath that smelly coat was a good working dog. From being accustomed to his failures and indifferent to his performance, I suddenly wanted to see him qualify. The demonstration over, Jago was returned to his unsuspecting owner. The dog promptly reverted to form and worked like his old self. He did not pass.

Two months later, his owner asked Sally Perry and me to help him train. At this point he had shown thirty times in Utility over an eighteen-month period without a single qualifying score. He was an irresistible challenge. At that time Sally had four Utility dogs, two sporting, and two working dogs, while I had two Utility sight hounds. Jago was stronger than any of us, but we hoped that he would not be smarter than all three of us.

Jago and owner would drive up the ninety miles from Los Angeles once a week. First he would go to Sally's, where she concentrated on mending the relationship between the dog and owner. The owner needed confidence that the dog would eventually pass. He also needed to dispel his considerable resentment over all those failures. He needed hope and the ability to love the dog. In addition to the four Utility dogs, Sally has a psychiatrist son, so she went to work on that aspect of the problem. When they were finished, I would meet dog and owner at a park to practice, a different park each week. Often a ring-wise dog will not act up except at an unfamiliar location, someplace that might be a Trial. Before showing any dog in a new class, it is valuable to practice in as many locations as possible, to keep the dog from being location trained and obeying in only one place.

My approach was more pragmatic than Sally's. I did not care if the owner actually loved the dog or not, just as long as he looked as if he loved him. "Come on, smile. Smile at him. Why should he work for you if you don't look happy? All right, relax the face muscles and try it again. If you look at him like you expect him to fail, then he will fail. He will live up to or down to your expectations. That is fine, fake it. There is nothing that says we can't fool him." With repetition, the handler's manner gradually shed its loser's depression. At the same time there was the problem of what to do about Jago's vast repertoire of ring tricks. The more a dog is allowed to misbehave in the ring, the harder it is ever to make him reliable. Jago's thirty tries at Utility had produced an impressive collection of nightmares for the trainer.

The obvious solution was the one I had seen transform him into a good working dog before, namely, a strong correction. Here we quickly hit a snag. I had seen Jago corrected by a two-hundred-pound man and he had not objected. But that was eighty pounds more authority than either I or Jago's owner had, and the dog made it perfectly clear that he intended to defend himself against anyone our size, which was pretty close to his size.

For our next practice I took along a throw chain that I had never used. They are of no use on a sight hound. But Jago was impressed by it. For two weeks I followed him through the exercises, throw chain in hand, waiting for him to goof off, and then correcting him. He eventually found a countermove. At the first clink of a chain he would drop prone and refuse to budge. He was dropping in the middle of the wrong exercises. That ended the chain's usefulness, but it had been useful. It had given us a means of correcting the dog without having to get within his fight-flight (attack) distance. He was working better except for collapsing at the clink of a chain.

The owner said he had once tried bouncing tennis balls off the dog for corrections. The dog was so heavily coated that he could never have felt a tennis ball's impact, but that reminded me of my hounds' least favorite toy. While they love the figure eight and bone-shaped toys, the hard rubber balls were rejects, just lying ignored in the yard. They made perfect training tools for Jago. When I bounced a ball off his rump for the first time, he produced a slight *Whuff* of surprise, and he decided to heel faster. Since my aim is not all that true, from time to time during the training I would miss the dog, and his owner would give a slight *Whuff* of surprise, but it was worth it. Jago shaped up until he refused to show us any of his old ring tricks. I have seldom seen a happier dog owner than Jago's on the day he qualified in Utility for the first time. Goals that are worked for the longest are often the most rewarding.

Between Trials we kept practicing. Showing at alternate Trials and practice matches is advisable for any dog working on a UD. So we took Jago to a practice match with real ring ropes and real ring help. His owner wanted the dog corrected from outside the ring, which I was reluctant to do. At ringside, Jago took Sunny by the throat, shook her, and casually tossed her aside. With a terrified and insulted yelp she bounded into my lap and shivered. She was undamaged except for her pride and her opinion of Jago. It had not done too much for my opinion of him, either. It changed my mind about the correction. We had nothing even as impressive as a tennis ball, so I borrowed an apple from lunch and stood at ringside willing the dog to blow it. He looked at the ring, decided that he was on safe territory, and declined to work scent. The judge looked a little surprised at having a spectator bash the dog in the butt with an apple, but Jago understood. He selected a scent article. Four shows later he finished his UD. The whole effort had taken twelve weeks and eight Trials.

What is the moral of this story? It is not that dogs are trained by bouncing rubber balls or apples off them. What helped Jago would ruin most dogs. We did learn a variety of things from working with Jago, though. He made us learn them.

First, there is no such thing as a hopeless dog. Unless the owner gives up, the dog will eventually pass.

Second, mere practice does not make perfect. Jago had received vast amounts of practice before we intervened. The quality of practice is much more important than its quantity.

> Bad practice makes a dog worse.
> Good practice makes a dog better.
> Only perfect practice makes perfect.

Third, smile and praise the dog, even if it is an act. If it is an act, do it well. The dog reads your expression. If you look angry, why should the dog play your game?

Fourth, fit the training to the dog. There are very few dogs with the combination of impervious coat, tough skin, and aggressive personality needed to benefit by the rubber-ball method. On the other hand, Jago's owner then wanted a Russian bear dog, so I saved the throw chain and rubber balls for the future.

Whether the dog is superaggressive, super-well-adjusted, eager, shy, cooperative, bright, or a little stupid, the training should be what works with him. The mark of a good trainer is the ability to study each dog and find an appropriate method for him.

The qualities of a good dog are adaptability, resourcefulness, observation, concentration, a spirit of fun, a will to play, curiosity, love for the owner, and respect for the owner.

The qualities of a good trainer are adaptability, resourcefulness, observation, concentration, a spirit of fun, a will to play, curiosity, love for the dog, and respect for the dog.

THE FINAL WORD ON TRAINING

It is finally time to admit that, in spite of the book's title, I have not been writing about conventional obedience work. The explanations of the steps taken to induce a dog to perform a particular exercise (what I call the cookbook sections) are a guide so that others can learn from my experience. Reading is quicker than learning by trial and error.

But the obedience exercises are simply a framework in which the dog and owner can learn about themselves and each other. This kind of learning takes place only if there is two-way communication. Many people do obedience training with the communication all one way, from person to dog. This minimizes the possible rewards of the experience. I strongly advocate learning: studying the dogs and ourselves, helping the dogs to learn, while letting them teach us and reveal us to ourselves. The dog is a mirror in which we can see ourselves if we make the effort.

While we are busy at work and at daily routines, the dogs have vast amounts of spare time in which to study us and our reactions. Like children, they have the advantage of free time to devote to the study of their favorite subject—us. We have all seen small children who manipulate distracted adults. This works because the fact that children are small does not make them less intelligent than adults. Once the forms of the social behavior patterns are learned—and these are learned very early—a child who is concentrating is more than a match for an adult whose attention is divided by outside interests.

Just as children can manipulate parents, dogs can manipulate their owners. What we do in training is pay attention to the dog, to bring to bear on him some of the concentration he is using on us. In doing this, the dog helps us to learn about subjects that are not generally thought of in connection with dogs, subjects like learning itself, socialization and habit formation, communication, social interaction, and motivation. These are a lot of dry and scholarly words for what makes each of us who he or she is. So in the end what one is studying, out on the training field with a friendly dog for help, is oneself.

12

At the End of a Dog's Life

The Chess Game

I started this book by talking about raising and training puppies. I will end it by talking about the final days of a dog's life. As the end of a dog's life approaches, we make a lot of critical decisions. A friend asked me if I remembered sending condolences when her first greyhound died. In the letter I compared the last weeks of a dog's life to playing a chess game with Death. In the game, we know we are playing against an invincible chess player. We know that we are inevitably going to lose. The object is to put off checkmate for as long as we can. If we play the game right and plan our moves well, we can see that the dog lives as long as he comfortably can and doesn't suffer at the end. If we play badly and make the wrong decisions, the dog may die sooner than he has to or may come to an unfortunate end. What follows are some of my planned moves in the chess game.

DEATH: I'll make the dog refuse food.
GAIL: At the end of a dog's life, I cook a wide variety of human food to tempt poor appetites. I do competitive cooking because I won't let a dog starve himself to death. When the cooking marathon is over and I can't find anything the

dog will eat, then I will make the appointment for euthanasia. In thirty years I have euthanized only two greyhounds who would still eat. Star was twelve and threw a clot to her spine that paralyzed her hindquarters. She was lying on a fleece on the floor of the vet's office eating treats I had brought for her. The vet said, "That's amazing." He was amazed that a dog in her condition would still be interested in treats.

When Sunny was fifteen and a half, she had become unsteady on her feet. I had once found her down in her small potty yard, trapped by the gas meter and unable to get up. As she became increasingly unsteady, I was afraid that she would go through the dog door, fall, be unable to get back into the air-conditioned house, and die of heat stroke. Temperatures can reach 115° in Sacramento in the summer. So I spent Memorial Day weekend at home with her and then helped her to the Rainbow Bridge on Monday. She was happily eating Milkbones on the way to the vet.

One of my greatest regrets was that the need to work away from home closed off some of the choices that I could otherwise make at the end of a dog's life. You can keep a dog alive longer if you can stay with him during the day and check on him periodically than if you are away for eight or ten hours at a job. One friend gets dogs to really great ages partly because she can stay at home with them when they get too feeble

to manage on their own. Now that I am retired, I can do the same, and it is a joy.

Tiger, Sunny, and Trip as teenagers. They did everything I ever asked of them, except live forever.

DEATH: The dog is on digitalis for his heart and won't eat.

GAIL: Ask your vet to lower the dosage of digitalis. Digitalis suppresses appetite. You can give only as much as the dog can tolerate without losing his appetite. The idea is to help his heart, not starve him to death.

DEATH: I'll make the dog leak urine.

GAIL: There is an entire sequence of counters for this move.

Dog doors. As animals age, they produce larger quantities of more dilute urine. They need to get outside more often than when they were young. This happens, by the way, to both dogs and people. There is absolutely no reason to get angry with the dog or person. The one to be angry with is Death. But the solution is free access to a potty area. Personally, I have restrooms spotted all over town. My dogs each have a living area connected to an outside area by a dog door. When I moved into my present house, it had decrepit doors and I thought about replacing them. Then I realized that I could install dog doors to my heart's content and wait to replace the doors until the dogs and I were through with the house. My old dogs' room has a Great Dane–sized dog door installed close to the floor so the dogs can just walk through when they are too old to jump through a higher door. And no, in twenty years, burglars have never used the dog doors to enter the house.

Vinyl beanbag beds. I make fleece-covered beanbag beds for my dogs when they are young. I had one large vinyl beanbag bed that Betty Lou and I passed back and forth for years depending on who had old dogs. Finally it cracked and died. I went shopping to replace it and couldn't find another. But then I walked past a table of vinyl at my local fabric store and realized that it could be sewed just like the fleece covers I had been making. So I made my own vinyl beanbag covers for incontinent dogs. Not liking the feel of vinyl myself, I toss a square of synthetic fleece (fake fur) over it and keep spares. Those can be washed as needed while the vinyl keeps the inside of the beanbag dry.

Real beds (for dogs that sleep with their owners). I always keep zippered vinyl covers on my mattresses. Even when dogs are young, they may throw up in bed, and mattresses are hard to dry. I cover the vinyl with a quilted fabric mattress cover like a Bedsack. The sheets go on over that. For a dog that sleeps in one place and is only slightly incontinent, a folded oversized bath towel will catch leaks. For more incontinent dogs, I recommend the disposable bed protectors that are sold for old people. They are absorbent on one side, plastic wrapped on the other, and they are about 30" by 36" square. Packages of these turn up fairly often in secondhand stores after their user has died. But they can also be bought at medical supply stores or mail ordered.

DEATH: I'll make the dog fecally incontinent.

GAIL: As an animal or person ages, nerve messages are transmitted more slowly from the brain to the hindquarters. This deterioration of nerve transmission is one of the reasons why old folks end up in wheelchairs a lot, and both people and dogs start falling down. It also produces fecal incontinence. The dog has very little warning when it has to defecate. It may have no warning at all or not even know it is happening.

To counter this, I try to keep my old dogs on a diet that produces very firm stools. It makes cleanup easier. Again, this kind of dog needs frequent and easy access to a dog door or other allowed potty area. If outdoors is absolutely not an option, you can make a litter box, or a designated potty area with a shower curtain covered with a washable fleece. The shower curtain protects the floor while the fleece can be thrown in the wash. If your dog has picked an indoor location of his own, don't punish him. Put a disposable bed protector on that spot. Put a towel over it and you may have a mini–potty area, a smaller version of the fleece-over-a-shower-curtain option.

DEATH: I'll make the dog weak in the hindquarters.

GAIL: This is caused both by decreasing muscle mass and the failing nerve transmission to the hindquarters. An unsteady dog needs good traction. Vinyl or tile floors may be out of the question. To get my old dogs through the kitchen to the back door, I lay out a row of rubber-backed bath mats. The bath mats give the old feet traction.

DEATH: I'll make the dog suffer from heat or cold.

GAIL: Old dogs often lose the ability to tolerate both heat and cold. Thanks to central heat and air, I can keep the house at decent temperatures. If the dog is not too unsteady on his feet, I make sweaters for him out of thrift store afghans. Old dogs often become emaciated. Their lack of body fat for insulation makes them lose body heat to their surroundings, which causes them to lose more weight. Sweaters can take the place of the lost body fat in insulating them from the cold.

Without air conditioning in hot weather, the dog needs to be cooled by being sprayed with water and put in front of a fan. That works in our low-humidity part of the country. Other measures may be needed for hot, humid climates. Kiddie wading pools are always good. I prefer four-foot-diameter pools. Bigger ones are too heavy to drain by dumping the water out of them. And you need to drain and refill them every few days to keep the water fresh and mosquito free.

DEATH: I'll give the dog pressure ulcers.

GAIL: I provide piles of synthetic fleeces or fleece-covered beanbag beds to prevent bursas and pressure ulcers. When I board dogs, I take fleeces to my vet to keep my dogs off his concrete. The first synthetic fleeces I ever used for the dogs were designed for use in preventing pressure ulcers on bedridden human patients. Pressure ulcers are caused by lying on hard surfaces, or being unable to move enough to keep blood circulation going, or by falling and struggling to get up, which causes friction between the skin and the floor or ground.

DEATH: I'll make your friends and relatives say that you should put the dog down.

GAIL: Nobody but the owner can make the decision of when it is time for euthanasia. I have had dogs that weighed half of their adult weight and looked like furry skeletons that lived happily with me for a year before the end. Sheena was perfectly perky and lived on Chinese takeout food for her last year. She had liver tumors that kept her from turning food into fat. I worried that a workman would see her and report me for dog abuse. When I took her to the vet, I blanketed her to keep from shocking the other patients' owners. She was a skeleton with fur. But she was a happy thirteen-year-old skeleton.

A corollary of this is don't make comments advocating euthanasia for other people's decrepit old dogs. The only time to advocate euthanasia is if the dog is suffering and the owner is having trouble letting go. Then, the only correct question to ask is, "Is the dog suffering?" As long as he isn't, then euthanasia isn't needed, no matter how decrepit looking the dog is.

DEATH: I'll make your dog die alone, or in a stranger's hands.

GAIL: I have had only two dogs die at home. One of them blew a heart valve. He was a dog that lived to eat. When I called him for dinner and he didn't come to meet me, I knew I would find him dead in his bed. The second one bled to death internally from a tumor while I was with him. For all the others, I have had to make the wrenching decision for euthanasia, but at least it lets me hold them and tell them what good dogs they are while they die. That is important. I have had three dogs die at vets' offices when I wasn't present, two of them euthanasias while the dogs were anesthetized and diagnosed with cancer, and one who was anesthetized to death for a routine tooth cleaning.

Those three showed me that I need to be there to hold them and wish them well on their way to the Bridge. I need to be there for the last move in the chess game. I wish that this were a game we could win. Sometimes, when Death threatens a young dog and we play very cleverly, we can win temporarily. Helping Kira live when she was born prematurely and was tiny and weak was one of my rare victories. I feared that she wouldn't live seven hours, or seven days, or seven weeks. So getting her to her seventh birthday and beyond was a win. Usually, the best we can do in the chess game at the end of a dog's life is to be very resourceful, to play the best we can, and to lose well, so that as the dog dies he is sure that he is loved. It helps to understand that what matters is how we play the end game, not the checkmate.

Life is eternal;
And love is immortal;
And death is only a horizon;
And a horizon is nothing,
Save the limit of our sight
—*Rossiter Worthington Raymond (1840–1913)*

Still, it hurts when they finally run beyond the limits of our sight.

13

Why We Do It

THANKSGIVING—THE OWNER
Patricia Gail Burnham

Let us give thanks
For warm puppies,
For beautiful adults,
For healthy veterans,
For loving homes
With sensible owners.
For the people who shaped
And protected our breed
Before us, and for those
Who will care for it
After our time.

For others who share
Our devotion to dogs,
And for the affection,
Honesty, and courage
Of our chosen breed.

For novice breeders
With their boundless enthusiasm,
And for longtime breeders
With their store of knowledge.
For understanding spouses
And tolerant neighbors.
For talented veterinarians
And caring friends.
For strangers who
Stop us on the street to say,
"What a beautiful dog."—
People who know nothing
About dogs
But who know everything about beauty
When it walks by them.

For tracking tests
In the rain.
And field trials
In crisp, fall weather.
For the excitement of dog shows,
And the intricacy
Of obedience trials.
For the fellowship
Of the dog fancy,
Of people whose hearts
Have been snared
By the quest for excellence,
Who, with the tools of
Genetics and training,
Strive to sculpt
Four-footed perfection.

THE DOG'S THANKSGIVING

Thanks to the great master
For kind owners
And warm houses.
For collars that don't pinch
And soft beds to dream on.
For cool water
And shade on hot days.
For tidbits of turkey
With a side dish
Of dinner rolls,
Or broccoli.

For liver at dog shows
Or perhaps a little
Cold roast beef.
For a light hand on our leash
And a gentle hand to stack us.

For rides in the car
And romps in the park.
For feeling needed.
For the company of our human.
For the opportunity to serve him
And to be with him.
To spend our lives
Within the reach
Of his gentle hands
And his understanding gaze.

Appendix 1: Title Abbreviations

The American Kennel Club and other dog organizations offer lots of titles a dog can earn, and they are adding new titles all the time. (Dog owners like their dogs to earn titles. I used to write Sunny and Tiger's names to try on titles that they were working in the way that a newly engaged girl writes her future married name to see how it will look.) So check with the AKC to see their list of current titles. When these titles are awarded, they are abbreviated and used with the dog's name. Below is a list of the conformation, obedience, tracking, Rally, and lure coursing titles. (I was going to include the agility titles, but agility titles reproduce like rabbits. By the time you read this there would be twice as many, so check with the AKC for them.) In addition to agility, there are titles for herding dogs, field trial sporting dogs, terriers, and protection work that would make this list twice as long as it is.

Obedience and Tracking

CD	Companion Dog
CD,TD	Companion Dog, Tracker
CDX	Companion Dog Excellent
CDX,TD	Companion Dog Excellent, Tracker
UD	Utility Dog
UDX	Utility Dog Excellent
UDT	Utility Dog Tracker
UDTDX	Utility Dog Tracking Dog Excellent
TD	Tracking Dog

TDX	Tracking Dog Excellent
VST	Versatile Tracking Dog
CT	Champion Tracker
OTCH	Obedience Trial Champion
HIT	High in Trial

The AKC also offers titles for Versatile Companion Dogs that have titles in three fields of training: obedience, tracking, and agility. The level depends on which titles the dog has.

| VCD1, 2 , 3, 4 | Versatility Dog 1, 2, 3, 4 |

Many breed clubs also offer Versatility Dog titles. The Greyhound Club of America offers two:

| VC | Versatility Dog (for dogs with Championship, Field Championship, and an obedience, tracking, or agility title) |
| VCE | Versatility Dog Excellent (for dogs with a VC title plus LCM, UD, TDX, or MACH) |

Show

| Ch. | Champion (the only show title) |

Other show abbreviations

BOW	Best of Winners
BOB	Best of Breed
BOS	Best of Opposite Sex
BIS	Best in Show

Lure Coursing

JC	Junior Courser
SC	Senior Courser
MC	Master Courser
LCX	Lure Courser Excellent
LCM	Lure Courser of Merit
F.CH	Field Champion
DC	Dual Champion (both a Champion and a Field Champion)

Racing

GRC	Gazehound Racing Champion
SGRC	Supreme Gazehound Racing Champion
ORC	Oval Race Champion
SORC	Supreme Oval Race Champion

Rally

RN	Rally Novice
RA	Rally Advanced
RE	Rally Excellent
RAE	Rally Advanced Excellent

Basic Behavior

CGC	Canine Good Citizen (an AKC title)
TT	Temperament Test

Organizations

AKC	American Kennel Club
ASFA	American Sighthound Field Association
CERF	Canine Eye Registry Foundation
LGRA	Large Gazehound Racing Association
NOTRA	National Oval Track Racing Association
NDR	National Dog Registry
OFA	Orthopedic Foundation of America
TDI	Therapy Dogs International
UKC	United Kennel Club

Appendix 2: A List of Talented Dogs

The dogs in our photos have been busily collecting titles.

Call Name	Registered Name and Titles
Arriba	Ch. Windwood Sweet Arriba, FCH, TD, TT, CGC, VC
Aurora	DC Fleetfield Rising Suntiger, SC, CGC, RN, VC, CD
BillyJoe	BillyJoe V. Siegestor, UD
Bubbie	Fleetfield ElSa Nighthawk, FCH, LCM, TT
Caboose	Rosewood Inside Track, UD
Chris	Ch. Suntiger Christopher, TD, TT, TDI, CGC
Dusty	DC Suntiger Sheena In Stardust, SC
Eureka	Ch. Huzzah Ishidot Get Up and Glow, UD
Fiver	DC Suntiger Fleetfield Black Hawk, CD, SC, CGC, GRC, RN, VC
Frolic	DC Suntiger Fleetfield Frolic, SC, CGC, GRC, RN, VC
Goldy	DC Suntiger Fleetfield Pure Gold, CD, SC, CGC, RN, VC
Halley	OTCH A Stardust Trail ot Vitosha, UDX, TD, NA
Jade	DC Suntiger Sheena's Jadzia Dax, SC
Jago	Am./Mex./Int./World Ch. Mount Everest Jancsi Jago, Am. UD, Mex. CDX
Jiggs	U-CDX Winstar's Root The Jigg Is Up, CDX, HT, PT, HTSS, HTS1, CGC, TDI, RA
Jirel	DC Suntiger Jirel of Joiry, CD, SC, VC, RN

Juliet	Fleetfield Fair Juliet
Kitty Hawk	Ch. Clairidge Kitty Hawk, CD
Lady	Suntiger Lady Shadowfast, F.Ch
Lancelot	Suntiger Sir Lancelot
Lily	OTCH The Merry Prankster, TD, UDX, OA, OAJ, JC, VCD2
Lottie	Ch. Chauffeured's Lotus Elan, UDX, TDX, LPT, NA, OA, CGC
Love	DC Suntiger No Greater Love, TDX, TT
Ringo	Ch. Suntiger Ringo Star CD, SC, RN
Riot	OTCH Sunfire's Causin a Riot, UDX6, TDX, OA, OAJ, MH, WCX, OBHF, TDI, CGC
Rush	Ch. Ellianne's Gold Rush, CD
Sasha	Bo-Rene's Cameo Sasha, Am-Can FCh, CD, TD, LCM II, TT
Saturn	Ch. Suntiger Heart's Delight, CD, SC
Sheena	Ch. Suntiger Sheena, CD
Souri	U-CD UKC/AKC Ch. Sierra Sch-Roo Mighty Mo, CD, CGC, TDInc
Star	Ch. Suntiger Star Snuggler, CD, TDI, CGC
Starlite	Suntiger Starlite
Star Traveler	Suntiger Star Traveler, CD
Sunnie	Rainbo's Here Comes the Sun, CD, CGC, PP
Sunny	DC California Sunshine Traveler, UDT, LCM, VCE
Taupe	DC Suntiger Sheena's Smoke Topaz, SC
Tempest	DC Suntiger Tempest Of Delight, SC
T.G.	Suntigress
Tiger	DC Midnight Shadow Traveler, UDTX, UCE
Timba	Ch. NeeChee's Foothills Timber, UD
Trip	Ch. Clairidge Light Fantastic, CDX, TD
Willie	Von Rojac's Will Shakespeare, UD, TDX

Index

Page references to illustrations are in italics.